REMINISCENCES ON THE ARMY FOR NATIONAL SALVATION

MEMOIR OF GENERAL CHU VAN TAN

Translated by Mai Elliott

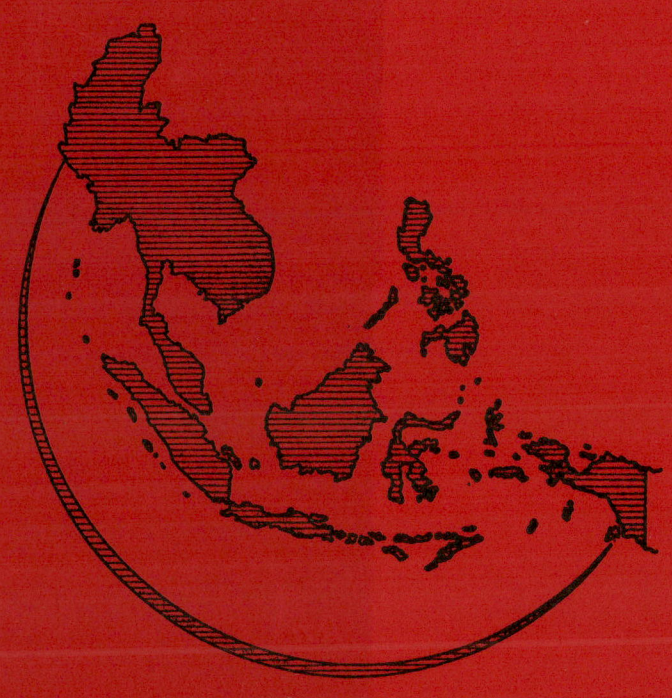

DATA PAPER: NUMBER 97
SOUTHEAST ASIA PROGRAM
DEPARTMENT OF ASIAN STUDIES
CORNELL UNIVERSITY, ITHACA, NEW YORK
SEPTEMBER 1974

PRICE: $6.50

WITHDRAWN

REMINISCENCES ON THE ARMY FOR NATIONAL SALVATION
Memoir of General Chu Van Tan

THE CORNELL UNIVERSITY SOUTHEAST ASIA PROGRAM

The Southeast Asia Program was organized at Cornell University in the Department of Far Eastern Studies in 1950. It is a teaching and research program of interdisciplinary studies in the humanities, social sciences, and some natural sciences. It deals with Southeast Asia as a region, and with the individual countries of the area: Brunei, Burma, Cambodia, Indonesia, Laos, Malaysia, the Philippines, Singapore, Thailand, and Vietnam.

The activities of the Program are carried on both at Cornell and in Southeast Asia. They include an undergraduate and graduate curriculum at Cornell which provides instruction by specialists in Southeast Asian cultural history and present-day affairs and offers intensive training in each of the major languages of the area. The Program sponsors group research projects on Thailand, on Indonesia, on the Philippines, and on the area's Chinese minorities. At the same time, individual staff and students of the Program have done field research in every Southeast Asian country.

A list of publications relating to Southeast Asia which may be obtained on prepaid order directly from the Program is given at the end of this volume. Information on Program staff, fellowships, requirements for degrees, and current course offerings will be found in an *Announcement of the Department of Asian Studies*, obtainable from the Director, Southeast Asia Program, 120 Uris Hall, Cornell University, Ithaca, New York 14850.

REMINISCENCES ON THE ARMY FOR NATIONAL SALVATION

Memoir of General Chu Van Tan

Translated by Mai Elliott

Data Paper: Number 97
Southeast Asia Program
Department of Asian Studies
Cornell University, Ithaca, New York
September 1974

Price: $6.50

© CORNELL UNIVERSITY SOUTHEAST ASIA PROGRAM 1974

International Standard Book
Number 0-87727-097-X

FOREWORD

As much as an individual can, Chu Van Tan personifies one of the major strengths of the Vietnamese revolution--the ability of the ethnic majority to work together in harmony and solidarity with the country's minorities peoples. The fact that as a member of one of these minorities, the Nung, he early attained, and has subsequently maintained, a position of great eminence in the leadership of the Vietnamese revolution, politically as well as militarily, is undoubtedly one of the more notable examples of this phenomenon.

It was Chu Van Tan's little guerrilla group--the Army for National Salvation--that in 1945 merged with another small unit headed by Vo Nguyen Giap to form the Vietnam Liberation Army, the force that was gradually to develop the strength and skill necessary to win the struggle for independence. Chu Van Tan played a major part in building up the base areas in the far north from which the Viet Minh first wrested control of territory from the Japanese and then from the French. (Incidentally, it was during the latter part of this period that one of his many duties was the responsibility for providing military protection against the Japanese to the American OSS groups then operating in this area.) And it was he who in 1945 became the Viet Minh's first Minister of Defense. Then and later as military commander of the Viet Bac Zone, the vast area embracing the six upland provinces of Tonkin that face on China's southern frontier, he played a leading role in training members of the minority groups which were to fight in the two crack divisions, the 312th and 316th, that established such a high reputation at Dien Bien Phu and in subsequent battles.

In recent years Chu Van Tan has continued to occupy top positions of leadership in the Democratic Republic of Vietnam--three-star general, Vice Chairman of the Standing Committee of the National Assembly, member of the National Defense Council and of the Lao Dong Party Central Committee, Secretary of the Viet Bac Regional Bureau of the Lao Dong Party and Commander of the armed forces in the Viet Bac. Up until four years ago he held the additional post of Chairman of the Administrative Committee of the Viet Bac Autonomous Zone, but despite a level of energy that has continued to amaze his colleagues, he then decided that this was more than he could manage and turned over that position to a younger leader, Brigadier General Bang Giang, a member of the Tay minority.

Any ethnographic map makes immediately clear the geo-political importance of the thirty-seven ethnic minorities of the Democratic Republic of Vietnam. Though numbering collectively only about 15 percent of its population, they occupy approximately two-thirds of its area, primarily the massive horseshoe of mountains and upland valleys fronting on southern China and northeastern Laos that ring the rice plains of the heart and sea face of Tonkin, where nearly all of the Vietnamese majority live. It was among the minority peoples of the six mountainous provinces of northern Tonkin that the Viet Minh established its first bases. Here dwell some of the major ethnic minorities--the Tay, Nung and Yao; and if Ho Chi Minh and his then predominantly Vietnamese

v

following were to be successful against the Japanese and their Vichy French allies it was essential that they enlist the support and cooperation of these upland groups. That they were able to do so, despite the traditional fear and animosity of these minorities towards the Vietnamese majority, constituted one of the first major achievements of the Viet Minh. The Hanoi government's continuing dedication to the progressive policies that have won the backing of these upland peoples for the revolution has clearly nurtured among them a growing sense of common national identity with the Vietnamese majority.

A recent indication of this solidarity was strikingly manifest during the bombings loosed against the DRV by the Nixon Administration in 1972. As had been the case in the bombings of 1965-68, schools, industries, government offices, and hospitals were evacuated from Hanoi and other cities and dispersed among the forests and caves of the upland areas inhabited by the ethnic minorities. In terms of the attitudes of the local population as well as of geography there could, I believe, have been no safer place to put them. For it is evident that the non-Vietnamese peoples who live there regard the government to which these facilities pertain as *their* government. Certainly that was the impression I had in September 1972 when I made a trip to the Viet Bac, a visit during which I had the privilege of meeting General Chu Van Tan.

This account of General Chu Van Tan covers the critical formative years of the Viet Minh when through the most arduous efforts, and despite savage and sustained repressive measures of the French and Japanese, it was gradually able to build up in northern Tonkin a substantial political following, strategically located base areas, and a formidable military capacity. Thanks to Mai Elliott's sensitive translation, his description of this period, so much of which he himself directly observed, comes through with remarkable intensity and vividness. Readers will benefit from her useful explanatory footnotes as well as from her carefully researched introduction describing the historical factors and social conditions that affected the wartime developments in the Viet Bac about which Chu Van Tan writes. Those who are interested in this fascinating and historically important period will undoubtedly share my gratitude to Mai Elliott for her excellent translation and enlightening introduction.

George McT. Kahin
July 1974

TRANSLATOR'S INTRODUCTION

Chu Van Tan was born in 1909 in Phu Thuong village, Thai Nguyen province, and came from a peasant family of the Nung minority. Poverty and privations were the norm among the people in his village. A large part of their meagre income was taken away from them through taxes and levies by the local officials and payment of high interest debts to the rich. Though Chu Van Tan's family was large and poor, his parents made a great effort to send their children to school, hoping that the acquisition of an education would help the family escape a life of toil and poverty and enable them to live one day in relative comfort. But, he observes, "it was in vain. Our life, like that of others in the mountainous region, became more and more difficult. Injustices were everywhere."[1]

Chu Van Tan attended a primary school in Thai Nguyen city for a few years. He had to interrupt these studies in 1929, probably because his family could no longer finance his education. After he returned to his village, Chu Van Tan said he felt he could not continue to live as before. "I hoped for some change, but did not know how to bring it about."[2] In 1934 revolutionaries arrived in his area to explain the evil of French colonialism and the objectives of the revolution, and to conduct training courses in elementary principles of communism, methods of clandestine action and organization of peasants. Chu Van Tan came from a family with a revolutionary tradition, his father having fought in the army of De Tham, a Vietnamese hero who put up a stubborn resistance against French conquest of the Tonkin highlands toward the end of the nineteenth century, and he was receptive. "I was deeply interested," he writes, "and immediately joined in revolutionary action."[3]

Chu Van Tan was admitted into the Indochinese Communist Party in 1934[4] and given the task of organizing the revolutionary movement in

---

1. Chu Van Tan, "With Uncle Ho," *Vietnamese Studies*, No. 15 (Hanoi, 1968), p. 59.

2. *Ibid.*, p. 60.   3. *Ibid.*

4. This and subsequent information on Chu Van Tan was obtained from his *Cuu Quoc Quan* (Reminiscences on the Army for National Salvation), and "With Uncle Ho"; from *Vietnam Advances*, No. 12 (Hanoi, 1963), pp. 23 and 27; Thach Son, "Bac Son Khoi Nghia" (The Bac Son Uprising), *Nhan Dan*, 19 August 1960; Duong Nhat Quy, "Cac Dan Toc Mien Nui Doan Ket Chien Dau Duoi Ngon Co Vinh Quang Cua Dang" (The Mountain Minorities United and Fought Under the Glorious Banner of the Party), *Nhan Dan*, 6 February 1965; and Tran Huy Lieu, *Cach Mang Thang Tam* (The August Revolution), Vol. I (Hanoi: Su Hoc, 1960). Some Western publications, basing their data on earlier French works which in turn were based on erroneous French Sûreté intelligence data, have stated that Chu Van Tan did not join the Communists until 1942 and implied that prior to that date he was the leader of a small band of bandits operating in the highlands of North Vietnam. (See, for example, *Who's Who in North Vietnam*, prepared by the U.S. Government from Central Intelligence Agency files and released by the Office of External Research, Department of State in November 1972. See also King C. Chen's *Vietnam and China, 1938-1954* [Princeton, N.J.: Princeton University Press, 1969], p. 87.)

1

the Vu Nhai area of Thai Nguyen province. Under his leadership, many protests were carried out against taxes and labor conscription for the construction of railway lines, and armed self-defense units were organized. In October 1940, as a result of the Bac Son uprising a War Zone (Chien Khu) was set up in the Vu Nhai (Thai Nguyen province) and Bac Son (Lang Son province), and Chu Van Tan was appointed to the Command Staff of this zone.

With the formation of the Army for National Salvation in 1941, Chu Van Tan became one of its commanders. In that same year he joined the North Vietnam Region Party Committee (Xứ Ủy Bắc Kỳ), and was put in charge of building up the Bac Son-Vu Nhai base. He led his unit through a difficult period of severe French repression launched in July 1941. In March 1942, after holding out for eight months in the forest, Chu Van Tan took his unit to the frontier region of China to escape French pressures, skillfully eluding the French Army. Two months after the Army for National Salvation withdrew to China, the French considered the Bac Son-Vu Nhai area pacified and reduced their forces. Chu Van Tan sent his unit back to its old Bac Son-Vu Nhai base in three waves--in November 1942, and in January and February 1943--with himself accompanying the last group. Under Chu Van Tan's leadership, this base was expanded steadily until it linked up with the one in Cao Bang province in March 1945.

Chu Van Tan joined the Indochinese Communist Party Central Committee in 1945 (he has been re-elected to this Committee at every Party Congress held since that date), and as preparations for the General Insurrection were set in motion, he was appointed to the Leadership Committee which was to direct the uprising and the seizure of power. After the August Revolution of 1945, he was appointed National Defense Minister in the Provisional Government headed by President Ho Chi Minh. He held this post until March 1946 when the Provisional Government was dissolved and replaced by a coalition government to include non-Vietminh elements. After the outbreak of hostilities following the French reconquest of Vietnam in 1946, Chu Van Tan became commander of the Vietminh forces in the Viet Bac, and Chairman of this zone's Resistance and Administrative Committee. In this capacity he helped the Vietminh hold firm in this crucial base area against repeated French attempts to clear it of Vietminh forces.

Since the restoration of independence, Chu Van Tan has continued to hold key positions in the DRV government. He has been Secretary of the Viet Bac Autonomous Zone's Party Committee since 1956, and up until 1970 he also held the position of Chairman of this zone's Administrative Committee. Currently he is also the Political Officer for the Viet Bac Military Zone, Commander-in-Chief of the Viet Bac Armed Forces, and Chairman of the Nationalities' Central Commission. He how holds the rank of Colonel General (Thuong Tuong) and is also a member of the National Defense Supreme Council.

Chu Van Tan has written many articles on the Viet Bac minorities covering a wide range of topics, embracing literature and art, economic production and development, and Party expansion and military questions. In 1964, his memoir on the Army for National Salvation was published under the title, *One Year on the China-Vietnam Border* (Một Năm Trên Biên Giới Việt-Trung). It was hailed as an important contribution to the history of the Vietnam People's Army. At the request of numerous readers who wanted to gain a deeper understanding of the Army for National Salvation, this memoir was expanded by Chu Van Tan and republished in 1971 as *Reminiscences on the Army for National Salvation* (Kỷ Niệm Cứu Quốc Quân).

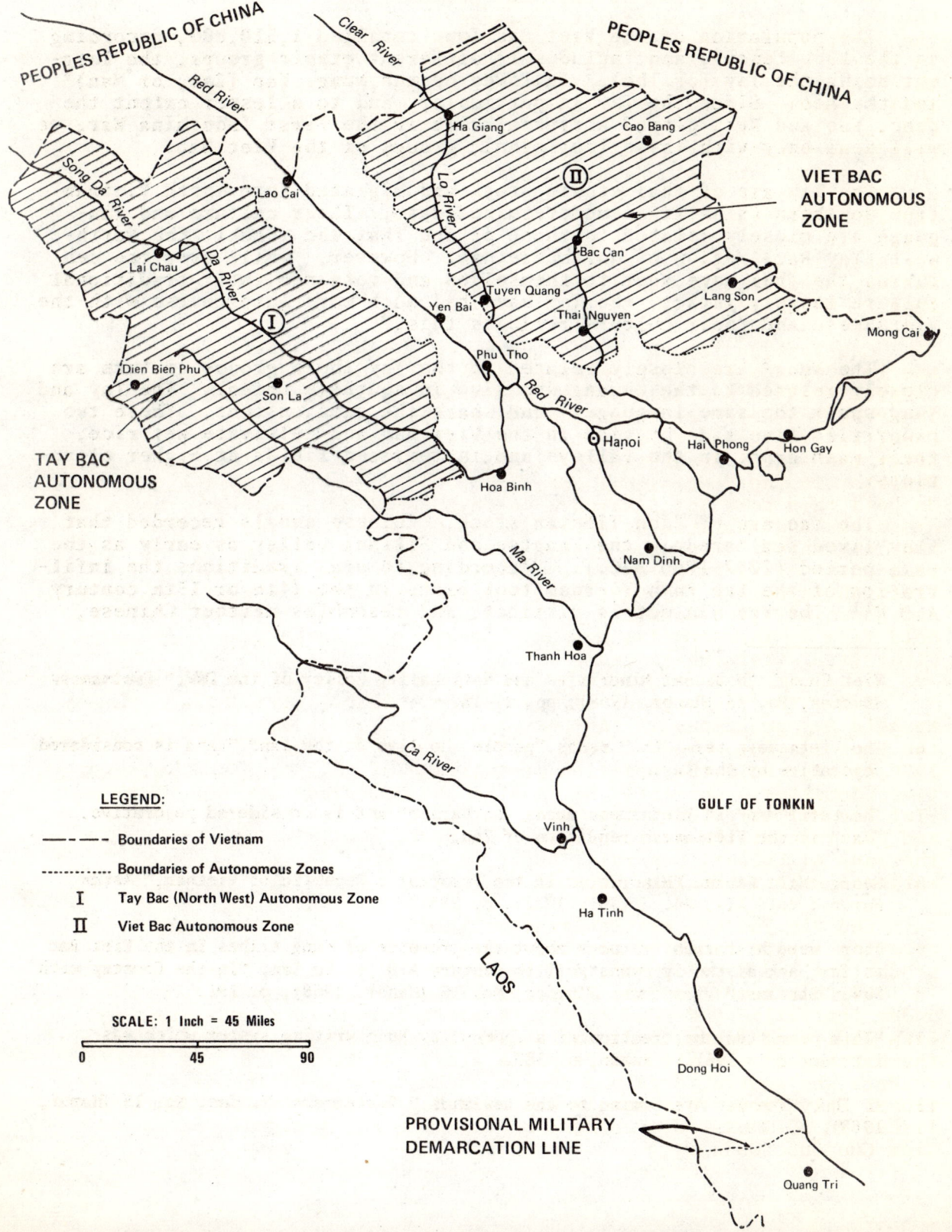

The Bac Son-Vu Nhai base which is the focus of Chu Van Tan's memoir is located in Lang Son and Thai Nguyen provinces in the highlands of North Vietnam. It is now part of an administrative unit called the "Viet Bac Autonomous Zone," which was set up by the Democratic Republic of Vietnam on 19 August 1956. This zone encompasses the old Viet Bac "Liberated Zone" established in 1945, and includes the six northeastern provinces of Lang Son, Cao Bang, Ha Giang, Tuyen Quang, Bac Can and Thai Nguyen (there last two were later merged into one single province called "Bac Thai").[5]

The population of the Viet Bac Zone totalled 1,510,000, according to the 1960 census, and includes 14 different ethnic groups, the largest being the Tay (or Tho),[6] followed by the Nung, Yao (Zao, or Man)[7] and the Meo. Since the Tay in particular, and to a lesser extent the Nung, Yao and Meo, played a crucial role in the First Indochina War, we will deal only with these four ethnic groups of the Viet Bac.

The Tay are of Thai ethnic stock and migrated into North Vietnam from southern China at an undetermined date. Their culture and language are closely related to those of the Thai who inhabit the Northwest (Tay Bac) region of North Vietnam. However, "while over the centuries the Thai have kept to themselves and retained their traditional culture largely intact, the Tay have had much more intercourse with the Vietnamese and their culture reflects this."[8]

The Nung[9] are closely related to the Tay (both groups in turn are closely related to the Chuang who live in southern China). The Tay and Nung speak the same language[10] and share the same customs. These two minorities live side by side in the Viet Bac and cultivate wet rice, their main crop, in the valleys and in terraced fields at higher elevations.

The Yao are of Sino-Tibetan stock. Chinese annals recorded that they lived scattered in the Yangtse and Sikiang valley as early as the Hsia period (2207-1766 B.C.). "According to oral traditions the infiltration of the Yao into Vietnam took place in the 14th or 15th century A.D."[11] The Yao dialect is distinct, and resembles neither Chinese,

---

5. Viet Chung, "National Minorities and Nationality Policy of the DRV," *Vietnamese Studies*, No. 15 (Hanoi, 1968), pp. 17-18.

6. The Vietnamese term "tho" means "people who live on the land," and is considered pejorative by the Tay.

7. The term "Man" in Vietnamese means "barbarian" and is considered pejorative. "Zao" is the Vietnamese rendition of Yao.

8. George McT. Kahin, "Minorities in the Democratic Republic of Vietnam," *Asian Survey*, Vol. XII, No. 7 (July 1972), p. 583.

9. There were historical records about the presence of Nung tribes in the Viet Bac as far back as the Ly Dynasty (11th century A.D.). Vu Can, "In the Country with Seven Streams," *Vietnamese Studies*, No. 15 (Hanoi, 1968), p. 191.

10. "This permitted the creation of a common Tay-Nung writing system which was introduced in 1961." Kahin, p. 583.

11. An Thu, "The Zao Are Coming to the Lowlands," *Vietnamese Studies*, No. 15 (Hanoi, 1968), p. 180.

Vietnamese, Thai, nor the Meo language. In their relations with other ethnic groups, the Yao use Chinese mandarin or the dialect of the ethnic group which is predominant in the area. The Yao live on mountain slopes and practice shifting agriculture. They grow rice, corn and millet.

The Meo belong to the Sino-Tibetan group and began migrating into North Vietnam in the nineteenth century in two waves. The first wave occurred at the beginning of the nineteenth century, and the second around 1845 at the time of the Tai-ping rebellion.[12] The Meo cannot stand the climate of the valley and prefer to live at the highest elevation and mountain summits. They practice slash and burn agriculture and grow mostly corn, their main staple. They grow little rice. Their cash crop used to be opium.[13]

Since the Tay and Nung were the largest ethnic groups in the Viet Bac and lived closest to the Vietnamese population in the Red River delta, historically they had the most extensive contacts with the Vietnamese. The following analysis of conditions in feudal times in what is now the Viet Bac applies mainly to these two ethnic groups.

The Viet Bac Area during the Feudal Period

In contrast to the policy of benign neglect that they adopted vis-à-vis the highland minorities of south-central Vietnam,[14] Vietnamese monarchs followed a more aggressive program of cultural assimilation in dealing with the minorities living in what is now the Viet Bac Zone. These minorities occupied a very strategic stretch of terrain lying between the Red River delta where the majority of the Vietnamese population was concentrated and the Chinese frontier. Their mountainous homeland was the traditional route used by invading Chinese armies who tried repeatedly to re-impose Chinese domination over Vietnam, and the hideout of dissidents or contenders to the throne such as the Mac in the late sixteenth century.[15] The control of these minorities living on the periphery of the heartland of the Vietnamese empire therefore became of critical importance to the Vietnamese monarchs.

According to La Van Lo, Vietnamese monarchs at first relied on local tribal chiefs to maintain control over the minorities. These chieftains were granted court titles and given complete authority over the areas under their domination. Under the Ly dynasty (beginning of

---

12. Edouard Jacques Joseph Diguet, *Les Montagnards du Tonkin* (Paris: Challamel, 1908), p. 129.

13. To increase production and help raise their standard of living, the DRVN has encouraged the Meo and Yao to resettle at lower altitudes. A large number of Meo and Yao have now been regrouped in such permanent settlements. See Kahin, p. 583, and An Thu, pp. 176-187.

14. The emperor recognized the autonomy of these minorities in return for tribute and recognition of the sovereignty of the Vietnamese monarchy.

15. John McAlister, "Mountain Minorities and the Viet Minh," in Peter Kunstadter, ed., *Southeast Asian Tribes, Minorities and Nations* (Princeton, N.J.: Princeton University Press, 1967), Vol. II, p. 819.

the eleventh century to the middle of the fourteenth century) Vietnamese princesses were given in marriage to these tribal chiefs to gain their allegiance and loyalty. During the Le dynasty (beginning of the fifteenth century to 1788), the *Tho ty*[16] system was instituted, under which those who had rendered meritorious services to the kingdom--mostly Vietnamese--were awarded court titles and sent to the highlands to set up latifundae and administer. Over time, they became assimilated with the local population and became an aristocratic elite, while remaining loyal subjects of the emperor. There were seven great *tho ty* clans, referred to as the "Thất tộc thổ ty." They were the Nguyen, Vy, Hoang, Ha, Be, Nong and Ma living in the provinces of Lang Son, Cao Bang, Ha Giang and Tuyen Quang.[17]

These *tho ty* enjoyed wider authority than their counterparts in the lowlands, and their position was hereditary. They controlled the economy of their domain through their supervision and distribution of public land, and were responsible for all political, military and legal matters. They collected tribute and taxes for the court, and in times of foreign invasion or internal rebellion, levied troops and led them into battle at the order of emperor.[18]

According to court decrees, the *tho ty* holding the title of *công* (duke) were granted a domain the size of a district; those holding the title *hau* (marquis) or *bá* (count), a domain the size of a canton; and those holding the title of *tử* (viscount) or *nam* (baron), a domain the size of a village. The *tho ty* had complete authority over their domain. In addition, they were also awarded by the court large tracts of land for their personal use, ranging from 200-300 hectares to a few dozen hectares--depending on their titles. This land was called *lộc điền* or "land granted by imperial bounty." Though this land remained in principle the property of the emperor, in practice it became the personal possession of the *tho ty* and their descendants since it was hereditary like the court title.[19]

The rest of the land in the domain was public land, and was supervised and distributed by the *tho ty* to the people for cultivation in return for the payment of taxes, military service and corvees. This land was kept by the same family, and handed down from generation to generation. However, if there were no male descendants at the death of the head of the family, or if the family failed to fulfill their obligations to the *tho ty*, the *tho ty* had the right to seize the land

---

16. *Thổ ty* is a Sino-Vietnamese term. *Thổ* means land, and *ty* or *tư* means private ownership, possession.

17. La Van Lo, "Buoc dau nghien cuu ve che do xa hoi o vung Tay, Nung, Thai duoi thoi Phap thuoc" (First Step in the Research on the Social System of the Tay, Nung and Thai Areas During the French Occupation), *Nghien Cuu Lich Su* (Historical Research), No. 68 (Hanoi, 1964), p. 38.

18. *Ibid.*, p. 39. According to Viet Chung, "in the 13th century, during the victorious resistance to Mongolian invasions, and in the 15th century during the national war against the Ming, the ethnic minorities largely contributed to victory. Credit for killing the commander-in-chief of the Ming troops, Liao Sheng, is generally attributed to Tay and Nung combatants of Quang Lang in Lang Son province." Viet Chung, p. 7.

19. La Van Lo, p. 40.

and distribute it to another family.[20]

In return for their right to cultivate the land, the villagers had to fulfill a number of services to the *tho ty*. For example, each year each *ho* (or household) had to take turns serving the *tho ty* for two or three months, ploughing, planting, harvesting, grazing draught animals, building houses, and performing other household chores. In addition, all able-bodied adults had to serve in the militia. Each year, the people had to provide the *tho ty* with basic commodities such as cotton, betel leaves and areca nuts, and supplied oxen, buffaloes, pigs and chickens for funerals, weddings and various festivals. Furthermore, they also had to offer to the *tho ty* as gifts the special products of the areas in which they lived. They also had to give to the *tho ty* part of the game they hunted in the forest. Failure to perform these services and obligations resulted in punishment--fines for small offenses, and seizure of land and expulsion from the *tho ty*'s domain for serious ones.[21]

Within his domain, each *tho ty* had complete authority over administrative and military matters. They appointed canton chiefs and deputy canton chiefs, as well as village chiefs and deputy village chiefs who took charge of administrative questions and conscripted laborers for public work projects and for service in the *tho ty*'s household. The *tho ty* also appointed military commanders who organized and trained the militia which drew on all able-bodied males who took turns cultivating the land, guarding the *tho ty*'s residence, patrolling and manning forts, and fighting in times of war or rebellion.[22]

The position and prestige of the *tho ty* was further reinforced by the role they held in the religion of their people. According to the oral tradition of the Tay in Ha Giang province, the *Tho ty* (also called *quang*) was credited with the clearing of land, transforming forest into ricefields, and protecting the first settlers against bandits and evil spirits. The *quang* therefore were worshipped by the people, and their protection sought through sacrifices and religious rituals. Their descendants were the intermediaries between the *quang* spirits and the people. They alone could communicate with the *quang* spirits and invoke their protection. For this reason, the *tho ty* were considered as the protectors of all living things within their domain. By the same token, they could beseech these spirits to destroy anyone who committed infraction.[23]

The people feared the power of the *tho ty* not only because they were afraid of having their land seized and being expelled from the domain, but above all because they were afraid that if they committed

---

20. *Ibid.*, p. 42. Also Nguyen Tuan Lieu, "May Net Tinh Hinh va Nhan Xet Ve Che Do Quang trong Dan Toc Tay o Ha Giang" (A Few Aspects and Observations on the *Quang* System Among the Tay Minority in Ha Giang Province), *Nghien Cuu Lich Su*, No. 44 (Hanoi, 1962), p. 21.

21. Nguyen Tuan Lieu, p. 21.   22. La Van Lo, p. 41.

23. Nguyen Tuan Lieu, p. 18. This myth of the origin of the *tho ty* probably derives from their fusion with the indigenous ruling group. Similar origin myths are found among the Black Thai whose ruling elite, the Lo Cam, are regarded as having a special relationship with the gods and as being divinely ordained to rule the people.

any offense the *quang* spirits would kill them and their families, and destroy their domestic animals and crops. Thus the *tho ty* kept the people in complete submission.[24]

This flexible policy of the Vietnamese monarchy appears generally to have earned the allegiance and loyalty of the minorities in the Viet Bac.[25] The *tho ty* system remained unchanged until new social forces introduced by the French occupation altered the Viet Bac society and brought about the decline of the *tho ty*.

The Period of French Occupation

Military Conquest

After their conquest of the Tonkin lowlands, the French recognized that unless they controlled the surrounding hills and mountains they could never succeed in pacifying the delta.

> Without this control small resistance units could always slip out for rest and regroupment and then filter back with new weapons and supplies. Perhaps more important, as long as resistance continued in the hills, the vast bulk of Vietnamese in the delta would have adequate psychological rationale for refusing to accept colonial rule as ultimate, final, and without alternative. Up through 1890 the French lacked the means to control these hills and instead merely seized strategic points along the frontier (Mong Cai, Lang Son, Cao Bang, Bao Lac, Ha Giang, Lao Cai) and tried to keep open the main communication routes out of the delta.[26]

French penetration began in earnest in 1890, but it did not go unchallenged. There were several pockets of resistance where small armed Tay bands harassed French communication lines and attacked isolated French forts.[27] The most important one was led by Cai Kinh, and

---

24. *Ibid.*

25. Revolts did occur, however. La Van Lo wrote: "The Vietnamese feudal class in its apogee scored a great accomplishment: it united people of all ethnic backgrounds to rise up and defeat many foreign invasions which occurred repeatedly in our history. The minorities' chieftains in general submitted themselves to the Vietnamese feudal court. However, there were times when a few chieftains in certain areas rebelled and fought against the court, but their main motivation was to oppose the abuses of the cruel king and mandarins who infringed on their rights and interests, or to support one dynasty against another, and not to oppose the Vietnamese Feudal State. The revolt of Be Khac Thieu in Cao Bang province at the beginning of the fifteenth century to oppose the Le Dynasty and restore the Tran Dynasty, and the revolt of Nung Van Van at the beginning of the nineteenth century, which spread to the provinces of Cao Bang, Lang Son, Thai Nguyen and Tuyen Quang, to protest against the corrupt Minh Mang court, illustrate this point. The revolt of Nung Tri Cao in the middle of the eleventh century was related to the movement of the Chuang people in Kwangsi who opposed the feudalists of the Sung court, and unrelated [to developments in Vietnam]." La Van Lo, p. 39.

26. David G. Marr, *Vietnamese Anticolonialism, 1885-1925* (Berkeley: University of California Press, 1971), p. 72.

27. Tran Huy Lieu, "Khoi Nghia Yen The, Khoi Nghia Cac Dan Toc Mien Nui" (The Yen The

operated in Lang Son province and a few districts in the northern section of Bac Giang province. This resistance lasted from 1893 to 1894 when it was finally crushed by an expedition commanded by Colonel Joseph Gallieni.[28] The most stubborn resistance occurred in Yen The, Bac Giang province, under the leadership of De Tham, a Kinh (or ethnic Vietnamese) peasant from Hung Yen province. His band was made up mostly of dispossessed Vietnamese peasants from the lowlands, but according to Tran Huy Lieu it would not have lasted as long as it did without the support of the local ethnic minorities.[29] Although De Tham was not killed until 1913, the French had by 1900 strengthened their control enough to consider "the 'pacification of Indochina' accomplished, according to official plan."[30]

Violent protests against heavy taxes and labor conscriptions erupted periodically in the highlands, but these were isolated incidents, not tied to any national movement of struggle, and were easily put down by the French. It was the Viet Minh who--with enormous organizational skills, perseverance and dedication--finally succeeded in fusing all these ethnic minorities into one single bloc and channelling their deep-seated resentment and antagonism toward the French into methodical resistance against French rule, and linking it with the movement in the rest of the country.

Economic and Social Transformation

The arrival of the French brought about a revolution in the patterns of land ownership. The French conquest and the fighting that ensued as the Vietnamese tried to resist French domination drove huge numbers of people from their villages. When these people returned to their villages they found "Frenchmen or French-protected Vietnamese in irreversible custody of their property."[31] This expropriation occurred in all parts of Vietnam. In the midlands and highlands of North Vietnam,

---

Uprising: The Uprisings of the Mountain minorities), Vol. II of *Tai Lieu Tham Khao Lich Su Cach Mang Can Dai Viet-Nam* (Research Documents on Modern Vietnamese History) (Hanoi: Van Su Dia, 1958), p. 62; and "Phong Trao Van Than Khoi Nghia" (The Van Than Insurrectionary Movement), Vol. I of *Tai Lieu*, pp. 187-193. "Such armed bands have come down in French history books as pirates and rebels, while more recent Vietnamese historians generally have hailed them as patriots and righteous armies (nghia-quan). Without wishing to get involved in this semantic quarrel . . . it should be stated in passing that the French had little justification for calling the kettle black, for labeling someone else as pirates, considering the manner in which they took over all of Vietnam. . . . On the other hand, present-day Vietnamese historians should be prepared to recognize that most of the leaders of these mountain bands operating after 1890 had motives which differed in degree, if not in kind, from representatives of the traditional elite like Pham Bach, Tong Duy Tan, Phan Dinh Phung and Nguyen Thien Thuat." Marr, pp. 72-73.

28. Tran Huy Lieu, *Tai Lieu*, Vol. I, pp. 187-193.

29. *Ibid.*, Vol. II, p. 62. Chu Van Tan's father was a partisan in De Tham's army.

30. Marr, p. 77.   31. *Ibid.*, p. 81.

>when French or native colonial units pursued De Tham and the various Chinese bands[32] operating in Yen The and the upper Red River valley, masses of peasants either fled or were forced, as part of the French pacification strategy, to leave their home districts. Failing even with this to put an end to the resistance, the colonial administration encouraged European planters to take over ownership of the vacated lands and bring in contract laborers from distant towns and provinces. By 1898 there was a land-grabbing rush in the midlands of Tonkin, the (French) governor general again taking advantage of traditional Vietnamese royal land prerogatives to parcel out vast permanent concessions to private Frenchmen, based on French private law.[33]

In addition to this seizure of land to establish plantations for French colons, the French were also seizing vast tracts of land to build roads and railroads to link the plantations and mines in the Viet Bac with the urban centers in the delta.

In areas unaffected by these seizures, the patterns of land ownership were also upset. As we had seen earlier, the "*lộc điền*" land granted by the emperor to the *tho ty* over time became the *tho ty*'s private property in practice, though in principle it still belonged to the monarch. The same was also true of the public land that was distributed to the villagers, since this land was handed down within the same family from one generation to the next. In 1931 through the application of the Civil Code in Tonkin, the French recognized the villagers' and *tho ty*'s ownership rights over this public land.[34] This legal property right allowed the people and *tho ty* to sell or mortgage their land. As economic pressures mounted, many *tho ty* and villagers had to sell their land to those who had prospered in the new political and economic order. This new pattern of land holding transformed the Tay and Nung societies and led to their fragmentation into poor and rich peasants.[35] Though the rate of fragmentation was on the whole lower

---

32. There were many Chinese pirate bands operating in the mountain areas of North Vietnam, the most important of which was the Black Flags commanded by a former Chinese Triad leader called Liu Yung-fu. "He sought refuge across the border in Vietnam in 1865 with several hundred followers after the defeat of the Taipings. His ranks swelled over the years until he in fact controlled the administration of the upper reaches of the Red River. His units, often called the Black Flags (Co Den), contained a hodgepodge of Vietnamese, Chinese and tribal contingents, fighting mostly for booty and survival but also from hatred for the Westerners and occasional feelings of class consciousness." *Ibid.*, p. 42. The fullest account of the Black Flags and their intervention in Vietnam can be found in Henry McAleavy, *Black Flags in Vietnam* (London: George Allen and Unwin, 1968).

33. Marr, p. 81.

34. Articles 551, 552 of the Civil Code applied by the tribunals of Tonkin in 1931, cited by La Van Lo, p. 42.

35. The rate of fragmentation depended on how deeply the cash economy had penetrated each area and how concentrated the ricefields were. La Van Lo writes that "in areas where the ricefields were relatively concentrated, the rate of fragmentation was the same as in the lowlands. Landlords formed 3% of the households but owned 30% of the land; rich peasants formed from 3% to 4% of the households but owned 10% of the land; middle and poor peasants constituted 90% of the population but owned only from 60% to 70% of the land. In areas where the ricefields

than in the delta, the fact that the landowners also held political power and abused it to enrich themselves and enlarge their holdings, created a situation that was quite oppressive.

This situation apparently also existed among the Meo and Yao who practiced shifting agriculture. In Bach Thong district, Bac Can province, for example, a landowner seized a large tract of hilly land in Na Leng (suitable for corn cultivation) to graze his cattle, and drove the Yao into the dense forest at higher elevation where they lived largely on wild tubers and gathered *dong* leaves[36] which they then sold in the market and used the money to buy some rice.[37] In the case of the Meo, it was not uncommon for the *chúa đất* (lord of the land, i.e., a rich and powerful man) to seize better plots of land and to force the villagers to settle on more arid land. For example, in Mieu Cao village, Ha Giang province, the ricefield belonging to the father of the girl who became the Chairman of the Village Cooperative after liberation was seized by a *chúa đất*. She and her father had to move to a very high and arid mountain peak.[38]

Thus, the economic power of the *tho ty* which had been based on their control of the land was destroyed. In some areas the *tho ty* became landlords and officials in the colonial administration, while in others they became dispossessed and bankrupt.[39] This loss of economic power was accompanied by the loss of political power, as the French in an effort to break the power of the *tho ty* "made the offices of district and province chiefs--the hereditary positions of the *tho ty*--appointive or elective. As a result many non-*tho ty* were placed in these positions."[40] A large number of the officials in the French administration

---

were more dispersed, the fragmentation rate was lower. The landlords, 1% to 2% of the households, controlled 6% to 10% of the land; rich peasants, 1% of the households, about 4% of the land; middle and poor peasants formed 95% of the population and owned from 80% to 90% of the land. There were areas where there were no landlords and no rich peasants." La Van Lo based these figures on a document of the Central Ethnic Nationalities Commission compiled in 1956-57. *Ibid*. Though the rate of fragmentation was low, it must be borne in mind that land in the mountain regions was more arid than in the lowlands and that the landlords and rich peasants usually owned the more fertile plots, leaving the less productive land to the poorer peasants who, because of the poor soil and primitive modes of production could barely subsist, especially since a large part of their income was taken from them in the form of taxes and levies.

36. *Dong* leaves are used for wrapping cakes.

37. "Na Leng Khong Con La Ruong Kho" (Na Leng Is No Longer a Dry Field), *Nhan Dan*, 26 March 1960.

38. Her father was subsequently murdered by the *chúa đất* who robbed the opium that he had planted and harvested. Nguyen Ngoc, "Mua Hoa Phien Cuoi Cung" (The Last Opium Crop), *Nhan Dan*, 28 August 1960.

39. La Van Lo, p. 42. The *tho ty* had lost their hereditary political prerogatives and no longer ruled as absolute leaders in their domains. They became simple officials within the French colonial administration.

40. Gerald C. Hickey, "Social Systems of North Vietnam" (Ph.D. dissertation, University of Chicago, 1958), p. 169. McAlister claims that this situation created considerable tensions between the *tho ty* and members of the new elite and that

came from the new class of rich peasants and landlords. Some of these families became extremely wealthy thanks to the salt and opium monopoly granted them by the French.[41] It was not unlikely that the peasants considered this new elite as illegitimate and resented their authority. And even if the peasants were prepared to accept them as the new leaders, their venality and corruption and the ruthless way in which they collected taxes and conscripted laborers undoubtedly did not endear them to the population.

Under the French colonial administration, the middle and poor peasants who produced on a small scale had to bear the brunt of the tax burdens and labor conscription. The taxes were numerous:

(a) head taxes, levied on all males from 18 to 60 years of age. (If a man was past the age limit but did not have the money to have his name removed from the roll, he would have to continue paying the head tax; this was the reason why many families continued to pay taxes for their relatives long after the latter's death);

(b) land and property taxes (*thuế điền thổ, thuế thổ trạch*);

(c) alcohol taxes;

(d) buffalo taxes;

(e) opium taxes levied on each Meo and Yao household regardless of whether they grew opium or not;

(f) horse taxes (levied on everyone who owned horses);

(g) kitchen fire taxes (*thuế bếp lửa*) levied on each Meo and Yao household (this tax presumably replaced the land tax which the Meo and Yao probably did not have to pay since they moved around from place to place and did not own any defined and fixed property).[42]

Usually the officials forced the people to pay more in taxes than they actually owed, and pocketed the difference. Failure to pay taxes resulted in beating and imprisonment. In addition, the villagers had

---

the resentment of the *tho ty* drove them to support the Viet Minh. He wrote, "[The *tho ty*'s] Vietnamese cultural background enabled them to play a vital part in the formation of the [Viet Minh] guerrilla zone. Since they were the only Vietnamese-speaking elite of any mountain minority, they were in an unparalleled position to work with the Viet Minh to organize a highland guerrilla base within their traditionally defined territory." However, McAlister offers no conclusive evidence to support his thesis. See McAlister, pp. 793-794.

41. La Van Lo, p. 43.

42. Information obtained from *Khu Quang Trung Trong Cuoc Van Dong Cach Mang Thang Tam O Viet Bac* (The Quang Trung Region in the Mobilization for the August Revolution in the Viet Bac Zone) (Hanoi: Viet Bac Publishing House, 1972), p. 7; and *Khu Thien Thuat Trong Cuoc Van Dong Thang Tam o Viet Bac* (The Thien Thuat Region in the Mobilization for the August Revolution in the Viet Bac Zone) (Hanoi: Viet Bac Publishing House, 1972), pp. 8-9. Both of these documents were compiled by the Commission for the Research of Party History in the Viet Bac Autonomous Zone. Part of the data also came from Thach Son, "Bac Son Khoi Nghia" (The Bac Son Uprising), *Nhan Dan*, 19 August 1960.

to pay for certain expenses incurred by the local officials. For example, each time the village officials had to entertain visiting mandarins and their retenue, or soldiers and their commanders who passed through the settlement, the officials divided the expenses among the villagers and forced them to pay, usually double what they had actually spent. In the case of the Meo and Yao who practiced shifting agriculture, each time they moved to a new area they had to offer gifts of meat, rice and wine to the local officials before they were allowed to stay and build their houses. After they had settled down, each family had to present to the officials 10 taels of opium per year as gift.[43]

The villagers had to perform as unpaid laborers on projects such as road and railroad construction, and building military outposts. They were supposed to receive a minimal pay, but the officials usually pocketed their salaries. They had to bring their own food to last them for the duration of the corvee and lose a long period of time which they would normally spend tending to their crops. Those who did not have enough food reserve at home to bring along had to borrow it from the rich at high interest rates. Working conditions were harsh and the laborers were frequently beaten by the supervisors. Many died from labor accidents; for example, during the construction of the road linking Nguyen Binh to Bao Lac in Cao Bang province.[44] These harsh conditions and abuses of the officials at times triggered violent protests, such as the revolt of the Tay in Lang Son province in 1920 under the leadership of Doi An.[45]

The peasants who rented land from the landlords and rich peasants had to pay high land rentals. Those who borrowed money or food from the rich were required to pay exorbitant interest rates, or to work for their creditors without pay for the equivalent of many more days than they actually owed. Another form of exploitation by the rich was to buy the peasants' crops in advance for a small sum, the peasants who

---

43. *Khu Thien Thuat*, p. 9.

44. *Ibid.*, p. 10. Hoang Thi Nghiem, a Tay girl from the Nuoc Hai area of Hoa An district, Cao Bang province, wrote that when the French built the road going from Cao Bang to Quang Yen, "They [the French] conscripted a lot of laborers. On the average, each villager had to go and work as a laborer once every two months, each time for 15 days. The rich families who had money bribed the village chief, and the village chief arranged an exemption for them and forced the poor to go in their place. Take my father, for example. Sometimes, he had just returned home when he had to leave again. Each time he came home, he looked more emaciated. But he was fortunate to come home alive. Many villagers were killed, crushed by rocks at the Ma Phuc pass [through which the road passed]. My mother in the end had to sell one *sao* [360 square meters] of ricefield cheaply in order to obtain 7 piasters which she used to get my father admitted into the militia so that he would be exempted from labor conscription." See *Nguoi Con Gai Cao Bang* (The Girl from Cao Bang Province) (Hanoi: Nha Xuat Ban Phu Nu, 1961), pp. 5-6.

45. After World War I, the French intensified their exploitation of the coal mine in Loc Binh and the tin mine in Van Linh (Lang Son province). Tay peasants were forced to work as miners and to build the railroad linking the mines with the Hanoi-Lang Son line, and with Quang Yen and the seaport. Taking advantage of this situation, a number of mandarins extorted money from the Tay who rose up in revolt to protest against labor conscription as well as against the heavy taxes. Tran Huy Lieu, *Tai Lieu*, Vol. II, pp. 84-90.

needed the money to tide them over until the harvest usually having no choice but to accept such unfavorable terms.[46]

The life of the people, insecure in the best of times, became even more miserable in times of crop failure or poor harvest. Then they had to go into the forest to dig up roots to subsist. Many were so starved that they died while digging for wild tubers.[47] Salt was always a problem, especially for the people living at high altitudes cut off from the economic activities of the valley. Many of them did not have enough money to buy it and had to use bamboo ashes as a substitute. The French used their salt monopoly to control the people; to be able to buy a can of salt, a villager was required to serve on construction projects as a conscripted laborer.[48]

This is how Le Quang Ba, a Tay from Cao Bang province who later became a brigadier general in the Vietminh's army, described his early life in his village located near Soc Giang, the district town:

> As soon as the harvest was gathered, we had to pay taxes to the "protectorate," not to mention local contributions exacted by the imaginative notables and rich people. And we soon found ourselves with empty hands. Long before the new harvest was brought in, we had to sell our chickens, one after another, in order to get something to eat. After the New Year Festival, the only food we had was wild plants and roots if we did not want to borrow maize or rice from the rich, at an 100% interest rate. . . . This miserable life was further aggravated by gambling, drinking, smoking of smuggled or "legal" opium. Gambling was open practice in market-places. Thefts were daily occurrences and armed robberies and murders quite frequent.
>
> As we lived not far from the authorities, I witnessed many a tragedy. Shackled men were thrown in prison on account of overdue taxes. Others came with poultry and pigs to bribe the mandarin and his acolytes in the vain hope of retrieving fields which had been seized by some village tyrants. Canton chief Thanh, who lived near our house, was the richest man in the region. He availed himself of his position to expand his land holdings, and for this purpose never hesitated to strip other people of their property in a most cynical manner.
>
> . . . I had no liking for the village notables. They often came to our house, scolding my parents for some overdue tax payment. They made me pay fifty cents or one piaster every time their signatures were required for some school document. Rice for a meal cost only two or three cents.[49]

General Chu Van Tan described life in his native village in Thai Nguyen province as follows:

---

46. *Khu Thien Thuat*, p. 12.

47. Thach Son, "Bac Son Khoi Nghia," *Nhan Dan*, 19 August 1960.

48. *Khu Thien Thuat*, p. 10, and Viet Chung, p. 10. Viet Chung wrote, "Among some tribes a bit of rock-salt was carefully kept in the house for the family to lick after each meal."

49. Le Quang Ba, "Reminiscences of Underground Revolutionary Work," *Vietnamese Studies*, No. 15 (Hanoi, 1968), pp. 27-29.

>Except for a few land-owners and rich peasants, the population lived
>in sordid misery. A Corsican colonialist had seized for himself over
>one hundred hectares of fertile land scattered throughout our region
>and its vicinity. He began by acquiring a plot of land near the
>upper stretches of a canal which he promptly diverted. As the plots
>on the lower ground were then deprived of water, the peasants had to
>sell them off. A few among them did try to resist, but their fields
>were soon surrounded by those of the foreign owner, and no longer
>accessible to their plough-animals. And they too were forced to
>abandon them.
>
>We were tormented by many other cares. Poll-tax took from each
>man half the price of a pig. Other contributions took a half of our
>income. Taxes, compulsory labor, high-interest debts finally ruined
>us. People in Phu Thuong used to say: "Whoever falls under the
>weight of a land-owner's granary will never get up." Very few could
>escape. And then there were the frequent floods which eroded the
>land so disastrously. Yet from Trang Xa to Lan Thuong, everywhere
>were gambling dens, drinking houses, opium shops. Natural calamities
>and social vices cooperated with the imperialists in keeping us in
>sordid misery.[50]

A Nung peasant from Trang Dinh district, Lang Son province, gave the following picture of life in his village:

>Under the old regime we were a people of hunger-stricken sharecrop-
>pers. Practically no Nung had any land for himself. We toiled hard
>for Tay landowners who grabbed half of our harvests. Every year we
>experienced three to four months of food shortage during which we fed
>on wild vegetables and tubers. . . .[51]

These class antagonisms and the resentment of the people of the Viet Bac toward the French administration[52] provided the Viet Minh with the opportunity to move into the area and set up their bases.

The Viet Bac Minorities and the Viet Minh

The Viet Minh very early on recognized the strategic importance of the Viet Bac highlands to the success of the revolution. The vast expanse of forests and mountains provided the ideal environment for the establishment of secure bases. The rugged terrain and the difficulty in communication made it difficult for the French to concentrate their forces to deal effectively with the revolutionaries. The position of the Viet Bac on the periphery of the Red River delta meant that cadres operating in the lowlands could retreat to the bases in the Viet Bac to escape French repression. In addition, the proximity of the Viet Bac to the Chinese border made it easy for revolutionaries to slip across the frontier into China whenever French pressures became too intense,

---

50. Chu Van Tan, "With Uncle Ho," pp. 58-59.

51. Vu Can, p. 200.

52. For example, describing the situation in Cao Bang province, Philippe Devillers wrote, "The population, the majority of whom were Tho [Tay], had always retained a rebellious spirit which the administration's often brutal policy had helped to reinforce." *Histoire du Viet-Nam de 1940 à 1952* (Paris: Editions du Seuil, 1952), p. 102.

as Chu Van Tan's unit did in 1942.[53]

Cao Bang province which was contiguous to the southern Chinese province of Kwangsi and easily accessible from Yunnan, where many exiled Vietnamese Communists were active while keeping their Communist affiliation secret to avoid Kuomintang arrest, was the first province in the Viet Bac to have an Indochinese Communist Party Chapter. It was set up in 1930 by Hoang Van Thu,[54] a Tay who had gone to Kwangsi in 1926[55] to join the revolution. In fact, Communist activities began there as far back as the 1920's and in 1929[56] a chapter of the Viet-Nam Cach Menh Thanh Nien Hoi (Vietnam Revolutionary Youth League)--the precursor of the Indochinese Communist Party (formed in 1930)--was set up.

In 1932, Le Hong Phong, an Indochinese Communist Party leader operating in Southern China, contacted Hoang Van Thu and Hoang Dinh Rong (a Party member of Tay origin who had been active in Cao Bang since 1926) to recruit cadres and send them to southern China for training.[57] The formation of new cadres was vital because the Party apparatus had been decimated by bloody repressions carried out by the French in 1931 in the aftermath of a wave of communist organized workers' strikes and the establishment of soviets in Nghe An and Ha Tinh provinces in Central Vietnam.[58] The Overseas Leadership Committee (Ban Lanh Dao Hai Ngoai) which had been set up by Le Hong Phong in 1932 to function as a provisional Central Executive Commmittee (Ban Chap Hanh Trung Uong Lam Thoi) also "paid great attention to the formation and consolidation of bases in Lang Son and Cao Bang provinces which would serve as springboards for expansion toward the delta."[59] Cao Bang became the conduit for cadres going to and returning from training in China, and the communication channel between the Party leadership in China and the remnants of Party organization in Vietnam.

Under the leadership of Hoang Van Thu and Hoang Dinh Rong, the movement--which had first taken roots among the Nung and Tay and then spread to the Yao and Meo living at higher elevations, with Tay and Nung cadres serving as carriers of the revolutionary influence--expanded gradually. The expansion was given great impetus during the Popular Front period in France (1936-1939) during which colonial rule in Vietnam was somewhat relaxed, with some measure of freedom for political

---

53. Two soviets, the Left River and Right River Soviets, were set up by the Chinese Communist Party in 1929-1930 in the southern portion of Kwangsi province near the border with Vietnam. Though these soviets were short lived, they left a reservoir of sympathy for the Communist Party among the ethnic minorities living in these areas. Vietnamese revolutionaries who crossed into these areas could therefore count on the support and protection of the local population.

54. Tran Huy Lieu, *Cach Mang Thang Tam*, Vol. I, p. 82.

55. "Comrade Hoang Van Thu," *Nhan Dan*, 20 January 1965.

56. Tran Huy Lieu, *Cach Mang Thang Tam*, Vol. I, p. 82.

57. "Dong Chi Le Hong Phong" (Comrade Le Hong Phong), *Nhan Dan*, 27 January 1965.

58. Huynh Kim Khanh, "Vietnamese Communism: The Pre-Power Phase (1925-1945)" (Ph.D. dissertation, University of Western Ontario, 1972), pp. 152-171.

59. "Dong Chi Le Hong Phong," *Nhan Dan*, 27 January 1965.

activities permitted. However, after the collapse of the Popular Front the French colonial administration launched an intensive repression campaign to root out Communist organizations in the province, and the cadres had to go underground. The movement recovered when the Japanese army invaded Indochina from southern China and the French position in the province was weakened.

The Bac Son Uprising

The Japanese invasion also sparked an insurrection in another part of the Viet Bac, in Bac Son district,[60] Lang Son province, near the border with Thai Nguyen province. Lang Son was the area of the Viet Bac where the French encountered a stubborn resistance when they penetrated into this part of the Tonkin highlands in the 1890's. It was also in Lang Son that the revolt of the Tay occurred in 1920 to protest heavy taxes and labor conscription to build railway lines.

The Communist-led movement developed early in Lang Son. In 1933, at the instruction of the Indochinese Communist Party leadership Hoang Van Thu set up Communist organizations in Bac Son district, with the help of cadres recently escaped from jail or recently returned from the border area where they had been hiding.[61] The first revolutionary cell was organized in Vu Lang village. From 1933 to 1940 mass organizations such as Thanh Nien Phan De (Youths Against Imperialism) and Mat Tran Dan Chu Chong Phat Xit (Democratic Front Against Fascism) were formed first in the villages of Vu Le and Vu Lang, and then spread to the entire district. The Communists organized many protests against labor conscription and taxes in 1938, 1939 and 1940, but these were easily put down by the French.[62]

In adjacent Thai Nguyen province, at the beginning of 1933 Hoang Van Thu who was then operating in the China-Vietnam border region sent cadres to La Bang, Dai Tu district, to set up grassroot organizations. According to Duong Nhat Quy, a Nung who took part in the Bac Son uprising:

---

60. The bad conditions in Bac Son explained the volatile situation which erupted into open revolt in 1940: "Under French occupation, the minorities living [in Bac Son]--the Man [Yao], Tay, Nung, Cao Lan, and Thai--led a miserable life. They did not have enough rice to eat, and had to dig up *dao* and *mài* tubers and to gather wild leaves in the forest to cook gruel. Many were so starved that they died next to the holes they were digging to find *mài* tubers. In the cold season, the chilly wind that blew down from the mountains and from the dense forest penetrated to one's marrows. The people did not have enough clothes to wear against the cold, and had to make blankets and clothes out of the bark of the *sui* tree. . . . On top of all this, the mandarins, the district chief and the village chiefs forced the people to neglect their fields and to go and work as laborers building roads, and recruited people to work in their households as [unpaid] servants. Head tax, buffalo tax, alcohol tax became heavier and heavier as time went by." Thach Son, "Bac Son Khoi Nghia" (The Bac Son Insurrection), *Nhan Dan*, 19 August 1960.

61. *Ibid*.

62. Tran Huy Lieu, "Phong Trao Chong Phat Xit Chong Chien Tranh Va Cac Cuoc Khoi Nghia Bac Son, Nam Ky, Do Luong" (The Anti-Fascist, Anti-War Movement, and the Bac Son, Nam Ky and Do Luong Uprising), Vol. X of *Tai Lieu*, pp. 10-11.

> We poor peasants understood then that . . . only the Party would
> bring land and a better life to the peasants of the mountain region.
> This was why many comrades and I joined the ranks of the Party. . . .
> After the Party cadres had propagandized and enlightened us, with
> their help after a while we set up the first group of Party members
> in this area. This group included Tay, Nung and Man [Yao]. These
> comrades were all poor and miserable people who had drifted here from
> Lang Son, and so when they were enlightened [by the Party] they ac-
> quired a determined revolutionary spirit.[63]

From Dai Tu, the movement spread to Dinh Ca and Vu Nhai districts. (Vu Nhai was under the leadership of Chu Van Tan.)

At the outbreak of World War II, the Japanese began to put increasing pressure on Indochina. The French decided to repair and extend the strategic road going from Thai Nguyen to Dinh Ca and Trang Xa, and on to Bac Son, Lang Son. To carry out this urgent project, wave after wave of Tay and Nung were conscripted to work on the road. Each person was conscripted to work from one to three months, usually without pay since their salaries were pocketed by the officials. After a short time at home, they were again conscripted. In order to drive them to work harder, the officials and supervisors did not hesitate to resort to violent means.[64] These abuses brought the resentment of the Tay and Nung to the boiling point, and they finally found an outlet for their pent-up frustrations and anger during the Japanese invasion.

Following the traditional invasion route from China, Japanese troops entered Lang Son province on September 22, 1940. After a one-day military encounter, the French Indochina Army surrendered. French colonial administration in the province collapsed in the aftermath of this defeat. Taking advantage of this situation, Party members in Bac Son--some of whom had recently escaped from the Lang Son jail in the confusion of the Japanese attack--led the people to attack the Binh Gia post and to ambush fleeing French Army soldiers to seize weapons and ammunition. On the morning of September 27, the local Party cell met to discuss the situation and decided to launch an armed insurrection to seize power in the district. This decision was reached without consultation with Chu Van Tan, who was then the Bac Son-Vu Nhai Party Secretary, with the North Vietnam Region Party Committee, or with the Central Committee.[65] The local Party cell apparently felt that the urgent situation required decisive immediate action, and in view of the difficulty in communication due to the confusing conditions at the time, decided to take action without waiting for instructions. A committee to direct the uprising and the attack on the district seat was set up. In the night of September 27th, over 600 people under the leadership of this committee attacked the Mo Nhai post in the district town and cap-

---

63. Duong Nhat Quy, "Cac Dan Toc Mien Nui," in *Nhan Dan*, 6 February 1965.

64. Tran Huy Lieu, *Tam Muoi Nam Chong Phap* (Eighty Years of Resisting the French) (Hanoi: Van Su Hoc, 1961 [?]), Vol. II, p. 52.

65. Though they did not consult the Central Committee, the local Party cell felt that they were acting in accordance with the resolution of the 6th Central Committee plenum of November 1939 which predicted that the Japanese would attack Indochina, and stated that "The Party holds the view that while the imperialists tear each other to pieces we must transform the Fascist aggression into a revolution to liberate the nation." See Thach Son, "Bac Son Khoi Nghia," *Nhan Dan*, 19 August 1960.

tured it. Documents and seals belonging to the officials were burned, to the great acclaim of the people, and the abolition of the French administration was announced.[66]

After the Japanese and the French Vichy government in Indochina arrived at an accommodation, the French were allowed to return to Bac Son. They recaptured the Binh Gia and Mo Nhai posts, and restored their administration. Fierce suppression of the insurrection followed, and the guerrillas had to scatter into the forest to avoid capture. Informed of the uprising, Chu Van Tan hurried to the delta to report to the North Vietnam Region Party Committee and request it to send a cadre to Bac Son to take charge of the situation. It was only in the middle of October 1940 that Tran Dang Ninh, the representative of the North Vietnam Region Party Committee, arrived in Bac Son.

At a conference held in Sa Khao, the Party decided to assemble its members and hard-core sympathizers into a "Bac Son guerrilla unit," set up a Command Staff for the Bac Son war zone (Chu Van Tan was one of its members), announce the dissolution of the local colonial administration, and adopt the slogan of "attack the French, drive out the Japanese, seize the property of the imperialists and reactionaries to distribute to the peasants." The Vu Lang school was attacked on October 25th, and the militia who had been assembled there by the French fled. Three days later a meeting was held at this school to prepare for the attack on the Mo Nhai post. Warned by spies, the French carried out a surprise attack, routing the guerrillas who fled into the forest.[67] This attack was followed by a severe repression which decisively put an end to the uprising. Although the insurrection failed, it was to provide the Indochinese Communist Party with the nucleus of an army and a base on the fringe of the Red River delta. In February 1941, this guerrilla unit was set up as the Army for National Salvation by the Central Committee, reinforced with new recruits, and placed under the command of Chu Van Tan, Phung Chi Kien and Luong Huu Chi (the last two were graduates of the Whampoa Military Academy in China, and were later killed in Cao Bang province).

Formation of the Cao Bang and Lang Son-Thai Nguyen Bases

Following the French defeat of September 1940, the authorities and troops in Cao Bang province became very fearful and demoralized. Taking advantage of this uncertain situation, the cadres intensified their activities. However, after reaching an agreement with the Japanese, the French were able to reconsolidate their position in the province. To put an end to this revolutionary agitation, the French launched a white terror campaign, and the cadres were forced to leave the settlements and flee into the forests and mountains. In this critical situation the Cao Bang Province Party Committee decided to send to China a group of forty cadres and youths who were being tracked by the French, in order to contact Party leaders and obtain new instructions. They

---

66. This and subsequent data on the Bac Son uprising was compiled from Tran Huy Lieu, *Tai Lieu*, Vol. X, and *Tam Muoi Nam*, Vol. II; from Chu Van Tan, *Ky Niem Cuu Quoc Quan*; from Thach Son, "Bac Son Khoi Nghia," *Nhan Dan*, 19 August 1960; and from Duong Nhat Quy, "Cac Dan Toc Mien Nui, *Nhan Dan*, 6 February 1965.

67. Chu Van Tan, *Ky Niem Cuu Quoc Quan*, pp. 9-10.

met Ho Chi Minh, Pham Van Dong and Vo Nguyen Giap in Chinghsi in southern Kwangsi[68] in early 1941.

At that time, Ho was preparing to return to Vietnam to take direct charge of the revolution and reconsolidate it following the devastating French repressions of 1939 which had virtually wiped out Party organizations in the urban areas (where the Party had switched to overt political action during the Popular Front period in France, from 1936 to 1939).[69] The cadres who had gone underground and moved to the rural areas at the instruction of the Indochinese Communist Party in the spring of 1939 survived this period of persecution. Although the Party's rural network had not been destroyed by the repression, this situation rendered necessary the creation of safe bases in the Viet Bac to which cadres in the delta could retreat in case the French intensified their pressure. Besides, the weakened position of the French in the aftermath of the Japanese invasion now made the establishment of such bases possible. The two sites that were chosen were the part of Cao Bang province close to the Chinese border which many cadres had been using as hideouts, and the Vu Nhai-Bac Son area where the uprising of 1940 had taken place and where remnants of the Bac Son guerrilla unit were operating.

Ho Chi Minh returned to Vietnam on February 8, 1941, and set up headquarters in Pac Bo, Ha Quang district, Cao Bang province. At that time, communication between the headquarters in Cao Bang and the Central Committee members operating in the delta was very tenuous and often cut off by French repression. A corridor linking Cao Bang with Thai Nguyen province, and going from Thai Nguyen to the delta and the rest of the country had to be opened to ensure better liaison and to serve as a funnel through which Viet Minh forces, which were being organized in Cao Bang, could be channeled southward to link up with the unit in the Bac Son-Vu Nhai base and carry out the general insurrection when the right opportunity arrived. Ho Chi Minh had told Vo Nguyen Giap while they were still in southern China preparing to return to Vietnam:

> The base in Cao Bang will open vast potential for our country's revolution. Cao Bang already has a solid revolutionary movement, and furthermore as it is close to the border, it will serve as a convenient base for liaison with the outside. But from Cao Bang we must move toward Thai Nguyen province and further south in order to have

---

68. Tran Huy Lieu, *Cach Mang Thang Tam*, Vol. I, p. 83.

69. According to Huynh Kim Khanh, ". . . the ICP abandoned its clandestine operations during the People's Front period and elected to concentrate its political activities in the overt and legal realm. . . . Only in the spring of 1939, when the ICP belatedly realized that the People's Front in France was teetering on the brink of total disintegration, did the Party give orders to its members to consolidate the clandestine section and 'withdraw into clandestinity.' This step was taken somewhat too late, however, by this time, several secret police agents had infiltrated the ranks of the Party and climbed up the Party's hierarchical ladder. . . . In September 1939, following the French government's official dissolution of the now 'anti-war' French Communist Party, the colonial regime resumed its persecution of Vietnamese Communists and swiftly destroyed most of the known Party's overt and clandestine organizations. . . . ICP urban networks were demolished virtually in toto. Two thousand party workers, including important leaders, were arrested." "Vietnamese Communism, pp. 302, 308-309.

contact with the whole country. If we can link the movement [in Cao Bang] with that in Thai Nguyen and the rest of the country, when we launch an armed struggle we can advance forward when conditions are favorable and hold our grounds when conditions are difficult.[70]

Ho convened the 8th Plenum of the Central Committee in Pac Bo in May 1941. It was at this conference that the decision was reached to set up the Viet Minh Front to draw and unite all social classes in the fight against both the French and the Japanese to liberate the country. The bases in Cao Bang and Bac Son-Vu Nhai were to be consolidated and the armed forces built up to prepare for the general insurrection to seize power.

To effectuate the link-up between Cao Bang and Thai Nguyen, Ho dispatched Vo Nguyen Giap and Le Thiet Hung (now a Major General) to Nguyen Binh district in Cao Bang province, where Party cells had been set up in the 1930's and where Viet Minh Front Committees had been formed.[71] They were charged with organizing the Southward March section (*Nam Tiến*) and opening a corridor from Nguyen Binh to Ngan Son and Cho Ra (Bac Can province), and then linking it with the towns of Cho Chu and Dai Tu (Thai Nguyen province). Ho instructed Giap to concentrate on military matters, and Hung on political questions. He also sent Hoang Van Hoan (at present a Politburo member) and a number of cadres to open a corridor from Dong Khe (Lang Son province) to Dinh Ca (Thai Nguyen province). At the same time he directed the Cao Bang Province Party Committee to expand Viet Minh organizations southward, especially from Nguyen Binh district into Bac Can province, and from Thach An district to Trang Dinh prefecture in Lang Son province.[72] Chu Van Tan and his unit meanwhile were directed to consolidate the base in Bac Son-Vu Nhai and to keep open the liaison route with the delta.

Ho's presence in Cao Bang gave the movement there a new impetus. Furthermore, the cadres who had returned with him from China spread out to re-establish contact with cadres who had remained in the province in order to maintain the movement and rebuild the Party apparatus which had been damaged by French repression. The Bac Son uprising had had a considerable impact in the province, and the cadres succeeded in recruiting a large number of people into National Salvation Associations. By the middle of 1942, the Viet Minh movement had spread to Ngan Son district in Bac Can province.[73]

In Thai Nguyen, after the Pac Bo conference Viet Minh organizations were set up in all areas of the province. However, in June 1941 knowing that the Bac Son-Vu Nhai base had been reinforced, the French launched a large-scale operation in the area. One section of the Army for National Salvation, led by Phung Chi Kien and Luong Huu Chi, re-

---

70. Vo Nguyen Giap, *Tu Nhan Dan Ma Ra* (Born from the People) (Hanoi: Quan Doi Nhan Dan, 1969), p. 34.

71. Tran Huy Lieu, *Cach Mang Thang Tam*, Vol. I, p. 82; and *Khu Quang Trung*, p. 12.

72. Vo Nguyen Giap, *Tu Nhan Dan Ma Ra*, pp. 89-90; and also from *Khu Quang Trung*, p. 12.

73. Data for this paragraph and for pages 23 to 25 were compiled from Vo Nguyen Giap, *Tu Nhan Ma Ra*; Tran Huy Lieu, *Cach Mang Thang Tam*, Vol. I; *Khu Thien Thuat*; and *Khu Quang Trung*.

treated and tried to make their way to Cao Bang in July 1941. They
were ambushed on the way and several men were killed (Phung Chi Kien
and Luong Huu Chi were captured and later died in jail). Chu Van Tan's
unit tried to hold on to their base, but unable to contact the Central
Committee members in the delta and the headquarters in Cao Bang (and
thus left without central direction), surrounded by the French and cut
off from the population (who had been resettled in "concentration villages" by the French)--and therefore from their source of supplies--Chu
Van Tan had to take the main body of his unit to China in March 1942.
The remainder of the unit was sent to Phu Thuong and Bac Son (Lang Son
province); Dai Tu, Phu Luong, and Dong Hy (Thai Nguyen province); Son
Duong and Yen Son (Tuyen Quang province); and to Huu Lung and Yen The
(Bac Giang province) to operate.

Two months after Chu Van Tan's unit left for China, the French considered the area pacified and withdrew the bulk of their forces, leaving
behind only enough troops to man outposts at strategic points in the
region. Chu Van Tan's unit began to filter back in November 1942, and
January and February 1943.

In January 1943 at the conference in Lung Hoang (Hoa An district,
Cao Bang province), Chu Van Tan met with Vo Nguyen Giap and Pham Van
Dong to discuss the opening of a corridor linking the base in Cao Bang
with the one in Bac Son-Vu Nhai. They decided to organize Southward
March units from Cao Bang and Northward March units from Bac Son-Vu Nhai
to effect the link-up. Following the directive to switch to political
mobilization, Chu Van Tan's unit split into three- to five-men cells in
order to fan out and set up grassroot bases (*gây cơ sở*) in Thai Nguyen
and Tuyen Quang provinces, and to push steadily into Bac Can province,
toward Cho Don and Cho Ra. In May 1943, Chu Van Tan succeeded in reestablishing contact with the Party's Central Committee operating in
the lowlands, and the communication channel between Party organizations
in the delta and in the Viet Bac was restored.

In Cao Bang province the appeals of the Party and the Viet Minh
Front to the youths to join the Southward March units were met with an
enthusiastic response. Nineteen units were organized, with the members
having to procure their own weapons. Each unit was sent to a different
area to make propaganda, recruit people into the movement, choose the
most dedicated and enthusiastic among them, train them for a short
period of time and then use them as new cadres to expand the movement
in the area. The Southward March routes were built up in this manner,
going through many mountains and valleys, through the settlements of
the Tay and Yao people.

In 1943, Ha Quang, Hoa An and Nguyen Binh districts of Cao Bang
province became "entirely Viet Minh districts" (*châu hoàn toàn Việt
Minh*), and National Salvation Associations were spreading in the other
districts of the province. Youths belonging to these mass organizations all joined self-defense units, and each district had several combat self-defense units. Many courses were conducted to train military
cadres. Parades and mock combat exercises were held to impress the
population, draw the hesitant ones into the movement and intimidate the
reactionaries.

In Bac Can province, the movement was spreading in four districts
and a Provisional Province Party Committee was set up. In Lang Son,
the movement was moving from That Khe toward Bac Son-Vu Nhai. In
August 1943, the Southward March unit from Cao Bang met the Northward

March unit in Phia-bioc, Bac Can province, and in December of that year, Chu Van Tan and Vo Nguyen Giap met for a conference in Nghia Ta (Bac Can province) to inaugurate the corridor linking the two bases. It was now possible for cadres to go from one base to the other without having to make the long detour into southern China.

However, the growing strength of the Viet Minh in Cao Bang and Bac Can did not escape the attention of the French. In November 1943 they launched a new wave of terror, and the corridor was severed. The new campaign was much wider in scope than the ones launched previously. The methods used were the same ones that they had applied in Bac Son-Vu Nhai in 1941. To cut off all contacts with the cadres, villagers in the more populated areas were relocated in settlements where they could be kept under surveillance, and forbidden to go into the forests and mountains. Many settlements were burned and levelled. Viet Minh sympathizers caught with propaganda literature were shot, mutilated and their bodies displayed to intimidate the rest of the population. Many cadres were caught and executed.[74] Existing posts were reinforced with more troops and new ones were built all over the province. Mobile patrols were formed which tracked down cadres and searched the mountains and forests for Viet Minh bases.

In order to prevent the movement from collapsing, Party members and militant National Salvation Association members were organized into "secret cells." They lived in the forest and at night came down to the villages where they received reports and food supplies from underground cadres and hard-core sympathizers, and gave new instructions. These cells hung on tenaciously and the movement began to recover.[75] Districts began to organize full time self-defense units which liquidated reactionaires and collaborators, and ambushed small patrols.

In July 1944, the Vichy government in France collapsed, and tensions between the French and the Japanese in Indochina mounted. A coup d'etat by the Japanese to overthrow the French seemed inevitable. In this situation, the Inter-province Committee for Cao Bang, Bac Can and Lang Son--which had been cut off from all contacts with the Central Committee in the delta and with Chu Van Tan's unit--convened a meeting in Lung Sa (Hoa An district, Cao Bang province) in August 1944 at which the decision to launch an insurrection in all three provinces was reached. All self-defense units were ordered to join the guerrilla units, and arms, ammunition and food were stockpiled. While these preparations were being feverishly pushed forward, Ho Chi Minh who had gone to China in 1942[76] returned to Cao Bang in October 1944 and imme-

---

74. See Vo Nguyen Giap, *Tu Nhan Dan Ma Ra*.   75. *Ibid*.

76. According to King C. Chen, when he arrived in southern China, Ho was arrested for carrying improper identification papers. He was accused of being a Japanese-French spy by the local authorities at T'ienpao, and jailed for over a year. The Indochinese Communist Party, under the name of the Vietnam Branch of the International Anti-Aggression Association, sent a cable to Sun Fo, son of Dr. Sun Yat Sen and president of the Legislative Yuan in Chungking, asking for Ho's release. They also sent a report to Tass in Chungking protesting Ho's arrest and declaring that this action of the Kuomintang had increased resentment toward China among Vietnamese revolutionists. The Chinese were then making plans to enter Vietnam to attack the Japanese, and so did not want to antagonize Ho's group whom they knew had mass support in Vietnam. General Chang Fa-k'uei, the Commander-in-Chief of the Fourth War Area, ordered Ho's release in October

diately ordered the postponement of the insurrection because the French, though weakened, could still muster enough forces to crush it without difficulty, especially since in no other area in the country was the Viet Minh in a position to rise up at the same time to force the French to spread their resources.

In Ho's judgment, the moment to launch insurrections had not yet arrived, yet in the new situation struggle by political action alone was not enough. His solution was to combine political action with military action which would be carried out to spread the influence of the revolution. Viet Minh units were then small and dispersed, and at his instructions the best fighters and weapons were assembled to form a concentrated unit, the "Vietnam Propaganda and Liberation Army" (Viet-Nam Tuyen Truyen Giai Phong Quan), which was put under the command of Vo Nguyen Giap. Within a month of its formation, in the winter of 1944, the unit attacked the posts in Phai Khat, Na Ngan and Dong Mu to seize much needed weapons and ammunition. The attacks had wide political repercussions, popular enthusiasm grew, and Viet Minh organizations began to spread. Meanwhile cadres and units from Thai Nguyen had been moving steadily into Bac Can and Lang Son provinces at the same time that the cadres and units in Cao Bang were spreading southward into these two provinces. By 1944 the revolutionary movement in Lang Son had been linked with the one in Thai Nguyen to the south and with the one in Cao Bang to the north. In March 1945, the Cao Bang base was again linked with Bac Son-Vu Nhai when the unit of Vo Nguyen Giap and the unit of Chu Van Tan met in Cho Chu (Thai Nguyen).

After the Japanese overthrew the French in March 1945, the French administration collapsed, and the Viet Minh moved rapidly to seize power in the Viet Bac--Cao Bang, Bac Can, Lang Son, Ha Giang, Tuyen Quang and Thai Nguyen provinces. On June 4, 1945, a Liberated Zone covering these six provinces plus adjacent areas in the provinces of Bac Giang, Phu Tho, Yen Bai and Vinh Yen, was set up at the direction of Ho Chi Minh. A Vietnam National Liberation Committee headed by Ho Chi Minh was also formed (this committee became the Revolutionary Provisional Government after the August Revolution of 1945). The Army for National Salvation and the Vietnam Propaganda and Liberation Army were merged and became the Liberation Army (Giai Phong Quan). Within the Liberated Zone, People's Revolutionary Committees were elected to carry out the ten-point program of the Viet Minh which included the seizure of land belonging to French colons and Vietnamese collaborators for distribution among the poor, the abolition of labor conscription and taxes (except for one light income tax), the reduction of rents and interests, and the postponement of the repayment of all debts.[77]

A week after the Viet Minh had seized power in Hanoi, two Liberation Army detachments composed of Viet Bac minorities marched into the

---

1943. However, the Chinese, fearful that Ho was a Communist, did not allow him to return to Vietnam. Ho lived under the surveillance of Hsiao Wen, an aide of Chang Fa-k'uei, and was not allowed to return to Vietnam until August 1944. Concerning Chang Fa-k'uei's reason for permitting Ho to return to Vietnam, Chen wrote, "As the Allied forces steadily advanced in Europe and the Pacific Chang's plan and preparation for entering Vietnam were in readiness. If the plan became reality, the only Vietnamese force that could cooperate with the Chinese . . . [would be] that of Ho Chi Minh." Chen, p. 84.

77. Information from *Khu Quang Trung* and Chu Van Tan, *Reminiscences*.

A Liberation Army detachment composed of Viet Bac minorities
in Hanoi after the August 1945 revolution.

capital on August 26, 1945. Le Quang Ba, a Tay from Cao Bang province, became the commander-in-chief of the Armed Forces of the Capital, while Chu Van Tan, a Nung from Thai Nguyen, was appointed Defense Minister in the government organized by Ho Chi Minh. During the resistance war that broke out after the French reconquered Indochina in 1946, two out of six divisions mobilized by the Viet Minh, the 312th and the 316th, were commanded by Tay generals. According to McAlister, they "were composed primarily of Tho numbering roughly 20,000 men in all," this constituting "approximately 20 percent of the Viet Minh regulars as of 1954 and about 5 percent of the total estimated Tho population in the early 1950's."[78]

When the French, intent on reconquering Vietnam by force, rejected all offers for a negotiated settlement and war became inevitable, Viet Minh forces withdrew back into their bases in the Viet Bac. There they regrouped, trained and prepared for the new phase of the resistance struggle which culminated with the French defeat in Dien Bien Phu, in another highland region of North Vietnam, the Tay Bac (Northwest) area. As McAlister points out, "without the Viet Bac Zone prepared during the Japanese occupation, the Viet Minh might have been exposed to the military superiority of the French and annihilated before another suitable base could have been established."[79]

---

78. McAlister, p. 796.   79. *Ibid.*

Mobilization of the Minorities

While non-communist Vietnamese parties usually ignored the minorities[80] which, in their view, were too remote and alien to be accorded a role in the national liberation struggle, the Viet Minh quickly realized the potential that these minorities could bring to the revolution. "Immediately after its founding, the Indochinese Communist Party . . . explicitly laid down its nationality policy as follows, 'To achieve the unity of all nationalities on the basis of equality and mutual assistance with a view to winning together independence, freedom and happiness.'"[81] From their long experience in dealing with the Vietnamese, the minorities must have greeted this declaration with considerable skepticism. However, when the Viet Minh actually treated the minorities with dignity and respect, showing that they attached great importance to their participation in the revolution, these minorities became convinced of its sincerity. This is how Chu Van Tan described his feelings after attending the Pac Bo conference in 1941 and meeting Ho Chi Minh:

> I was full of self-confidence: I had grown mature during the journey. With the knowledge I had gathered, with weapons, documents and a correct line of action as my equipment, I was certain I could do better. . . . I was elated by the thought that I, a mere cadre of a national minority, had met the leader of our Party, of our people, who happened to be one of the leaders of the Comintern! Equality among the nationalities, revolutionary comradeship, these were no longer empty words! I was completely freed from all inferiority complexes.[82]

The Viet Minh movement first penetrated among the Tay and Nung and then was carried to the Yao and Meo who lived at higher elevations. Viet Minh support among the minorities was confirmed by Major A. K. Thomas, the leader of the OSS group operating in the Viet Bac in 1945 with the collaboration and assistance of the Viet Minh. In his "Report on Deer Mission" (the code name of the operation), Major Thomas wrote: "The people [of the Viet Bac] are principally of three types--Annamese, Tho and Man [Yao]. . . . The Tho are strongly VIETMINH in sentiment. The Man hill tribes . . . are also VIETMINH in political sentiment."[83]

The Viet Minh realized that in order to achieve success it was necessary for them to recruit and train local people as cadres. A Party document stated: "Provinces with minorities' population should organize committees specializing in mobilizing them, form and train cadres of ethnic background and let them develop the national salvation

---

80. The Vietnamese Quoc Dan Dang Party (Kuomintang), for example, was active in the highland region of North Vietnam, but recruited its members from the Vietnamese population living in the area.

81. Viet Chung, p. 11. This statement was contained in the Indochinese Communist Party's Program of Action of 1930.

82. Chu Van Tan, "With Uncle Ho," p. 69.

83. Major A. K. Thomas, "Report on Deer Mission," in *Hearings Before the Committee on Foreign Relations on Causes, Origins, and Lessons of the Vietnam War, May 9, 10, and 11, 1972*, 92nd Congress, 2nd Session (Washington, D.C.: U.S. Government Printing Office, 1973), p. 263.

movement in their own areas; only in this way would we be able to obtain quick results."[84] Cadres from the minorities were recruited usually through family or friendship ties, trained in short courses and then sent back to their areas to work. When a cadre moved into a settlement, if he did not have any relatives or friends in the village, he set about winning the sympathy and trust of a villager, and then contacted other families through this person. The most ardent sympathizers were trained to become cadres and to lead the local movement. After that, the cadre moved on to another settlement where he could count on the kinship and friendship ties of the people he had recruited in the previous settlement to gain an entry into the area. At the same time, the villagers he had recruited would proselytize their own relatives and friends scattered in various villages. In this way, the network spread, and since the cadres in most instances were bound by friendship or blood ties to the people, the villagers were not prone to betray and denounce them to the authorities.[85]

The cadres recruited from the minorities were successful because they understood the situation in their own areas, knew local customs and habits, had prestige among the people and could win their confidence and get them to do what was needed. Outside cadres usually only came in to consolidate the local movement and to provide further training to the local cadres.

The minorities of the Viet Bac did not speak a common language. The *lingua franca* was usually Chinese mandarin or the dialect of the largest ethnic group in any given area. A large number of Tay spoke Vietnamese, and Nung and Yao had a basic knowledge of it, but most did not. To overcome the language problem, Viet Minh cadres learned the dialects of the areas in which they operated. Vo Nguyen Giap, for example, spoke Tay and Yao, and Pham Van Dong was fluent in Tay.[86] To propagate Viet Minh programs and policies, documents, bulletins and leaflets were translated into the local dialects, using a very simple and concise style so that these politically unsophisticated people could understand them and remember them easily. For example, the Viet Minh Program was translated into five-word verses called the *Việt Minh Ngũ Tự Kinh* (adopting the format used in the old Confucian Classics Primer, the *Tam Tự Kinh*, which consisted of three-word verses) so that the people could chant them and recite them by heart. In addition, songs and poems were composed in the local dialects to exalt the revolution and the struggle for national liberation, and these the minorities also learned by heart. Mobile propaganda teams went around explaining the *Việt Minh Ngũ Tự Kinh* and articles printed in the official Viet Minh newspaper, *Viet-Nam Độc Lập* (Independent Vietnam), and taught revolutionary songs to the minorities.

To raise the political consciousness of the people, the cadres taught them simple questions and answers which they could memorize easily:

    Q. We are poor, we wear ragged clothes, we are sick and malnourished, who causes this?

    A. It's because the French imperialists and Japanese fascists oppress and exploit us.

---

84. Van Kien Dang, 1939-1945 (Party Documents), cited in *Khu Thien Thuat*, p. 73.

85. *Khu Thien Thuat*.   86. Kahin, p. 586.

Q. If we want to have enough to eat and be happy, what should we do?

A. We must unite tightly with the Viet Minh Front to make revolution, rise up to drive out all the French imperialists and Japanese fascists, overthrow the reactionary government, and set up a people's revolutionary government.

Q. What benefits will we enjoy if the revolution succeeds?

A. We will have equality; men and women will be equal, there will be no oppression. We will have enough to eat, warm clothes to wear, the peasants will have land to till, and there will be no exploitation. We won't have to pay head taxes. . . . We won't have to do labor conscription work.[87]

The Viet Minh also organized mobile exhibits of pictures to show the crimes of the Japanese and French, and the heroic deeds of the Chinese Red Army in their fight against the Japanese. *Lien Hoan* (get-together) parties were held where people of different ethnic backgrounds met and fraternized in order to forge unity and friendship between them and overcome the divisiveness spread by the French. In addition, cultural classes were conducted to combat illiteracy, so that more and more people could read Viet Minh documents.

In order not to antagonize the people, the cadres were instructed to observe local customs and habits strictly, in all circumstances. Ho Chi Minh himself set the example, adopting the clothing and living style of the minorities in the areas where he stayed. He also laid down the "Four Recommendations" and the "Five Interdictions" which all cadres must follow. The "Four Recommendations" were:

1. To help the population in their daily work: husking and milling rice, fetching water and firewood, looking after the children.

2. To get acquainted with local customs and habits, to strictly respect all "taboos" observed in the region and by the family with whom one is staying.

3. To learn the local dialect, to teach the local people to sing, read and write, to win their sympathy and little by little to conduct revolutionary propaganda.

4. To win the population's confidence and support through one's correct attitude and discipline.[88]

The "Five Interdictions" were:

1. Not to cause any damage to the crops and fields, not to deface or impair the population's furniture and household articles.

2. Not to insist on buying or borrowing what people don't want to sell or lend.

3. Not to forget one's promises.

---

87. *Khu Thien Thuat*, pp. 21-22.

88. Le Quang Ba, "Reminiscences of Underground Work," p. 47.

4. Not to violate local customs, habits and religious beliefs.

5. Not to divulge any secrets.[89]

By adhering to these rules and using these methods, the Viet Minh succeeded in mobilizing the minorities of the Viet Bac and bringing them into the national struggle for independence and social emancipation. The Viet Minh success stemmed largely from the fact that they issued appeals which reflected these minorities' aspirations. In these areas of grinding poverty where exploitative taxation and labor conscription had added such a heavy burden to the life of the people, promises of a better life and an end to the abuses of the French administration struck responsive chords. The French, in practicing their divide-and-rule policy, concentrated so much on the negative aspects of the relationship (the mistrust and antagonism) between the Vietnamese and the minorities, that they tended to forget that feelings of patriotism and nationalism did exist among the minorities, especially among the Tay, the most Vietnamized of all ethnic groups in the Viet Bac. Or they tended to forget that in the case of the minorities who did not identify with the Vietnamese as strongly as did the Tay, resentment of French intrusion and abuses was so great that it could outweigh any feelings of mistrust that these minorities might have had against the Vietnamese. This was demonstrated by the enormous sacrifices that these minorities were willing to make for the Viet Minh cause, and by their determination, in the face of great odds, to help carry the struggle for national independence to a successful conclusion.

Acknowledgments

I would like to express my deep gratitude to Professor John M. Echols, Acting Director of the Cornell University Southeast Asia Program, who saw the value of Chu Van Tan's memoir and gave his approval to this translation project. I am also greatly indebted to Professor George McT. Kahin and my husband David Elliott for their encouragement and assistance in editing the translation and the introduction.

Mai Elliott
July 1974

---

89. *Ibid.*, p. 48.

REMINISCENCES ON THE ARMY FOR NATIONAL SALVATION

(Memoir of General Chu Van Tan)

Hanoi
Nha Xuat Ban Quan Doi Nhan Dan
(People's Army Publishing House)
1971

INTRODUCTION

The Army for National Salvation was one of the armed units which were the precursors of the Vietnam People's Army today. Born after the glorious Bac Son insurrection and during the dark years of our country then living under the yoke of the savage colonialist rule of the French and Japanese imperialists in league with the reactionary feudalists, the Army for National Salvation--led by the Party, protected and supported by the people--carried out an extremely heroic struggle full of difficulties and hardships to "sustain the rifle shots of Bac Son" and to build up the revolutionary base in order to advance toward national insurrection. Starting in 1944, the Army for National Salvation--along with the Vietnam Propaganda and Liberation Army--fought, performed missions, contributed to the establishment of the first Liberated Zone, and did their utmost to prepare for the successful August Revolution. Many comrades in this armed unit sacrificed their lives in the course of the struggle; many other comrades today have become outstanding leading cadres and commanders of our Party and Army.

Comrade Chu Van Tan was one of the men who had directly contributed to the glorious activities of the Army for National Salvation since its formation. He has recounted many stories about the Army for National Salvation which have appeared in newspapers or published in book form. In 1964, the People's Army Publishing House issued his book, *One Year on the China-Vietnam Border*, which recorded a phase in the activities of the Army for National Salvation then receiving the utmost support of friendly China's Party and people.

Along with other memoirs which have been published by the People's Army Publishing House--such as *Born from the People* by comrade Vo Nguyen Giap, *Under the Glorious Banner of the Party* by comrade Song Hao, *From the Mountains and Forests of Ba To* by comrade Pham Kiet--the book *One Year on the China-Vietnam Border* of comrade Chu Van Tan have helped the readers understand the glorious tradition and the extremely difficult but also extremely heroic evolution of our people's revolutionary armed forced under the very ingenious and very enlightened leadership of our Party.

At the request of readers who want to understand more fully about the Army for National Salvation, the People's Army Publishing House proposed to comrade Chu Van Tan that he supplement his memoir. Although very busy, comrade Chu Van Tan expended a large amount of time and effort to meet this request, and handed to us the book *Reminiscences on the Army for National Salvation*.

We are happy to introduce this book to the readers, and are very grateful to comrade Chu Van Tan, as well as to many agencies--in particular the Central Commission for the Research of Party History--and to many comrades and citizens, to whom our revolution is indebted, who have contributed their efforts to help us issue this book.

November 1971
People's Army Publishing House

REMINISCENCES ON THE ARMY FOR NATIONAL SALVATION

World War broke out in September 1939. In Indochina, along with the issuance of the mobilization order, the French carried out a fascist policy,[1] did their utmost to terrorize the revolution, and implemented their wartime economic policy designed to suck up all the human and material resources to support their fascist war.

In the face of a changing situation, our Party directed all Party committees and cadres operating under legal and semilegal cover to withdraw into secrecy, sustain liaison with the population, and maintain their bases and forces in the urban areas, but at the same time to direct the focus of their activities to the countryside in order to transform it into a vast base area for the revolution.

In May 1940, the German fascists attacked France. Over a month later the French reactionary capitalists surrendered to the German fascists. Taking advantage of French defeat, the Japanese fascists entered Indochina, seizing for themselves the prey they had been coveting for a long time. On September 22, 1940 the Japanese fascists moved their troops to attack Lang Son, and at the same time they landed 6,000 troops in Do Son (near Haiphong). After a few engagements in the Vietnam-China border area, the cowardly French army fled. Decoux, the Governor General, hurriedly followed the example of his cohorts in France, knelt down in submission and offered Indochina to the Japanese.

From them on, the Vietnamese people came under the domination of two enemies, the French fascists and the Japanese fascists. Faced with this situation, the Vietnamese people had only one way open to them, and that was to rise up in struggle in order to save themselves.

The Bac Son-Vo Nhai region where the revolutionary movement had been in existence for a long time, was also terrorized. A number of Party members and non-Party member revolutionaries were arrested. But the Party infrastructure and revolutionary organizations survived and continued to expand.

When the Japanese troops attacked Lang Son, the French army retreated and fled through Binh Gia and Bac Son, toward Thai Nguyen. The enemy administrative network in the areas through which the French army fled was badly shaken: the That Khe district chief fled, the Na Sam district chief was captured by the people, the French representative in Binh Gia threw down his weapon and fled, abandoning his outpost. The people's revolutionary fervor was at a boiling point. Many people ambushed enemy troops to seize their weapons. A number of canton and village militia chiefs, militiamen, province troops and Vietnamese soldiers serving in the French regular army sided with the revolution. A

---

1. 1939 marked the end of the Popular Front government in France. During the Popular Front period, from 1936 to 1939, colonial rule in Indochina was somewhat relaxed and some degree of political freedom was permitted. After the collapse of the Popular Front, the colonial administration in Indochina embarked on a policy of repression and launched a "campaign of white terror." (Trans.)

number of Communist Party members, native of Bac Son-Vo Nhai, who had been imprisoned in the Lang Son jail since 1939--such as comrades Nong Thai Long, Vuong Van Ne (alias Thanh), Rue, Duong Van Thuc, Duong Van Tu, etc., escaped from jail. They met with the local comrades on the morning of September 27, 1940, to assess the situation, and together decided to launch an armed insurrection, set up a Command Staff to lead the insurrection, and appoint a committee in charge of the attack on the Mo Nhai post.

Right that night, over 600 people--including members of all the ethnic minorities, the Tay, Yao, Nung and Kinh[2]--from Huong Vu, Bac Son, Tam Hoa, Chieu Vu and Tran Yen villages, along with a number of canton and village militia chiefs, militiamen, and Vietnamese soldiers serving in the French army who had sided with the revolution, converged toward the meeting place. Besides sticks and spears, the insurrection forces had close to thirty rifles.

Exactly at 8:00 P.M., the insurrection forces split up into three prongs and advanced to attack the Mo Nhai post (that is to say, the seat of Bac Son District). The insurrection began. After ten minutes of intense fighting, the district chief and the soldiers in the post fled, and the insurrection forces seized the district seat.

At the news of this victory, all the ethnic minorities poured toward the Mo Nhai post, and formed a huge meeting. The comrade representing the Command Staff of the insurrection reported to the people the results of the first attack, and announced the dissolution of the imperialist government. Immediately, registers, papers, certificates and seals belonging to the enemy were burned in public. Everyone was filled with joy and cheered wildly.

On September 28 and 29, the insurrection forces carried out two consecutive ambushes in Canh Tiem and Sap Ri passes, destroyed over ten Frenchmen, including a captain, and seized a number of weapons.

The insurrection frightened both the French and the Japanese. Because of their reactionary nature, the French compromised with the Japanese fascists in order to have a free hand to suppress the Vietnamese revolution. The Japanese fascists, realizing that an immediate overthrow of the French was not to their advantage, reached a quick agreement with the French colonialists and used them as tools to suppress the insurrectionary forces.

The French colonialists dispatched troops to reoccupy the Binh Gia and Mo Nhai posts. The insurrectionary forces had to withdraw into the forest. White terror began.

Informed of the insurrection, the North Vietnam Region Party Committee sent comrade Tran Dang Ninh[3] to Bac Son to take direct command of the movement.

In the middle of October 1940, a Region Command Staff was set up with Tran Dang Ninh as leader. It put forth the slogan of fighting the

---

2. "Kinh" is a term used to refer to Vietnamese of the delta areas. (Trans.)

3. Tran Dang Ninh was a member of the North Vietnam Region Party Committee, and head of the Rear Supply Section during the Resistance, from 1948 to 1949. (Trans.)

French and driving out the Japanese, announced the dissolution of the local administration, confiscated certificates and seals, burned the registers of the local officials, formed a guerrilla unit, eliminated secret police gang leaders, made propaganda to explain Party policy to the people, and organized the masses to make them ready to deal with the enemy. Our guerrilla forces were rather large then, and took Don Uy, Bo Tat, Sa Khai, Nam Nhi and Vu Lang as their base areas.

The French colonialists concentrated about 100 militiamen and occupied the Vu Lang school, with the aim of spreading their terrorism. On October 25, 1940, the revolutionary forces divided into two spearheads and advanced to attack the Vu Lang school. In the face of the intimidating power of the revolutionary forces, the enemy soldiers fired a few shots in the air and then fled.

Three days later. . . . On October 28, 1940, the revolutionary masses organized a meeting in the Vu Lang schoolyard, and prepared to reoccupy the Mo Nhai post.

After regaining control over the majority of the militia and canton militia chiefs, the French colonialists used local secret policemen as guides to lead Bordier--the owner of the Dinh Ca plantation--and soldiers from the Mo Nhai post through a shortcut to attack our forces from the rear. The revolutionary masses dispersed into the jungle. The guerrilla unit dispersed in all directions.

The enemy marched into Vu Lang, shooting and killing the revolutionary masses, and burning down villages and settlements. They ordered the people "to atone for their sins" by cutting off the heads of the cadres and bringing these to them. The canton and village militia chiefs went through villages and settlements with bullhorns and demanded that the "Communists" surrender to the French.

In November 1940 the 7th Central Committee Plenum was held. The reality of the Bac Son uprising made our Party see clearly that, beneath two layers of repression and exploitation perpetrated by the French and Japanese, "a revolutionary high wave would certainly rise up, and the Party should get ready to assume the sacred mission of leading the oppressed people of Indochina to take armed and violent actions in order to regain their freedom and independence."[4] Even though our country "did not as yet find itself in the face of a situation in which direct revolution was feasible," in view of conditions prevailing in the world and in our country at this time, our country's revolution could break out with localized uprisings in areas where conditions permitted (such as Bac Son), which could then lead to a general insurrection to seize power in the entire country.

With regard to the question of spreading the impact of the Bac Son uprising, after listening to comrade Tran Dang Ninh's report, the Plenum passed a resolution to maintain the Bac Son armed forces, set up guerrilla units, carry out armed missions, and when necessary fight to protect the lives and property of the people, and expand the grass-root bases of the revolution, using the Bac Son-Vo Nhai area as the nucleus under the direct leadership of the Central Committee.

---

4. Party Documents (January 25, 1939—September 2, 1945), Su That, Hanoi, 1963, Section B: The Political Situation in Indochina. (Footnote in text.)

Under the care of the Central Committee, and after being reinforced with a number of cadres from the Bac Giang military training school and from the delta, the Bac Son guerrilla unit was reassembled. The Bac Son guerrilla command staff at this time included comrades Hoang Van Thu[5] (alias Van), Luong Van Chi[6] (alias Giao or Huy), and myself, with Thu in general charge. At first, the command staff was stationed in Don Uy (near Vu Lang), but later on it gradually withdrew to Vu Le and Khuoi Noi.

In this period, with the policy line of secret action and armed propaganda, the Bac Son guerrilla unit split up into cells to rebuild the Party infrastructure and reorganize the masses. Military training was spread to every village. It was at this point that the guerrilla command staff received instructions to prepare for a new mission.

---

5. Hoang Van Thu, a Tay, was born in 1906 in Diem He district, Lang Son province. He left school in 1926 and went to China to join the revolution. He lived in Kwangsi province, in southern China, where he earned his living as a metal worker. He took part in the Le Hong Phong training course in Lungchou and was admitted in the Indochinese Communist Party in 1930, after which he returned to the Viet Bac area and was instrumental in developing Party organization in several provinces in this zone--such as Cao Bang, Lang Son and Thai Nguyen. As the Secretary of the North Vietnam Region Party Committee and a member of the Party Central Committee, he was one of the key cadres who provided leadership to the Party during the difficult period of repression after the fall of the Popular Front in France. He was arrested by the French in 1943 near Hanoi, where he had been sent by the Central Committee to lead the movement in the capital following the arrest of Nguyen Khang, a member of the Standing Committee of the Hanoi Party Committee. He refused to provide information to the French, even after months of torture. The French executed him in May 1944. He is considered one of the heroes of the revolution, and commemorative services are held in his honor every year in the DRV. (Trans.)

6. Luong Huu Chi, a Tay, came from the same province as Hoang Van Thu. He was a close friend and an old classmate of Thu's in Lang Son, and left school to go to China with Thu. He studied at the Military Academy in China, and took part in revolutionary activities in Kwangsi. He was captured by the French in 1941, and died in jail of malaria. (Trans.)

TRIP MADE BY ICP CENTRAL COMMITTEE FROM VU NHAI TO ATTEND PAC BO CONFERENCE (MAY 1941) AND RETURN TRIP

LEGEND:
——▶ Trip to Pac Bo
---▶ Return Trip

SCALE: 1 Inch = 29.2 Miles

CHAPTER I

Since the conclusion of the 7th Party Central Committee Congress, the Central Committee had sent cadres abroad on many occasions to reestablish contact with the Communist International and with Party organs overseas. Going abroad was very difficult then. Once a comrade managed to reach Lungchou (China) and waited for two months without being able to meet liaison agents, and had to come back. It was difficult enough for one person to go, but to travel in groups was even more difficult.

At the beginning of 1941, we received the instruction to secure a route and to protect Central Committee members going on mission. It was only long afterward that I found out this was an extremely crucial mission: these comrades were on their way to attend the 8th Party Central Committee Congress convened by Uncle Ho.

In February 1941, comrades Truong Chinh[1] (alias Son), Hoang Van Thu (alias Van), Hoang Quoc Viet[2] (alias Chinh), and Tran Dang Ninh arrived in Vo Nhai. They stopped in my village to rest for a short time. After that they went to the Bac Son Guerrilla Command Staff Headquarters in Khuoi Noi to make further preparations.

It was in Khuoi Noi that Thu transmitted to us the decision of the Central Committee to change the name of the Bac Son guerrilla unit into

---

1. Following is a biographical sketch of Truong Chinh which appeared in *Vietnam Advances*, No. 3 (Hanoi, 1962), p. 23. "Truong Chinh, Chairman of the Standing Committee of the National Assembly of the Democratic Republic of Vietnam, was born in Nam Dinh in 1907. His revolutionary activities dated back to 1925-1926. In 1927 he joined the Revolutionary Youth League and took part in the founding of the Indochinese Communist Party. In 1930 he was arrested by the French colonialists and condemned to twelve years of detention. In 1936 following the victory of the Popular Front in France he was liberated. From 1936 to 1939 he worked for the founding and the consolidation of the Indochinese Democratic Front. From 1941 to 1951 he was Secretary General of the Indochinese Communist Party; from 1951 to 1956 Secretary General of the Vietnam Workers' Party, and from 1956 member of the Political Bureau of this Party. From 1958 to 1960 he was Vice-Premier and President of the State Scientific Research Committee of the Democratic Republic of Vietnam. He was elected deputy to the National Assembly in the May 1960 general elections and re-elected member of the Central Committee and the Political Bureau of the Vietnam Workers' Party at the Third Party Congress in September 1960." (Translator's Note: The name of the Party was changed from Indochinese Communist Party to Vietnam Workers' Party (Lao Dong) in 1951. Truong Chinh at present is still the Chairman of the Standing Committee of the National Assembly, and a member of the Politburo.)

2. Hoang Quoc Viet was born in 1905 in Bac Ninh province. He attended the Practical School of Industry in Haiphong in 1922, but was expelled in 1925 following a strike. He went to work in factories and mines, and joined the Thanh Nien Party in 1928. He was arrested in 1930 and sent to Con Son Island. He was released in 1936 during the Popular Front period in France. He became a member of the Indochinese Communist Party Central Committee in 1941. Since 1950 he has been President of the Vietnam General Confederation of Labor. (Trans.)

Army for National Salvation.[3] The Central Committee had held this intention since 1940. The insurrectionary forces had gone through a filtering process after months of hard and bitter struggle and now there was exactly one platoon left.

On February 14, 1941, the AFNS 1st Platoon was formally set up in a ceremony held in a clearing in Khuoi Noi, near a stream which ran through the jungle of Vu Le village, bordering on the two districts of Vo Nhai and Bac Son. In the afternoon, we assembled on the old platform of a house belonging to the two brothers Lo and Lieu. From Vo Nhai came Nong Thai Long,[4] Nhi Phung and myself (at that time I was assuming the name Ba). From Bac Son came Binh,[4] Quoc Vinh, Duong Van Thuc,[4] Duong Van Tu,[4] Hoang, Tan, Rue,[4] Van Sang, Hac Chap and Pho Sang. From the delta came Nguyen Cao Dam (alias Do), Binh Dac, But, Hoang Van Thai (alias An),[5] old Mr. Sinh (i.e., Manh, native of Thai Binh province), Luong Van Chi (alias Giao), etc. The entire platoon consisted of twenty-four men--cadres and Party members from the delta and mountain areas who had matured in the Bac Son insurrection and who had been active in the life and death struggle against the enemy.

The jungle stream gushed with joy in greeting to the revolutionaries from all places who gathered here. Thu attended the ceremony as the representative of the Central Committee.

Thu was a Tay from Lang Son province. He was skinny, but he was used to trekking through the mountain areas, and could climb hills and ford streams very well. He was a frequent visitor at my house. To me, he was like an elder brother--I was close to him, and at the same time I had a great respect and affection for him.

In a calm and deliberate manner, Thu stepped in front of the lined-up troops. In a clear voice, he said, "We are living in a situation in which we have lost our country and our homes have been destroyed. Our fatherland is reeling under the French and Japanese bandits. Even though the Bac Son uprising failed temporarily, it demonstrated our people's indomitable spirit which is rising and which nothing can crush. The insurrection has created a revolutionary armed force for our people. We must preserve and expand this precious capital. For this reason, the Central Committee has decided to form the Army for National Salvation. As members of this army, you should adhere to the tradition of the Bac Son Guerrillas, and bear hardships. You should maintain secrecy well."

On the mission of the AFNS, Thu pointed out clearly: "The AFNS should carry out armed missions. When necessary they should fight to resist repression, protect the lives and belongings of the people, expand the revolutionary base and build up guerrilla base areas. Your base areas will be the places where our comrades will come to study and train. As Bac Son is in an important location, you will also have the

---

3. Hereafter referred to as AFNS. (Trans.)

4. Nong Thai Long, Binh, Duong Van Thuc, Duong Van Tu, and Rue escaped from the Lang Son jail during the Japanese invasion of 1940 and led the Bac Son uprising. (Trans.)

5. Hoang Van Thai is now a Lieutenant General and the Deputy Chief of the Joint General Staff of the People's Army of the DRV. (Trans.)

task of providing security for the Party cadres passing through this area."

After passing on to us the instructions of the Central Committee, Thu handed us a beautiful flag with a yellow star and fringes--a gift from the women of Hanoi. After that Luong Van Chi read the five pledges[6] of the AFNS. Then in the name of all the brothers, I promised "to carry out the tasks assigned to us by the Party. . . . The AFNS will not be deterred by hardships and difficulties, nor will we be afraid to lay down our lives. We are determined to build and expand the movement."

After the ceremony, Thu and I returned to the headquarters. On the way, Thu told me I had been appointed to the North Vietnam Region Party Committee, and said that the Central Committee members this time would go on to attend the 8th Party Congress and that we had been assigned the task of providing security for the delegation on their way to the conference.

I was as familiar with the roads in this section of the country as I was with the lines on the palms of my hands. My work as a surveyor and a lumberjack to deceive the local security police had led me into the deepest jungles and the most isolated paths. Comrade Tai, a local cadre, and comrade Lam, a native of Lang Son province and a member of the AFNS, were also chosen for this task. They were the "earth gods" (*thổ công*)[7] of the areas the Central Committee comrades would go through.

It was a great honor for the men chosen for this special mission. We were both happy and worried--we were happy that we had been assigned the first task directly given to the AFNS by the Central Committee: to provide security for the Central Committee on their way to attend a congress which was crucial to the fate of the entire country. We were worried because we knew that the journey would be fraught with difficulties and dangers. We would have to climb hills, cross streams, pass many enemy posts at a time when they were spreading thousands of troops and security policemen to surround us. At all costs we must provide security for the Central Committee comrades!

I promised Thu, "We are determined to protect the Central Committee and ensure their safety going to and returning from the conference."

Lowering his voice, Thu said, "On this trip we might meet the International representative."

I detected intense feelings and a great confidence in these words of his. I thought of the forthcoming journey with excitement. "But how about my work back here? My work in the unit, especially since it has just been formed?"

---

6. The five pledges were: (a) we will not betray the Party, (b) we will remain absolutely loyal to the Party, (c) we are determined to struggle and revenge our comrades who have sacrificed their lives, (d) we will not surrender to the enemy, (e) we will not harm the people. (Footnote in text.)

7. *Thổ công* or "God of the Soil" is used to refer to someone who is very familiar with the terrain of an area (like the *thổ công* who knows every square inch of the earth under his control). (Trans.)

As if he could guess my concern, Thu said right away, "The Central Committee has appointed Chi to stay behind and take charge. He has the mission of keeping the road from Bac Son to Dinh Ca open, and training the AFNS. I have talked with Chi."

Chi--whom we usually called Giao--had operated with Thu abroad. He had studied at the Military Academy in China. He had helped us along and given us guidance in military and political matters. This was why we called him Giao ("Teacher"). He was a Tay, with hooded eyes and an aqualine nose. He was of small stature and looked every inch a "scholar." However, his movements were quick and energetic and very military.

Absorbed in our thoughts and talk, before we knew we had reached the headquarters. In the headquarters, the brothers were weaving baskets in preparation for the journey.

* * *

There were nine men in the group: the four Central Committee comrades, Truong Chinh, Hoang Van Thu, Hoang Quoc Viet and Tran Dang Ninh whom we usually referred to as "the brother with the big head"; a representative from the Central Vietnam Region Party Committee (comrade San); a representative from the South Vietnam Region Party Committee (comrade Thao); and to guide and protect the delegation: comrade Tai, a local cadre; comrade Lam, an AFNS soldier; and myself.

Our baggage consisted of a few baskets containing clothes with secret documents hidden inside. Our food consisted of a few pecks of dry roasted glutinous rice. My weapon was a special type of rifle: a Dop rifle with the butt removed, with only the trigger mechanism and the barrel in place, and a clip of five bullets. I took along two handkerchiefs to wrap around my hand when I fired in order to insulate it from the scorching barrel. During the day, the rifles and bullets were hidden in a wool blanket wound around the carrying poles of the baskets. Sometimes we would move in secret; other times we would move openly, disguised as traders, going toward That Khe and then on to the border at night.

We started our journey in the late afternoon, a few days after the ceremony setting up the AFNS. We crossed the Van Ha forest. When it was pitch dark, we passed through the Loong settlement, followed the mountain path full of sharp and pointed rocks, went through the Phie Khao settlement and reached Bo Tat, a hamlet at the entrance to Vu Lang village, which lay in an area where we had an infrastructure (cơ sở). The group stopped to rest for a few days here, to reconnoiter the road and to find out more about the existing situation. From here on was an area where we had not set up any revolutionary infrastructure and where enemy soldiers carried out frequent patrols. We must move very fast, and within one day and night go from Bo Tat to the bank of the Van Mich river. This leg of the trip was long, and we would have to cross several kilometers of the main road linking Bac Son with Binh Gia. We would also have to go through the villages of Ban Que, Ban Sao, Van Thuy and Rang Mong, swarming with enemy agents searching every nook and cranny.

From Bo Tat we went to Na Tou, crossed Lung Chon, and stopped to rest at the edge of the forest. We waited for it to get pitch dark before we proceeded to Ban Que, and then crossed a section of the highway, and turned onto the route leading to Ban Sao and Van Thuy. We were all elated for having successfully made it through a dangerous leg of our journey. But we were all tired. Ninh, who was normally weak physically, began to develop a fever.

That night, it was pitch dark. Comrade Tai went ahead to find the path, the rest of us followed closely behind, the man walking behind grasping the shirt of the one in front. The comrades from the delta were unfamiliar with forest paths and stumbled and fell often. At each crossroad, I had to run ahead to check, and then run back; I waited for all of them to pass by and then followed behind.

We had to cross Rang Mong; this was the most dangerous part of our trip. There was only one single path which ran through the settlement, and on both sides rose steep rocky mountains. There were many reactionary officials in this village. If we were detected here, there would be no way out for us. We had to sleep on a high mountain peak on the way to Rang Mong, in order to cross this dangerous section the next day.

The next day, just as we were about to make it through Rang Mong, we heard cocks crowing. My heart skipped a beat: it was almost daylight. Comrade Tai who appeared as nervous as I, said in his quickened breathing: "Hurry up, comrades! If it becomes light, we'll have a difficult time!"

Ninh was then as hot as a glowing charcoal. He was in fever, a terrible fever, but he held on to the man walking in front of him. Hoang Quoc Viet's feet were sore, and he limped along with great difficulty. But knowing that each minute we made haste meant a minute less of danger, we focused all our strength on our feet and tried to walk as fast as we could, with our eyes open wide to check on all four sides. An hour later, we passed through Rang Mong!

In the early morning, we went to the forest to change our clothes because they had become filthy after a night on the slippery paths and the steep slopes. We resumed our march immediately thereafter. There were isolated settlements on the way, and we met many people going back and forth. We split into two separate groups. Thu, Lam, Tai and myself pretended to discuss trading problems in the local dialect. The other comrades, especially the two from Central and South Vietnam, had no choice but to remain as quiet as grains of paddy (*im như hạt thóc*). This was a Nung area. Normally, if one spoke the Vietnamese dialect, this would be a dead giveaway. But to speak Vietnamese with a Central Vietnamese accent would be even more of a giveaway.

That evening, we reached Pac Cap, the congruence of three branches of the Van Mich river. Our group went to the house of two Nung peasants who knew comrade Tai. This family cheerfully arranged a place for us to sleep, and then helped us to prepare food. Ninh who was already ill and had had to walk all day and all night in the mountain and forest, exposed to the wind and fog, was in a high fever and could not eat. We were all worried; we still had a long way to go and we feared that Ninh's illness would worsen.

Tai went out to reconnoiter the road and met some villagers who told him that the canton militia chief frequently searched the road from Pac Cap to Po Co. This meant we could not take the land route. The Central Committee comrades decided to go by river to avoid danger. From here on, we would have to go by raft along the Van Mich River to the Ban Trai bridge in That Khe. It was better to go by river because there were fewer enemy posts and fewer villages to go through. It was less dangerous than the land route. Comrade Tai was very familiar with the river and knew every rock, every cataract in its course. In the evening we found four small rafts, each made of a few bamboo trunks. We tied the four rafts into two larger ones--one to carry four of us, and the other five. Comrade Tai cut down a few bamboos and arranged them into a platform on one of the rafts so Ninh could lie down without getting wet.

At dusk, we boarded the rafts. A new problem cropped up: who was going to pilot the rafts? Only Tai knew how to do this well. I was not very familiar with this. We talked it over for a while, and then decided on the following division of labor: on the first raft, comrade Tai would pilot the raft, while comrade Lam stood at the rear; on the second raft, I would pilot while Thu stood at the rear. I would both pilot and provide security. The others would not be able to replace us.

Having acquired a great deal of experience on the river, comrade Tai told us, "If the raft overturns, just cling to it, don't let go of it and try to swim. If you let go of the raft, the current will carry you away."

The Van Mich river had many rocks, many cataracts and falls in its meandering course. The two rafts moved in the night, bobbing and pitching. Each time the rafts bumped into the mountain slope, the people aboard were thrown back and forth, and lost their balance. Negotiating each cataract was a challenge. The torrent gushed swiftly along. The shimmering water reflected the night sky. The two rafts were like two leaves floating on the river. My raft followed in the wake of Tai's raft. As I navigated the raft, my hands and feet were in constant motion, and I opened my eyes wide to peer in front of me. I saw the skill with which Tai navigated his raft and negotiated each wave. Normally his small and slightly stocky body did not look very striking, but now he looked very steady and in full control, his legs flexed and straightened up again with the bobbing waves. Each time we approached a cataract, he signalled to us. Many comrades had to bend very low and cling to the bamboo pole. The current rushed along, the raft plunged into the water and then reared up again. The water swirled and gushed.

We continued in this way, and at midnight arrived at a landing place a few hundred meters from the Van Mich post. To avoid the post, we disembarked and went on foot through a small village, past the main road, crossed the mountain and then turned toward Hat Quang. Comrade Tai meanwhile piled one raft on top of the other, and transported Ninh by the water route to Hat Quang to wait for us.

The twisting road was only over one kilometer long, but it caused us a lot of trouble. It was midnight then and none of us was familiar with the road. We groped along, trying to follow the instructions Tai had given us. When we were close to the village, we held our breath and slipped past. About an hour later we reached Hat Quang. As we edged our way down the narrow river bank, we saw Tai waiting for us. We were overjoyed and asked as we stepped aboard the raft, "Has Viet got here already?" We were usually very concerned about Hoang Quoc Viet because his eyesight was bad, he limped and his health was not good.[8] We rechecked our group and discovered that Viet was missing.

---

8. These resulted from mistreatment during imprisonment by the French. (Trans.)

We were scared. It was so quiet I could hear my heart beat madly. The comrades selected Lam and me to go and find him.

We searched for a long time, checking one bush after another without finding him. We returned to the raft to report. Everyone was disappointed. We looked at each other. Our throats constricted and we were close to tears. One comrade said, "If we wait here till morning we will be seen, and our great mission will be ruined. Perhaps we have no choice but to. . . ."

However, the Central Committee members decided to let me go and look once more. Thu reminded me, "Try and find him no matter how dangerous it is!"

I considered that an order. Besides, there was a strong bond of affection between us revolutionaries, and also Viet's devotion and assistance to the Bac Son movement had given me strength and clarity of mind. I remembered all this very well. Hoang Quoc Viet came to us when the skies and mountains of Bac Son were still cloaked in gloom. He came from the delta, but wherever he went--whether it was a Tay, or a Nung, or a Yao area--he managed to maintain a firm foothold in these mountain and jungle regions which seemed so full of insurmountable difficulties. He was even more successful than we in proselytizing the ethnic minorities in these remote places. When the movement in Dinh Ca was strongly pushed forward, he went with us to Trang Xa, and then down to Dai Tu and La Bang to set up our infrastructure.

I turned into the twisting path and groped my way back to the landing place where we had disembarked earlier. When I reached a three-way intersection leading to the village, I lay down and put my ear to the ground: I could hear a dog barking. Guessing that someone was near the village fence, I crawled toward it. When I was about fifty steps from the fence, I could see a shadow in the thicket; I clucked my tongue as a signal. The other answered in the same manner. That was him! That was one of us!

I was overwhelmed with joy. I crawled quickly forward, grabbed his arm affectionately and said softly, "Well, brother Viet! The other comrades have been waiting for you till their eyes are about to fall out from the straining and peering!"

Then, in order to gain time and to make sure he would not get lost again, I lifted him on my back and said, "Let us hurry! They're waiting for us." I carried him and ran all the way to the raft.

The others were impatiently waiting for us. Seeing me and Viet, they became animated. Some comrades forgot the enemy was nearby and clapped their hands and cheered. The sound reverberated and was carried very far. Someone hushed them and reminded us all to maintain secrecy.

Comrade Tai hurried us onto the rafts. The others did not have time to ask any further questions, and pushed off in great haste in order to pass through the area surrounding the Van Mich post before daylight.

We spent the whole next day on the rafts. We were all exhausted, especially the navigators who had to row all day, all night, without a moment of rest. Even though we were tired and worried, we had great fun. Each time we reached a deserted stretch of water, comrade Truong Chinh asked us to sing--if we knew any revolutionary songs--or to tell stories. Thu related many exciting stories about the Long March and the battles the Chinese Liberation Army had fought against the Japanese. The two comrades from South and Central Vietnam sang revolutionary songs. I also sang some ethnic minority songs. Ninh was still in a high fever and kept asking for water. Once in a while when we asked, he would answer in his feverish breathing, "I can still make it, let's go on!" or "I'm very tired but I can go on." I was very moved by his words. He was fighting an unfortunate and terrible illness. He too had contributed a great deal of effort to the Bac Son movement. He had helped to rebuild it and to set up a strong and solid guerrilla base. When Bac Son went through a difficult period, the Party sent him up to guide and help us, and he had actively participated in the organization and formation of the Bac Son Guerrilla Unit.

That evening we docked and went to a house on the edge of the river to fix dinner. The couple who owned the house were very kind and did their best to help us. We reembarked right after supper in order to reach Ban Trai at midnight. A few kilometers past Ban Trai was the shortcut to the frontier.

When we were near the Ban Trai ferry landing, it suddenly turned windy and rained very hard. The rafts were hurtling along between two sheets of icy water. At times the strong wind seemed to want to lift the rafts from the river and hurl them far away. We clung tightly to the rafts as the sky and river dumped frightening volumes of water over our heads. The weaker comrades shook with cold.

When our rafts docked on the right bank of Ban Trai, Ninh was unconscious and did not respond to our calls. His hands and feet were icy. Knowing that he could not go on, the Central Committee comrades decided to send him back. We told comrade Tai to carry Ninh to a nearby hut--the local people sometimes stayed in the hut to watch over their patch of corn--and try to revive him, and then find a way to take him back to the delta. We left the rafts to go on foot. From here to the border, both Lam and Thu were familiar with the route.

It was raining and windy. When we had to say goodbye to Ninh we all wept. Tears welled up in our eyes. I felt sorry for him and worried that he might not survive. He had made it through so many dangerous legs of our journey only to have to turn back now.

Comrade Tai put Ninh on the raft and ferried him to the left bank. We watched the river and the frail raft in the rain and wind, and our hearts felt heavy. However, we had great confidence in the nautical skill of Tai. The raft docked. We followed each of his movements. He gently lifted Ninh on his back and carried him to the corn patch.

We only resumed our journey after comrade Tai had disappeared from view. (A few months later, when we returned to Vo Nhai and asked about Ninh, the comrades there told us that thanks to Tai's devotion and the villagers' care, Ninh recovered from his illness and came to Vo Nhai on several occasions to look for the Central Committee.)

About three kilometers from Ban Trai was the route leading to the border. We went past the Pac Cam militia post and arrived in Kim Ly,

Na Khau and Na Ke--Thu's old base of operation[9]--at around 3 o'clock in the morning. When we reached Na Cai, we would be about 10 kilometers from the China-Vietnam border. The owner of the house we went to was overjoyed when he saw Thu and found out that we were Party cadres. He asked us about all sorts of things. He offered us water and then opened a can of honey for us to eat to regain our energy. Knowing that this was a safe place, the Central Committee comrades took out their documents soaked with rain water and dried them near the fire. They talked with the head of the household while they dried their papers. Some comrades were so exhausted they did not bother to change their clothes, and lay down and went to sleep.

We resumed our journey the next night. We turned into Kim Ly village, a solid revolutionary base area, for a visit. The majority of the people here were Nung and Tay. At the sight of comrade Thu and us, they all flocked to see us. Every family wanted comrade Thu to stay with them for a few days. When they found out we had to leave right away for an urgent mission, they reluctantly let us go and wished us good luck. The meeting with the people there moved us and infused us with energy and enthusiasm.

From here onward, the route took us through mountains, but to us the obstacles were insignificant.

The night was far advanced and it was very dark. Grassy hills interspersed with mountains in an unbroken line. When it was past midnight, we reached a high mountain peak, on which was a stone slab indicating the border between Vietnam and China. So, after four days and four nights of continuous travelling, after many worries and hardships, we had completed the most dangerous part of our trip. We all felt elated; we talked with animation and laughed loudly.

We arrived in Ban Khiec, a Chinese village next to the border. The peasants there treated us with affection. When they saw Ly (another alias of Hoang Van Thu) and us coming, they welcomed us warmly and asked for news about the Vietnamese revolution, talking noisily and excitedly. They decided to slaughter a horse to treat us. When the brothers said they did not want to see the people waste so much food on them, the villagers said, "We'll eat most of it anyway, and the amount you'll be able to put down is so insignificant that you needn't worry!"

The people in this area had a special sympathy and affection for Thu. Anyone who came in contact with him loved him. He took charge of all liaison with the local cadres and managed to obtain passes for us to go to Lungchou.

After a few days' rest in Ban Khiec, we resumed our trip. When we arrived in Lungchou, we contacted the local comrades and asked for passes to go to Chinghsi. We were on the road for five long days. On the way, a few things struck me about China. First, the life of the Chinese people was miserable and the situation was very complicated. Wherever we went we heard the people curse the oppression and exploitation of the Kuomintang, and long for the Communist Party like parched land longing for rain. Second, the revolutionary spirit of the Chinese

---

9. Hoang Van Thu was active on both sides of the border among the minorities in the 1920's and 1930's. (Trans.)

people was intense. Wherever we went, we met ardent sympathizers of the revolution. The people in the border region understood quite a bit about the situation of the Vietnamese revolution. They loved us and helped us to the utmost of their ability.

In Chinghsi, we learned that the site of the Congress was not in China, but in Pac Bo settlement in Ha Quang (Cao Bang province). We went south from Chinghsi. After two days on the road we arrived at Liutung (Duong Lau) and again reached the China-Vietnam border marker.

* * *

The wind blew strongly and continuously.

From on high, we looked down toward Pac Bo and saw a few people on the Vietnam side of the border. Being familiar with guerrilla activities, we immediately guessed that those men were guerrillas standing guard to provide security. We were right. Le Quang Ba[10] (alias Le) and Hoang Sam[11] (alias Son Hung) ran toward us, greeted us with joy and led us to an opening in the mountain. Phung Chi Kien, Vu Anh[12] and Dang Van Cap[13] were waiting for us. They all smiled happily when they saw us. Then we all clambered onto terraced ricefields and walked away from the opening in the mountain. Halfway up we saw a tall and gaunt old man, with a sparse black goatee and a nimble gait. When we reached him, he cheerfully shook hands with all of us and asked about our health and our trip. When we told him about Tran Dang Ninh, his face clouded with sadness and worry. He asked us for more details, and told us to be sure to inquire how Ninh was doing on our way back. At that time, I did not know what the old man was doing. He was advanced in age but he was still very alert and nimble, and full of concern for everyone. I did not dare to ask, and it did not even cross my mind that he was the representative of the International. But the image of the "Old Leader" was engraved in my mind from that moment on. The old man guided us as he walked on. He led the Central Committee comrades to an opening in the mountain--there was a flat rock we could sit on--past a hammock and then into the cave. The living quarters were located about a hundred meters from the ricefield embankments.

---

10. Le Quang Ba, a Tay from Cao Bang province, was born in a family of peasants. He first became interested in Communism in 1926-27 and joined the Indochinese Communist Party in 1932. He was a member of the first Party cell in Ha Quang district. He went to southern China and met Ho Chi Minh there in 1940, and returned with Ho to Vietnam in 1941. Along with Vo Nguyen Giap he organized the first unit of the Vietnam Propaganda and Liberation Army. After the August Revolution, he became the Commander-in-Chief of the Hanoi Capital Armed Forces. He was the commander of the 316th Division in Dien Bien Phu. He is now a member of the Central Committee and Chairman of the Committee of Ethnic Minorities. (Trans.)

11. Hoang Sam, a Vietnamese born in Thailand, was sent to Cao Bang by the Party following his expulsion from Thailand for engaging in revolutionary activities. He was fluent in Tay and Nung dialects. He became the Deputy Chairman of the Haiphong Administrative Committee in 1955, and is currently Secretary of the III Region Party Committee and Commander of the III Region. (Trans.)

12. Vu Anh became Deputy Minister for Heavy Industries in August 1965. (Trans.)

13. Dang Van Cap is the President of the Vietnam Oriental Medicine Association. (Trans.)

The old man invited us to sit down and said, "Let's rest and relax for a while. You comrades have just come from far away, you must be very tired."

However, the Central Committee comrades had already pulled out their pens and papers, and were ready to plunge into work.

Ceremony setting up the Army for National Salvation in September 1941. (First man on the left is Chu Van Tan.)

A meeting of the Army for National Salvation directed by Chu Van Tan (standing with hand pointing).

CHAPTER II

It seemed we had just arrived in Pac Bo a short while ago, and yet it was already time to leave!

I was instructed to take the Central Committee members, along with weapons and ammunition back to the Bac Son War Zone.

When we arrived in Pac Bo I was still inexperienced, but now on my return, I felt stronger, like a bird which had acquired more feathers and more wings and which--given new strength--could now soar very high. I felt very happy for having had the chance of meeting comrade Nguyen Ai Quoc, the Party leader, the man whom I had admired and longed to meet, and in whom I had placed so much faith.

When we came to Pac Bo we had only a Dop 5 rifle with the butt removed to make it easier to carry, but now on our return we had pistols, rifles and hand grenades. In addition, we had priceless documents, among which was the 8th Resolution of the Central Committee.

When we left Vo Nhai, only three of us were from the AFNS, but on our return we had with us many cadres who had been assigned to our ranks as reinforcements. Among them was Phung Chi Kien, a Central Committee member. He was still young, but his talent was precocious. I met him near the mountain opening the first day we arrived. In the days that followed, I saw him again during the training sessions. Listening to his stories, I was full of admiration and affection for him. Bit by bit I learned that Phung Chi Kien was from Dien Chau, Nghe An province, and had spent over ten years abroad. He joined the "Resistance Reserve Youth Force Association" which was an organization set up by the Party overseas to assemble all patriotic youths. He had spent some time in the San Dau guerrilla base, and then studied at the Red Army University in the Soviet regions (of China). He was skilled in military matters, and spoke good Chinese. In 1939, when he was still in China, he held the position of Company Commander in the Chinese Red Army. The picture of him as a young commander in a Chinese Communist guerrilla base gave me even greater confidence.

Having Phung Chi Kien assigned to Bac Son, to the AFNS, was an honor and I felt grateful to the Party Central Committee and to the old man Thu Son for their great concern for this war zone.[1] I was moved when I thought of the Old Man.[2]

All the past events, all the memories concerning the old man Thu Son--the man with the kind and bright eyes, with the sparse goatee, and the nimble gait--appeared before my eyes.

---

1. "Ông cụ Thu Sơn," or "Già Thu" (Old Man Thu Son, or Old Thu) was Ho Chi Minh. (Trans.)

2. Ông Cụ, "Old Man," means an old and venerable man. Here it is used as a mark of affection and respect. (Trans.)

During the entire time the Central Committee members held their meeting, the other North Vietnam Region Party Committee members and I attended a course of Marxism-Leninism arranged by the Old Man. My level of understanding was still low, but I concentrated on the documents and tried to understand what they said. I was happy and at the same time moved to be near the Old Man. He told us many things about countries from Asia to Europe. I suddenly remembered what my classmates used to tell each other when we were still in school: "A few revolutionaries from our country had gone abroad." I wanted to ask [whether the Old Man was one of these revolutionaries] but remembering Hoang Quoc Viet's injunction about maintaining secrecy, I felt I should not be too curious.

Outside study hours, the Old Man frequently came to see me and find things for me to do, or asked minutely about the Bac Son-Vo Nhai movement. Once, he came over and asked softly, "Can you write?"

"Yes."

"Then bring some paper and a pen over here. From what you've told me about Bac Son, I'll read a poem and you can write it down."

I wrote down the poem and took it back to Bac Son. Unfortunately, it became lost. Now I can only remember that in general the Old Man praised the revolutionary movement there.

It was not once but many times that he called me over to give me advice in general and in particular about Bac Son. He talked about the international revolutionary movement to encourage me, making me realize and giving me great confidence in the strength of the revolution in our country and in the world, the greatness of the Russian Revolution and the expanding strength of the anti-Japanese war zones of the Chinese Communists.

One day, I went to the cave opening, found a rock and sat down to read a book. With my back leaning against a tree, I tried to think but could not keep my eyes open and almost dozed off. Suddenly I heard a noise; the Old Man was approaching. He said, "Well, make an effort. You've just sat down to study, and yet you're about to go to sleep."

I woke up with a start. When I looked around, I saw only the back of the blue shirt he was wearing. After he reminded me, he immediately went back to work. His appearance, his gestures and words plunged me deep in thought. He was busy with the conference, and yet he paid attention to me sitting near the cave. He was solicitous to me, but did he extend his solicitude to all the others, I wondered? When I asked, the comrades in the group all told me that he frequently came to them and urged them to study. He said only these few words softly to me, but I was so engrossed thinking about them that I became wide awake. I told myself that he had a lot more to do and was more tired than I, yet he constantly took care of me, therefore I must do my best to be worthy of his love and concern.

Living near him every day made me feel contented and relaxed. In addition, the Old Man told us many stories which enriched our knowledge. I noticed that he had a wide and profound knowledge. I told myself I was lucky to be able to come here to study. Giao and the other brothers in the AFNS who stayed behind in Bac Son did not have my chance, therefore I should study well so that when I returned I could tell them all the things that the Old Man had taught me and advised me.

During our night-time activities, sometimes the Old Man told us about his past activities. He told each story in a few sentences, and did not talk very long. He assigned comrade Phung Chi Kien to tell us about his participation in the 8th Route Army (in China), in the Long March, and in the victorious battles against the Japanese in China. Anyone who had an interesting or exciting story could talk about it. I talked about the fighting in Bac Son.

Each time I went with comrade Le Quang Ba to visit the villages in Pac Bo, I asked him about the Old Man. Ba revealed that the Old Man was Nguyen Ai Quoc himself. This made me respect the Old Man even more, and I was confident that the revolution was close to victory.

One day, reconnaissance agents informed us that the French in Soc Giang post were leading troops into our area on patrol. A few comrades picked up their rifles and left. The Central Committee comrades divided up the documents to take along. After we left our quarters, we walked away from the mountain cave. The Old Man told us, "There is a three-way intersection on the top of the mountain, one of the paths lead to China. Once we get there, there is nothing the French can do to us."

I had not expected him to be so familiar with the geography and topography of this area.

He carried only his typewriter and gave the rifle and documents to us. I said, "Please keep the documents and give me the typewriter."

He replied, "Just keep the documents and rifle, and let me carry the typewriter."

I was happy [that he had so much confidence in me], but at the same time I was a bit perplexed. "I am young, so it is natural for me to carry the rifle, but how come he gave me such important documents to carry? He must trust me a lot! But why is it he only kept the typewriter?" I wondered.

He and his typewriter were inseparable. When I was near him, I rarely saw him use a pen. He had a stack of white typing paper next to him, and he just sat and typed day after day. I never saw him write a draft in longhand. I only saw him type, reread what he had typed, and then type again.

He was a disciplined man, and followed a fixed schedule of eating, sleeping and working, doing everything in its own time, and he deviated from this schedule only if the situation became tense. If he said he would do something, he set about doing it right away. If he reminded one of us to do something, he immediately proceeded to show him how to go about doing it.

The house on stilts was as small as a hut made of bamboo in the jungle. In front of the house was a Hoa Ma tree in bloom, full of yellow blossoms. Every morning he woke us up to do exercises. The Central Committee comrades and he went to the terraced ricefields. The Old Man did T'ai-chi exercises beautifully. I loved T'ai-chi, so I watched him and then went into the jungle to practice in secret. He took such good care of his body, no wonder he was in good health and remained alert and nimble. I noticed that he could squat in the fashion of the local people for a long time. When he climbed mountains, he stepped along briskly. I was busy with my studies, and rarely had the occasion to go mountain climbing with him. One afternoon, we went with him to visit a cave. It was a day of the fourth Lunar month, and the Hoa Ma trees were in full radiant bloom with clumps of yellow flowers. The forest and mountain resounded with the songs of nightingales and blackbirds. It was sunny and warm, the warmth of Spring turning into Summer. Uncle Ho[3] and we walked along; on one side of the trail rose non-rocky hills and on the other side rocky mountains. In the distance a waterfall flung its water in the air, like a spray of white blossoms. The Old Man leaned on his stick. He went to visit the forest and then the cave, and even went into areas that the local people were afraid to penetrate. Once in a white he turned around and reminded us to stay close to each other in order not to get lost. As we followed him, each time we passed an area with a strategic topography, he would point out to us how we could deploy and fight the enemy there.

When we were deep in the cave, he said, "The people here are still superstitious, and they don't dare to go in here because they are afraid of ghosts and wild beasts. But we are Communists and we don't believe in ghosts and spirits. There is nothing but cold air in this deep cave."

He was interested in educating us whenever and wherever he could. He never wasted a moment. If he was not talking with the Central Committee comrades or with us, he would go to visit the security unit or the people. He educated the local youths carefully. When you looked around, the scene seemed innocuous enough; small boys grazing buffaloes, and young boys and girls singing love songs--but in actuality they were at that very moment gathering information for the revolution, and protecting the headquarters. They were the eyes and ears of the revolution. The Old Man frequently told us: "One cannot carry out a revolution by oneself. We need a lot of people, we need the whole nation. If we want to have the support of all the people, the cadres everywhere should do their best to win the people over, propagandize, educate and encourage the people." He also reminded me in private, "The ethnic minorities are alike wherever they live. Once they have put their trust in someone they remain loyal to the end. You come from an ethnic minority, and it must be easy for you to understand the minorities, but you must always be careful in your work."

These teachings were illuminating to me. I thought of the brothers in the AFNS back home, and I told myself, "When I get back I'll have to tell them everything in detail."

I engraved in my mind everything he taught me, and I felt that spending a day with him was like spending years studying. Before I met him I knew my level of understanding was low and was very concerned. I wondered how much responsibility I could take on. I was not afraid at all to sacrifice my life, but I believed that if I was given a position of leadership I would not be able to take charge. After I met him, I had confidence in myself and felt I could perform any task the Party assigned to me.

---

3. Hoang Quoc Viet mentioned that at the start of this conference in Pac Bo, "At first, all of us called Uncle Ho comrade, then Cụ (venerable old man), but later Truong Chinh and Hoang Van Thu used the appellation "Uncle." We found this word suitable to our feelings, and since then, we addressed our leader by the affectionate appellation that we are using now." "Our People, a Very Heroic People," in *A Heroic People, Memoirs from the Revolution* (Hanoi: Foreign Languages Publishing House, 1965). (Trans.)

We were all eager to hear him talk, not only about his own personal experience, but also about the situation in the world.

During the time the Central Committee held their congress, I studied documents, including the latest one--that is to say, the Central Committee Resolution No. 8 and the Viet Minh Program. While the Central Committee met, we studied--and this went on until the congress ended. I heard that after reviewing the insurrection in Bac Son and in the South,[4] and the insurrection of troops stationed in Do Luong,[5] the congress gave the following assessment: "In spite of the fierce French repression, our people refused to retreat. The insurrections have had a widespread and profound impact in the whole country. These insurrections were the opening shots, signalling the beginning of the national insurrection. They were the first steps of the Indochinese people's armed struggle." The congress pointed out that "we must build up many guerrilla units and bases. When conditions permit, we would launch guerrilla warfare, but we must maintain armed propaganda units and build up our infrastructure." The conference affirmed:

> The French colonialists and the Japanese fascists will die. The Indochinese Revolution will end with an armed insurrection. In order to launch this armed insurrection, we must focus on the following factors:
>
> 1. The national unity achieved by the National Salvation Front.
>
> 2. The people can no longer bear living under the yoke of the French and Japanese, and they are ready to make sacrifices in order to move toward insurrection.
>
> 3. The ruling cliques in Indochina have reached a crisis of all-encompassing proportion, from the economic as well as political and military points of view.
>
> 4. The objective factors favorable to the insurrection in Indochina would be: the Chinese Army defeats the Japanese troops; Revolution breaks out in France or Japan; the democratic bloc achieves victory in the Pacific; the Soviet Union achieves victory; revolution breaks out in French colonies; turmoil breaks out in Japan; and in particular, Chinese or English-American troops enter Indochina. With respect to the National Salvation Front, even though our Party has succeeded in mobilizing many struggles, even though insurrections have broken out in Bac Son, in the South and at Do Luong, and even though the Bac Son troops are still active, the forces in the entire country have not been unified. In order to have a national force capable of launching and consolidating an insurrection, our Party must:

---

4. The insurrection in the South (Nam Kỳ Khởi Nghĩa) took place in November 1940 in the provinces of Gia Dinh, Cho Lon, Tan An, My Tho, Can Tho, Vinh Long, Soc Trang and Bac Lieu, under the direction of the South Vietnam Region Party Committee (Xu Uy Nam Ky). This insurrection triggered an exceptionally savage repression by the French colonial authorities which decimated Party organizations in the South. Rebel areas were bombed, thousands of people were arrested, over 100 cadres were executed and countless others were sent to Con Son Island. (Trans.)

5. This mutiny of Vietnamese troops serving in the colonial army occurred on 13 January 1941 in Do Luong, Nghe An province, Central Vietnam. (Trans.)

(a) Expand and consolidate existing National Salvation organizations, instilling in them a spirit of struggle and sacrifice and making them ready to launch the insurrection.

(b) Expand the organizations into the provinces where the movement is still weak and into ethnic minorities regions.

(c) Train the cadres to make them determined and ready to make sacrifices.

(e) Train the cadres to make them capable and experienced to lead and cope with all changes in the situation.

(g) Organize small guerrilla cells and guerrilla units operating regularly. We must proselytize enemy soldiers. At present, although our Party forces have not spread vigorously to every area of the country, time and space will work in our favor.[6]

The Old Man and the Central Committee guided us to study on the spot, so that we could understand the task of fighting the French and Japanese and saving our country. Our minds became clearer and clearer as we progressed in our studies. All the things we had longed to comprehend were explained to us in detail. It was gratifying, like rain after a severe drought. All these things illuminated the way for the Bac Son movement and for me in my activities in the years that followed.

Before we left, the Old Man called the North Vietnam Region Party Committee comrades over, and had separate instructions for each one of them. He typed the resolution in several copies and gave them to the Central Committee comrades. He said, "You take this one, and this one will serve as a report to the International." Then he handed documents to each one, and they accepted their documents with happiness.

We gathered our squad, distributed weapons and ammunition, reviewed our password, repeated the slogan, "carry your weapons at the ready, but do not shoot indiscriminately," and got ready to get on the road. The brothers going to Bac Son split up into two groups, each group going in a different direction. A number of comrades took the Central Committee members back through the old route, from Pac Bo to Chinghsi, to Lungchou and then on to Bo Cuc where they would wait. This group included Truong Chinh, Hoang Quoc Viet, Hoang Van Thu, Phung Chi Kien (alias Phung) and Dang Van Cap (alias Truong Van Minh). A number of other comrades, such as Lam, Hai Tam (Be Son Cuong), Phung Hec, Ma (Ma Thanh Kinh), etc., were under the command of Hoang Sam and myself. Besides weapons, we also carried a number of secret documents. From Pac Bo we would go to Soc Giang, Dong Ngan, Mo Sat, Hoa An, and then to Lung Hoang to meet the comrades in the Cao Bang Province Party Committee who would make arrangements for us to go from Hoa An to Dong Khe, That Khe, Na Ma, Pa Lau, Tan Trang and on to Bo Cuc where we would join up with Truong Chinh's group to make preparations for the return trip to Bac Son. Going back with us was comrade Mac Van Hai, a native of That Khe, who had operated for many years in China. He acted as our guide. He was in charge of the shortcut from That Khe through Van Mich.

* * *

On the 6th day of the 5th Lunar month (June 1941), we said goodbye to Pac Bo and the Old Man Thu Son, and set out.

The group going through China was joined by Cao Hong Linh when they reached Chinghsi.

---

6. Excerpt from the 8th Resolution of the Central Committee. (Footnote in text.)

We were enthusiastic when we came to Pac Bo, and now on our way back our enthusiasm was even greater. On the road, the more I thought about the things I had learned, the more I missed Pac Bo and the Old Man.

When we reached Ha Quang—Dong Ngan, we saw masses of people standing about as if they were attending a festival. Some sang courting songs. We could not tell what the festive occasion was all about, and were suspicious. We hid in the bushes, and observing proper military procedures we crawled forward and watched in secret. We could not make out the lyrics of the warm courting songs of our homeland, and only heard faint echoes of the melodies from where we were. The first group of people who met us smiled happily and told us that they had organized the singing in order to deceive the enemy, protect and welcome us, and help us make our way through safely. We were elated and walked among the people, our confidence in the revolutionary masses strengthened.

When we arrived at Bo Cuc, we saw Truong Chinh, Hoang Quoc Viet, Hoang Van Thu and Phung Chi Kien waiting for us. They were happy to see our armed unit getting through safely, and looked very pleased.

Here, we had the chance to visit our relatives on both sides of the family in their villages--not only kinship ties but also revolutionary ties bound us intimately together, for the influence of the revolution had penetrated deeply among the people in this area.[7] For me, a revolutionary visiting relatives in such a situation, my joy was beyond words. There was a strong bond between the two countries--Vietnam and China--as well as between my family's native places on both sides of the border, and there were also strong feelings of affection between my family and the relatives on both the maternal and the paternal sides. Here, everyone down to the little children knew Hoang Van Thu. Everyone was happy to see us getting through unharmed. They all wished a rapid victory for the Vietnamese revolution.

We were detected while going through Na Khau and Na Ke. The village militia chief thought we were bandits, and sent the militia out to block the road. The Central Committee sent comrades Lam and Mac Van Hai to reason with them. Hai said, "We are not bandits, we're only borrowing the road and passing through." At the same time he hinted to the village militia chief that we were numerous and well armed, and that if he touched us he would be wiped out. He was frightened, and let us pass. That day we went to Khau S'lin, a mountain sharp and pointed as a bamboo shoot, to sleep.

The next night we had to go through That Khe and circled the foot of Khau Phin mountain. When we crossed the That Khe River, the current was strong and swift, and the water reached above our waists. We linked arms, and guided each other across. We went around the foot of the mountain, and headed straight for That Khe and Po Co, and on to Van Mich. Van Mich was over 40 kilometers from That Khe, and we must try to get there in one night.

Walking at night, besides observing the road all around us and

---

7. The Chinese Communist Party set up a soviet in the Lungchou area of southern Kwangsi (inhabited mostly by the Chuangs who are closely related to the Tay and Nung) in 1929. This Left River Soviet was short lived (it collapsed in 1930) but had a deep impact among the people of this area. (Trans.)

being on the lookout for unforeseen dangers, we had to pay attention to Hoang Quoc Viet and help him. "Fat" Ma was assigned to accompany Viet.

The third night, we were on the last leg of our trip. When we were in a hamlet of Binh Gia village, we saw a group of people returning from somewhere and carrying over ten torches. We were then walking in the terraced ricefields, and since there was nothing else we could do, we avoided them by climbing up the hill. "Fat" Ma followed us, but Viet was too slow and could not keep up with us.

We sat down and checked to see whether we had everyone before resuming our journey, and noticed then that Viet was missing. "Fat" Ma and Dang Van Cap went searching for him but could not find him. I guessed he must have gotten lost at the terraced ricefields, and retracing my steps I went down the slope. He was going up and I was coming down, but I did not see him until I was right next to him.

He said, "I thought you had gone very far, so I was going to climb up to the mountain, sleep there and then take the main road back the next day!"

We had lost almost an hour.

Around midnight, going through the Pac Nang Pass, we could see the Binh Gia fields ahead of us. The moon was bright. We had to cross a bridge. We lowered ourselves to the ground and peered toward the bridge. We saw a few militiamen stretched out on the bridge, lying still. If our eyes had not been sharp, we could not have made them out.

I said, "Even though they are there, we must go through."

Our unit went ahead and got on the bridge first. Surprised, the two militiamen stood up with a start and stammered a question. Comrade Lam and I held them tight and told them what we wanted to do. One of them struggled free and ran, yelling as he ran, "Help!" Comrade Lam had his arm locked tightly around the neck of the second one, and reasoned with him as they walked along, so he agreed to guide us through. I signalled to the comrades walking behind us to cross the bridge quickly. Our whole group crossed the vast fields of Binh Gia village without running into any difficulties. We did not release the militiaman until we reached Tam Canh, on the edge of the Bac Son territory. We let him go and told him how to report to his superiors without incurring punishment and without harming us. His release was so unexpected for him that he thanked us profusely and promised to do as we had instructed him.

We crossed Tam Canh and as we reached Quynh Son settlement (in Bac Son district), we ran into another group of militiamen. Knowing we had been detected, we called out to them not to shoot, and said we would wipe them out if they opened fire. Knowing that we were revolutionaries, they got out of the way and let us proceed to Lung Pan. This was a revolutionary base, and old Mr. Van and his family were reliable sympathizers. He made arrangements for us to eat and sleep. We met the brothers from the AFNS who had been waiting here. They had come from the Tan Lap area, and included Luong Huu Chi, Ha Khai Lac and Dam (alias Do), as well as the rest of the unit.

As the man in charge of the Bac Son guerrilla base, Chi gave a report on the situation in Bac Son from every point of view, from the time we left to accompany the Central Committee comrades to the Party conference, to the present. The consolidation of the infrastructure and of the movement was proceeding well, and for this reason the movement in Bac Son-Vo Nhai had pushed strongly ahead and this area had become a political corridor to the delta. The AFNS had been given military and political training, and was well disciplined and organized. However, the cadres had not been very careful about maintaining secrecy. The elimination of spies and secret police gang leaders had not been executed neatly. Meetings had been held publicly. A number of our cadres had come out into the open and were being watched by the secret police and the imperialists.

After that, Thu communicated the new resolution of the Party to all the brothers in the AFNS. The cadres and fighters were encouraged and enthusiastic.

To implement the Resolution of the Central Committee, we discussed the plan to consolidate the Bac Son movement. Right after that the Central Committee set up a new Command Staff for the Bac Son war zone, and appointed comrade Phung Chi Kien as General Commander. I was the Deputy Commander and Chi was the Political Officer. The Command Staff of the Bac Son Armed Forces was put under the leadership of the Standing Committee of the Party Central Committee.

We were assigned the task of taking the Central Committee members to Bo-py-a where they would take up temporary quarters. Before leaving they reminded us that we must "resist white terror and keep open the liaison route with the delta. At the same time we must prepare a second secret route so that when necessary the Central Committee could retreat safely." After that, we parted. A number of local cadres led the Central Committee members to the base area in Bo-py-a, while we went to Khuoi Noi with the unit. The National Salvation Unit was reconsolidated under the direct command of comrade Phung Chi Kien. After being reinforced with a number of cadres and informed of the new Party policy, the AFNS followed a new line of action. On the one hand, we organized military and political training, stocked food supplies and expanded the military training of self-defense forces in preparation for resisting white terror. On the other hand, we consolidated the infrastructure and organized a corridor of liaison, using the masses, to link the base area with the delta.

We discussed starting training courses to strengthen the military cadres, including those coming from the delta provinces. The Command Staff assigned me to Vo Nhai to resist white terror, and also to maintain firm the movement there; at the same time I was to stock up food in case the Central Committee and the AFNS had to retreat. Besides consolidating existing communication routes, I also had to find a secret route so that when necessary the Central Committee could move down to the delta easily.

CHAPTER III

I returned to Vo Nhai.

During the time I accompanied the Central Committee members to the Party Congress, I still had not broken all ties with my family. By the time I returned, I had been absent from February to June 1941. Back home during this time a number of comrades who tried to eliminate secret police gang leaders were uncovered. In Vo Nhai, a number of comrades who operated openly were also uncovered. The enemy tracked them down relentlessly. A number of them fell into the enemy net. The families of some comrades were also terrorized. Some people from Phu Thuong and Trang Xa refused to sit still and let the enemy come to take them, and fled into the mountains. In addition, a group who had attended the 8th Central Committee Plenum were detected on their way back (due to the betrayal of a fellow named Cong).[1] The enemy panicked and, gathering their troops, carried out a search operation from Lang Son into Bac Son, and advanced from Thai Nguyen into Vo Nhai. They wanted to kill two birds with one stone: first, to track down the leading cadres and the nerve organs of the Party in order to destroy the Communist movement in Indochina, and second, to strangle the struggle movement in Bac Son.

The enemy built posts as they advanced, and split up their troops to search each part of the jungle. On our part we remembered Uncle Ho's instruction in Pac Bo, and using the Viet Minh program we had just brought back with us, we did our best to propagandize and organize the people, to give them confidence and make them determined to act. We succeeded not only in expanding the movement into a wider area, but also in making it sink deeper roots among the population.

Vo Nhai fought back.

At that time, soldiers from Thai Nguyen and Lang Son poured into Bac Son to terrorize it because they suspected that Communist Chinese troops had moved there.

Dinh Ca and Trang Xa were terrorized to the same extent as Bac Son. Columns of fire rose from burning houses. The sound of old people and children weeping and crying was hard to bear. The sight of destroyed villages and settlements intensified my hatred for the enemy and increased my concern for the Central Committee. I wondered how they were doing in Bac Son, and whether Kien and Chi managed to protect them. Were they safe? I was in Trang Xa, and it was not possible for me to find out everything about the situation in Bac Son. The villagers who went to the markets in Bac Son and Dinh Ca told me a little about the situation there. Where we were we only saw the enemy fiercely poking and searching everywhere. Some of the villagers were worried and discouraged.

---

1. An agent of the French Sûreté who infiltrated the Party during its phase of overt political activities in the Popular Front period. (Trans.)

It was the planting season then in Trang Xa, but it rained a lot and flood waters poured in, flooding even the streams that were usually dry. A pitch dark night without stars or moonlight in July 1941, a number of brothers from the AFNS wanted to go to Dong Tac and Dong Tham villages to collect the rice that the people had donated. Enemy soldiers and secret policemen had let it be known that they would come and burn down these villages. Before the brothers went into the village, they saw shadows moving ahead, so they hid behind big trees and rocks to find out whether those were soldiers. They strained their eyes and peered into the night, ready to cope with the enemy. On closer look, they saw clearly two men--one limping and the other of large stature--walking in front. They whispered to each other, "That looks like Quoc Vinh!" Then they saw the men head toward the house of Bao, a revolutionary sympathizer. The brothers were also heading in the same direction. It was a chance meeting. Happy and moved, they rushed out to welcome the newcomers. They recognized each other in joy and excitement. The large man was Quoc Vinh, and the other was Hoang Quoc Viet, followed by Thu and Truong Chinh. The brothers were overjoyed at the arrival of the Central Committee members and told each other, "We'll get some help now!"

Viet said, "Comrades, please take us to your headquarters."

"You've just got here from up there, so you must be tired. Rest a while," one of the AFNS comrades replied, "and then you can come to our headquarters."

It turned out the Central Committee members, in lucid anticipation, had left Bac Son early and succeeded in slipping through the enemy's tight encirclement. And luckily, when they arrived in Trang Xa they ran into the brothers going to collect rice. The Central Committee had left Bac Son, but Phung Chi Kien and Luong Huu Chi remained in Khuoi Noi to lead the people to resist enemy terrorism.

* * *

Darkness had not lifted, and morning light had not dawned. The Leo mountain, lying to the Northeast of Trang Xa village, was about 400 meters high, and stretched all the way to Quang Lung. We set up our headquarters in the mountain, and from there advancing forward or retreating would be easy for us.

When it was almost light, a comrade from the AFNS came running back and reported, "Brother Viet has come back!"

When I heard this, I was overjoyed and ran out of the hut to welcome them. Usually, whenever the brothers went down to the villages to get rice, they split up and came back separately. But this time, there were more people coming back than when they left. Looking closer, I saw Truong Chinh, Hoang Quoc Viet and Hoang Van Thu. Our joy, of course, was boundless. The arrival of the Central Committee in Trang Xa was exactly what we had fervently hoped for. Viet said, "It was admirable of comrade Quoc Vinh to dare guide us through.

Quoc Vinh was from Bac Son, and it was the first time he had made the trip to Trang Xa, but he was very clever in avoiding all enemy patrols and watch towers, and managed to protect the Central Committee comrades and take them safely to their destination.

Thu grasped my hand and said, "The enemy is getting fierce up there.

I was moved. Their presence meant we would get direct assistance from the Central Committee. I wanted to find out more about the situation but I thought they must be tired from a trip full of tension, so I asked them to lie down and rest.

The next day we had the chance of working with the Central Committee. It was then that we found out about the true situation in Bac Son. At first the Central Committee and the protecting unit were stationed in Bo-py-a, but later on they had to move to the Vu Lang area. Political and military training for the brothers proceeded normally. However, lying in the middle of the enemy's encirclement--the Japanese and French were sending out spies to gather information day and night-- the Central Committee could not stay in one place, and had to be constantly on the move. Once, while they were asleep at night, villagers came in to tell them that enemy soldiers had entered their area. In the middle of the night, they had to grope their way along the mountain slope and move to Lan Rao, a village surrounded by rocky mountains. There was only one path leading to the village. They were sure they had found a safe place to hold training classes. In the morning, looking out from the village in all four directions, they saw only grass and trees and the moldy green color of the mountains. That evening, a stranger walked into the village. The comrade on guard duty was from the delta, and did not speak the local dialect. Seeing the stranger, he questioned him, but the man pointed to a house and said, "I live here, I'm going home!" The fellow slipped through the sentry post, but was detected when he reached the settlement. (The Central Committee comrades were then holding a meeting.) Comrade Quoc Vinh, in charge of providing security for the meeting, stared fixedly ahead and then suddenly cried out, "Who's going there? Why was that man let through?" He leaped from the steps and ran after the stranger. The "hound" seeing he had been detected fled!

So, their presence there had been discovered. They sent people after the man to catch him but he was gone. They had no choice but to leave and follow comrade Quang Long who was their guide. As they neared the trail, they spotted enemy soldiers coming in. Fortunately, the soldiers were led by a villager whom they had forced to act as their scout. Seeing someone he knew, the man jerked his hand and motioned comrade Quang Long to step back. Quang Long ran backward. If it hadn't been for this villager, he would have run right into the enemy. Quang Long hurriedly stepped back into the jungle and the whole group stopped. Quang Long reported to Hoang Van Thu. Kien pulled out his pistol, and ordered the brothers in the security unit to prepare to fight. The villager yelled to the soldiers, "Listen, Mr. officials, please hurry! It's getting dark!" The group knew that that was a signal for them to step aside and avoid a confrontation, but where could they hide? After guiding the soldiers and their commanders to the fields, the villager secretly returned to where the group was and scolded them: "Why did you take this route? If you don't know your way about you'll be killed by them one of these days. You'd better follow this route. . . ." That said, he told Quang Long how to guide the group away. They reached Ban Loong (in Vu Le district) safely. But they could only stay there for a few days and then had to move again.

Faced with such a situation, the Central Committee decided to return to Trang Xa, where we were stationed.

So, Bac Son was going through a difficult period. However, I was confident that with the 8th Central Committee Resolution lighting the way, and under the guidance of Phung Chi Kien and Luong Huu Chi, Bac

Son would sail through this turbulent time and would become consolidated and strengthened as a result.

"Now, it's the turn of Trang Xa," Thu said to me, smiling. "Please report."

Encouraged, I reported to the Central Committee the things we had accomplished--how we had proselytized the people in accordance with the Viet Minh Program, how we had stocked up over one hundred pots of rice in our storehouse, what results had been achieved in our resistance against enemy white terror, and how we had cleared communication and liaison routes. I concluded, "There are now two or three routes to the delta. The Central Committee can go back and forth any time they want."

Thu asked to reconfirm it, "Are the routes to the delta well protected?"

I was positive. "We guarantee your safety."

The three of them--Truong Chinh, Viet and Thu--nodded their heads and looked at me intently. Thu told me, "Now just follow the program that has been set forth. We have to study further a few more situations."

I caught the hint, and withdrew so they could work.

From then on the Trang Xa war zone had a new mission: to protect the Central Committee, and at the same time to safeguard the liaison and communication routes from here to the delta, and ensure that letters from the delta arrive safely here. The Central Committee worked in an atmosphere of urgency. They were very busy, but never forgot to give guidance to the Vo-Nhai and Trang Xa area. Later on, Thu told me the Central Committee would go down to the delta to expand the movement. I was happy for the sake of the movement in the delta, but I was sorry to see the Central Committee leave after such a short stay in Trang Xa.

Watching the comrades working day and night, I did not want to disturb them with my opinion which I felt was naturally limited to my own area of operation. I thought that the situation in the whole country--not just in Trang Xa--required their attention.

*   *   *

Two days later.

A liaison comrade arrived from Bac Son with two urgent letters: one addressed to the Central Committee comrades and the other addressed to myself. Looking at the two rolled-up notes, I noticed right away that they both originated from the same place. "Coming from Bac Son, they must originate from Khuoi Noi where Kien's and Chi's headquarters are located. I wonder what has happened there!" I took the letters right away to Thu. Then, standing there, I opened mine and read it. Yes, the letter was from Khuoi Noi and it was in Phung Chi Kien's handwriting. I read at a quick glance, "The situation in Bac Son is difficult; please come at once to discuss what to do."

I looked at Thu reading his letter. His brows were knitted. Having spent much time near him, I understood that this meant the letter was making him search hard in his mind for a solution. He looked up, and then looked down at the piece of paper again. Seeing me also carrying a letter, he asked, "Did the letter say much?"

I answered, "They're having difficulties up there and ask me to go there immediately."

Thu turned around and went in to see Viet and Truong Chinh. They read the letter and discussed it. A while later, Thu gave me a letter from the Central Committee to take to Phung Chi Kien in Khuoi Noi. He said, "The situation in Bac Son is really difficult. The Central Committee has weighed everything carefully. The letter explains it all clearly. Tell them to persevere and consolidate the infrastructure and use it as a solid base for resisting terrorism. If it becomes too difficult they should withdraw in order to keep their forces intact."

I rolled the letter inside a section of banana leaf,[2] sealed the two ends, pushed it inside my bushy hair, pulled a cap over my head all the way down to my ears, and set out immediately. It would take me a day to go from Trang Xa to Khuoi Noi, going across mountains.

The flood waters rushed down the streams, and blocked the way in many places. I carried the letter on my head. I felt as though my head and my heart were on fire [burning with the urgency of the situation]. Kien and Chi must be anxiously waiting for me. The Central Committee had left Bac Son and moved to Trang Xa. Two-thirds of the National Salvation forces were left in Bac Son. Trang Xa and Bac Son were far apart, and communication was difficult. The situation in Bac Son was taking a turn for the worse. We must maintain our political infrastructure firmly and at the same time preserve our armed forces intact. These thoughts dogged me as I walked.

In order to avoid the watching eyes of the secret police, I waded through the stream, oblivious of the flood waters which hit my face. I was wet from head to toes. The letter was the only thing that remained dry.

I arrived in Khuoi Noi at dusk, but Kien and Chi and a number of comrades had left.

*   *   *

The next day, on my way back to Trang Xa to report to the Central Committee about the situation in Khuoi Noi and about the things that a number of AFNS brothers who stayed behind had told me, I passed through Dinh Ca, and discussed with the AFNS operating there a plan to deal with the enemy terrorism.

These brothers were staying on the top of a mountain, about a kilometer behind my father's house. Comrades Nong Thai Long, Hoang Thuong, Tien and about a squad were present. However, the secret police agents who were spying in the area detected us and went to report to the soldiers in the Dinh Ca post.

Unaware, we continued our meeting, which lasted into the night, in an atmosphere of urgency. I told the brothers about the situation in-

---

2. Messages were usually written on thin and tiny pieces of paper for easy concealment. (Trans.)

side and outside the country, and also talked about the general situation in our war zone, and then discussed a plan to counter enemy terrorism. Each man expressed his opinion, and the plan was approved unanimously. Comrades Nong Thai Long and Hoang Thuong accepted the task of contacting Van Sang who was then the Squad Leader in Bac Son to tell him and the brothers up there--as well as the local villagers--to deal with the lies and distortions that the secret police agents were spreading against us. I instructed Nong Thai Long further: "They must concentrate their efforts on maintaining firm the infrastructure. If they have difficulties, Mr. Van Sang should bring the brothers down here."

I asked Hoang Thuong about the situation in Lam and Phat villages. He said, "It is still quiet there. The enemy so far hasn't stirred yet.

I stayed in the headquarters there to rest, but couldn't go to sleep. I wondered how far Kien and Chi and the other brothers had gone for the last few days and nights, where they had stopped to rest, and whether they had encountered any difficulties along the way. I hoped they managed to slip through safely. I had heard that this time Chi would try to go to the area where the Old Man was staying. This would be a good thing.

I passed a night full of bad dreams.

It was not complete daylight yet. In the middle of this deep forest, darkness still clung to the trees and leaves. All of us were still asleep. Suddenly I heard whispers coming from the direction of the stream. It seemed I even heard rifles being loaded. I gently poked the man lying next to me in the ribs, and asked quickly in a low voice, "Was that the noise of rifles being loaded?"

He remained very quiet, listening intently to every sound outside. Then he sat up with a jerk. "You're right!"

"Get up quickly! We've been detected!" I yelled to the brothers, "Pick up all documents and get ready to fight!"

I jumped up, rushed to the door, and by habit automatically loaded my rifle. I rushed outside. It was still dark, but I could hear footsteps and the thud of nailed boots coming down from the top of the hill. I knew the enemy was coming in from two directions to attack our camp by surprise. They had split into two groups: one was coming up from the stream below, led by the secret police, and one was coming down from the hill, commanded by a Frenchman. I thought, "They've split up into two prongs to catch us in a pincer movement. Well, we'll take advantage of their own scheme to foil them!" I aimed in the direction of the sound coming from the two advancing groups, and fired a shot in the space between the two advancing columns. My goal was to make the group coming down open fire on the group coming up, and the group coming up open fire on the group coming down. The enemy fell into my trap, and fought each other fiercely. Taking advantage of this opportunity, we retreated safely.

I hid behind a tree to watch a well-matched battle between the enemy soldiers, and at the same time was at the ready to protect the brothers. I was most concerned about Mr. Tien, a Kinh from the lowlands who had just come here and was not as familiar with the forest as we were. I wondered whether he had managed to catch up with the other brothers.

It was broad daylight. The two enemy columns fired at each other for a while and then withdrew. They cursed each other like mad. The group near the stream pulled out first. The one coming down the hill rushed into our camp to search. But the hut was empty! They had no choice but to withdraw. However, they did not dare to go back in the main direction, and had to stomp out a new trail with their nailed boots. I did not want to shoot them. If I opened fire, I could have killed a few of them!

All the soldiers had left.

I went down to the stream and suddenly saw a bunch of vegetables someone had soaked in the stream. I figured out that this bunch of vegetables had saved our lives! When the soldiers saw the vegetables, they loaded their rifles. We heard this noise and slipped out of the hut in time to escape their pincer movement. If it had not been for this bunch of vegetables, they would have come in quietly and surrounded us, and who knew what could have happened. Comrade Hoang Thuong had mentioned to me that he had just returned from a mission in the settlement. It must have been Thuong who plucked these vegetables and soaked them in the stream to keep them fresh in order to cook some soup the next day. All that was past and gone--now I must go and find them. So thinking, I went to the places we had agreed in advance to retreat to if something happened, but no one was there.

Suspecting that Hoang Thuong had fled to his father's house, I went down to Lam village. Thuong's father had married a cousin of mine. I asked him, "Did any of us come down here?"

He looked me up and down, and said in a worried tone of voice, "Early this morning I heard rifle shots, and guessed that you people had fired them. Is the situation serious?"

I told him briefly about what had happened.

"Aya!" he immediately asked, "did anything happen to Thuong?"

"I've looked all morning without finding him. Perhaps he's returned to Trang Xa. Today is market day in Dinh Ca, why don't you go to the market?"

"I'm not going to the market today."

"Go and keep your eyes open. The soldiers certainly go to the market."

Then I discussed with my cousin-in-law how to gather information at the market place. "If you know any woman who goes to the Dinh Ca market, then ask her to do it for you."

It was only then that he agreed. Nowadays, no one found going to the market a pleasant experience. Everywhere they went, they saw only militiamen and province troops. I ate at the home of Cam Voong, a sympathizer. Then I went to his garden well shaded with trees and foliage to sleep and regain my strength. But my mind was in a turmoil, and I could not go to sleep. "I was overconfident and careless and allowed the enemy to attack our camp by surprise. Now the brothers are all dispersed and lost." This worry and anxiety made me sit up with a start. "Could it be that they've gone to Phat village? From here to there, the mountain route is only over two kilometers long. Who knows, maybe Nong Thai Long and Duong are resting contentedly there." Thereupon, I slipped out of the garden, and walked along the foot of the mountain. The path was tortuous and thick with undergrowth. I crossed over to Phat village, and went to the houses of Uncle Pinh and Sister Bi Ooc. No one was there. Uncle Pinh took some rice into the bush for me to eat and told me to come and spend the night at his house. But I was too agitated, and taking the rice I returned to Lam village to wait for Thuong's father and a number of villagers to come back from the Dinh Ca market with the news.

After a long time, I went back to the garden to lie down. But I was restless, and anxiously waited for their return. I cannot describe how agitated I was. Thuong's father did not come back till late in the afternoon. He related with satisfaction, "They were talking noisily all over the market place. 'Alui! the Communists only fired to trap us. Our side just shot at each other. The First Lieutenant almost got killed! The Adjutant has been dismissed!'"

He took a kettle to the kitchen to boil water, lit a pipe, exhaled the smoke in a thick cloud in front of his face, laughed with great satisfaction and continued, "The secret police agents were blaming each other. They said, 'We were frightened out of our minds when we surrounded the Communists. Our encirclement was tight but we didn't catch any of them. When we turned around to go back, we saw the footprints they had made when they passed through. We shook with fear! It was lucky they didn't shoot at us. It was only after we reached Dinh Ca that we knew we were safe!'"

Our policy of not shooting at the soldiers who were forced to go on operation had produced good results. This was a lesson for us to use later on in our efforts to sow dissension in the enemy ranks. I guessed that Thai Long's group had slipped through the forest safely and returned to Trang Xa. Tien must have arrived safely too.

I told Thuong's father, "If they had shot any of us, they would have cut off his head and displayed it on a stick. So, we can put our minds at ease."

Thuong's father puffed a last smoke on his still glowing pipe and said worriedly, "The arrival of the soldiers in this area means something will happen. Stay here and I'll fix you something to eat. Go back tomorrow."

"That will not do. I'm very worried, and I must go back right away."

"Alright, if you see Thuong, tell him to be careful. You too must be careful."

* * *

I examined the footprints around my father's house, and not noticing anything suspicious, I came in. I took this opportunity to visit my father because I had heard the enemy was going to arrest him and put him in jail. They had already told him so many times. They held the power. The reason the local officials had not dared touch my father was because he had great prestige in the village and also because they were using him to induce me to come home.

He was very happy when he saw me enter. He killed a duck and prepared food. Sipping his wine cup, he said, "They said they'd take me away, but I'm not afraid to die."

I looked up; his eyes were bloodshot as though he was angry at the memory of the day when the secret police came here in a menacing manner and wanted to arrest him and take him away. He picked up with his chopsticks the best morsel, put it in my bowl, and said with affection, "Eat my son. Today we can sit and eat together. The next time you come back you might not see me again."

He drank another cup and said, "When I was 16 years old I took up arms to fight the French. I was in the army of Mr. Hoang Hoa Tham then.[3] I'm old now, I can't do anything any more, so you must do it."

I said, "They will burn down our house sooner or later. If you have anything of value, give it to someone to keep for you. Otherwise it will just feed the fire, Father."

He shook his head. "I don't care about losing the house. I don't regret anything. I'm only worried . . . I'm only afraid they will dig up our family graves up on the mountain."

I felt great love and sorrow for my father. I said, "Don't be afraid, Father. Even if they dig up the graves, nothing will happen. Thu has told you so himself. As long as the Revolution succeeds nothing matters. When this happens, everyone--not just our family--will have enough to eat and warm clothes to wear, and no one will be able to bully us."

My father had great respect for Hoang Van Thu. In everything, if he was told "Thu said so," he listened right away. It had been such a long time since I came to visit him last, but now it was time for us to part again because of the enemy's terrorism. I talked with him, related stories I felt would do him good, and told him about the frantic struggle of the enemy and the prospects for the movement. He said to me, "I'm not worried about myself. I'm old, and for me, to die is only natural. The secret police might have gotten wind of your presence here. Early this morning I heard rifle shots in that direction. Be on your guard when you go, my son."

I did not dare tell him about what had happened that morning. It would not do him any good to know.

After supper, I said goodbye to him and returned to my headquarters.

---

3. Hoang Hoa Tham, better known as De Tham, the "Tiger of Yen The," was a peasant from Hung Yen province. Based in the mountain areas of Yen The, and with no more than two hundred armed men, De Tham led a resistance movement against the French in the 1890's. With this meager force, he managed to keep the spirit of resistance alive for many people in North Vietnam, until his assassination in 1913. The French pursued him relentlessly, and by the end of 1909 had reduced his followers to a couple of men. Still unable to catch him, the French spent considerable time and money in keeping him from recruiting a new group and in trying to have him assassinated. This tactic succeeded in 1913, and De Tham's head was delivered to the French for a bounty. See David Marr's *Vietnamese Anticolonialism* (Berkeley: University of California, 1971). (Trans.)

I did not get back until 9 or 10 o'clock at night. I slept in the fields and waited until the next morning to return to our camp.

The brothers were getting up when I entered the hut. They all shouted with joy. Truong Chinh asked, "Why did it take you so long to come back?"

I had been gone for two days! During the time I was away, news had come in from Dinh Ca, and Viet, Truong Chinh and Thu were burning with worry and anxiety, especially when they saw Nong Thai Long and the brothers from Dinh Ca arrive without me.

Thu immediately criticized me severely. "You should have returned right away after you completed your mission. But you lingered on, and let such an unfortunate thing happen."

I sincerely admitted my error, and then reported in detail to the Central Committee about all the events in Khuoi Noi.

CHAPTER IV

It was sunny. The autumn sunlight filtered through the leaves in the Khuon Manh forest. The huge tree trunks rose straight and tall. Bamboo shoots sprouted at the foot of bamboo trees. A cool breeze rustled the leaves. The lush rice and corn patches stretched in a gentle grade to the water edge. White pebbles gleamed in the stream bed. The age-old forest hugged both sides of the stream, like two huge and protective arms.

This afternoon, many women of the Man [Yao] ethnic minority came to the stream bank together. They had heard that there would be an important ceremony, so they asked for permission to come and listen to the cadre talk. They knew this cadre well, and loved him very much. He limped and walked with difficulty, but he worked very hard. What he said--everyone agreed--was accurate. The French in the posts, the soldiers, the secret police, the village officials, like hunting hounds were sniffing everywhere, but he did not leave and stayed on among the villagers to tell them how to deal with the enemy who were burning down their houses and destroying their villages, and how to cope with those who were the running dogs of the French. The women told each other, "The cadre is coming. Let's listen to him. He'll tell us a lot of interesting things."

At that time, we were living through days and months of relentless enemy attacks from all four directions and on every front--political, military, as well as economic. Through the betrayal of Cong and Hai[1] the French imperialists found out about our operation and our strength. In contrast to the previous occasion when they reoccupied the Mo Nhai post with 20 province troops, and when they attacked the Vu Lang school by surprise with 40 soldiers and militiamen, the enemy this time mobilized a much larger force. A column from Lang Son advanced through Binh Gia to attack the villages of Huong Vu, Huu Vinh, Tan Lap, Vu Lang and Vu Le, sowing calamity on the heads of the Bac Son population. Before enough time had elapsed to make people forget about this hateful action, a second column--consisting of province troops, militiamen, secret police, canton security chiefs and cruel rich people--advanced from Thai Nguyen through Dinh Ca to terrorize the villages of Trang Xa, Phu Thuong, Lau Thuong, La Hien and Lang Muoi in Vo Nhai district. They relentlessly surrounded and searched the villages, and swept through the forest and settlements without letup. They burned down houses, wrecked the hamlets, terrorized the people and herded them into fascist concentration camps in Na Pheo, Dinh Ca, Lang Giua and Dong En, in order to carry out their scheme of "draining the water to catch the fish," and tried to cut off all contacts between the people and the AFNS. Difficulties piled up, but with the leadership of the Central Committee, we were doing our utmost to overcome them in order to propel the movement forward.

---

1. These two were lackeys of the imperialists, and had infiltrated the Party to sabotage it. (Footnote in text.)

Truong Chinh and Hoang Van Thu had returned to the delta. Hoang Quoc Viet stayed behind to help us devise a plan to deal with the enemy's terrorism and to organize a resistance force. Before a month had elapsed, a letter from Thu suddenly arrived, asking Viet to return to the delta immediately. Viet could not prolong his stay any longer, so he made preparations to implement the directive of the Party. Before going back to the lowland, Viet set up--in the name of the Central Committee--a second platoon of the AFNS. (The platoon that had been set up in Khuoi Noi previously was referred to as the AFNS First Platoon.)

The village women were right. Hoang Quoc Viet did come that day. The members of the AFNS had gathered in the fields and lined up in two rows. In this critical movement, even if only one man took up arms to fight the enemy, this would be worth rejoicing. But that day, not just one man--but dozens of people--[took up arms to fight the enemy]. They included the remnants of the AFNS First Platoon--the comrades who had met the challenge in the Bac Son base--plus a number of comrades who had recently joined the ranks.

It was the 15th of September 1941. The Second Platoon of the AFNS attended the ceremony which formally set it up. The majority of the platoon members present that day had joined after the enemy's surprise attack on the command headquarters of the AFNS in Dinh Ca at the beginning of July 1941. Practically all of them came from families that the imperialists had herded into concentration camps. Many of these families had been fiercely terrorized by the enemy. For example, comrade Thoong's family and comrade Trieu Khanh Phuong's[2] family of six were jailed in Dinh Hoa where they slowly died of hunger and disease. Comrade Phuc Quyen's mother was beaten to the point of insanity. The enemy also dug up his ancestors' graves--as well as mine--poured gasoline on the remains and burned them. In the pagoda and in the communal house of Cau Ran hamlet in Phu Thuong village, Delorque (?) and Sinh-- two security agents notorious for their cruelty--and their henchmen day and night were doing their best to torture old people, women and children, especially the families of the men and women who were serving in the revolutionary base, hoping to shake up the morale of the AFNS and dampen the spirit of struggle of the population.

The sufferings of each individual piled up together became a common hatred and resentment. All shared the same hatred for the enemy and the same desire for revenge through common action. For this reason, they loved each other and were ready to share everything with each other. In danger they were prepared to sacrifice their lives to save their comrades-in-arms.

The sun slanted toward the West. The autumn light spread over the rice and corn fields stretching along the banks of the Khuon Manh stream.

I looked at Nguyen Cao Dam. He looked like he had regained his strength somewhat. The enemy bullet which had pierced his shoulder and entered his chest, and the days and nights he had spent hiding in the forest not long ago, had sharpened his hatred for the enemy. Dam's story--from many points of view--was an experience from which we could derive a useful lesson. It seemed to me I could still see the story unfold before my eyes.

---

2. Trieu Khanh Phuong, a Yao, is now a member of the Viet Bac Region Party Committee, and Deputy Chairman of the Viet Bac Zone's Administrative Committee. (Trans.)

After the group of Phung Chi Kien and Luong Huu Chi withdrew from Bac Son, the comrades who stayed behind gathered together and formed a squad under the leadership of Dam, Tan and Rue. Their task was to maintain firm the infrastructure and resist the terrorism of the enemy. They divided into three cells, headed by Dam, Thuc and Van Sang. Each cell was in charge of a critical area. Dam, along with Quoc Vinh, Tan, Rue and Thai were stationed in Phie Khao.

At that time, the fields were a golden sheet of ripening rice stalks.

Local security agents sprouted like weeds. They led soldiers to terrorize Phie Khao. A number of villagers were frightened and did not dare to let the cadres stay in their houses. Dam's cell and their camp had to move to the Mo Re cave, which was as small as a house on stilts built on only eight support columns.[3] Their weapons consisted of two Dop 3 rifles and one Dop 5 rifle. One day, comrades Hoang, Thuc and Dung went from Bo Tat to Don Uy to establish contact with the local infrastructure and then go down to Huu Vinh to collect rice. There were only five men left in the cave.

The leaders of this cell found the situation unsettling. The cave was located near the house of a fellow called Thai who had been behaving in a suspicious manner lately. They wanted to move their camp, but Thai told Tan and Rue, "We don't have to move! There's no need to do so now! I have just been down to the village and I got a chicken to cook rice soup. There is nothing to fear."

So, they decided to stay an extra night. The next day, Thai's brother--Dao--led militiamen to the cave entrance and yelled to Thai to come out and surrender. The soldiers did not dare to rush into the cave because they knew the comrades were armed. Thai glanced furtively at the rifles in the hands of Tan and Rue, and said, "Don't shoot! There are a lot of soldiers out there!"

Seeing Tan and Rue hesitate, Quoc Vinh snatched their rifles and was about to rush out to fight with the soldiers, but Tan and Rue stopped him: "Let's wait and see! We can't just save our own lives, we must save everyone in the cell."

There was nothing for Quoc Vinh to do but to stare in anger at the cave entrance. His brows were knitted.

Before the soldiers could call him a second time, Thai went out. He was brazen and unabashed: "They have surrounded us! If we don't come out, we'll die. If we come out, our lives will be spared."

It was then that Tan and Rue realized they had been "raising a bee in their sleeves,"[4] and that they had fallen into Thai's trap. They had not been firm about moving their camp the previous day. Now they realized this, but it was too late.

---

3. In Bac Son, to be able to build a house with eight support columns and a tiled roof is nothing out of the ordinary. (Footnote in text.) This indicates that the Bac Son area is now prosperous. (Trans.)

4. An expression meaning to trust someone who turns out to be a traitor. (Trans.)

Quoc Vinh rushed out of the cave, on the heels of Thai. But he did not come out to meet the soldiers as the traitor Thai had done. Instead, as he emerged from the cave he slipped into another path. With a quick glance he saw that the soldiers were only blocking the main route. The shadow of a large man also appeared and quick as an arrow, he plunged down the mountainside. Tan and Rue only had time to shout, "Comrade Dam!" when a burst of rifle fire resounded. One bullet plunged into Dam's back, near his shoulder. Seeing that Dam kept on running, Thai told the sodliers, "He'll die, leave him alone. These two fellows Tan and Rue--they're the leaders. You must catch them alive!"

The soldiers surrounded the Mo Re cave. Thai and his brother Dao, and the militiamen took turns calling on the AFNS brothers to surrender. They called out the name of each man, and threatened to "come in and get them if they did not come out." They yelled for a long time, but no one emerged, so they went to Chieu Vu to get some grenades to throw in the cave. The explosions reverberated in the forest and mountains.

Tan and Rue retreated deeper into the cave. Near noon, the militiamen groped their way down the cave and opened fire. It was only then that Tan and Rue gave up and came out of the cave. The enemy led them away.

Dam was quite seriously wounded. Blood soaked the shirt he was wearing, but he kept on walking, groping his way through the forest toward the camp of the other AFNS cell. It was very late at night. As he approached the camp of Duong Van Thuc and Hoang, he stopped dead in his tracks; inside the hut soldiers were interrogating and torturing comrade Hoang. It turned out that Hoang was caught by the enemy when he went to Huu Lung village to collect rice. They then led him back to the hut to torture him, in the hope of finding out where Duong Van Thuc was. Dam hastily climbed on a rocky mountain. The shouts of "Thuc! Thuc!" and the sound of blows and kicks that the enemy was showering on Hoang drifted up to where Dam was hiding. He felt as though the blows were falling on his own chest. It was agonizing for him because there was nothing he could do to save his comrade. The soldiers beat Hoang until their arms hurt and they had to stop to gasp for breath but he still did not utter a word. So they had to take him away. Dam stayed where he was, convinced that Duong Van Thuc had also been captured by the enemy.

After a long time, when he could no longer hear the sound of blows and kicks, and the voice of the soldiers interrogating Hoang, Dam knew that the soldiers had left and he came down. Surrounded by forest trees, Dam walked alone, tortured by the thought of what had happened. He criticized himself for having lost his vigilance in dealing with Thai, and regretted that he had not been able to save his comrades from the enemy's claws. His pain grew as he thought about this. How many men were left in his squad? Quoc Vinh escaped from the cave, but did he manage to reach a safe area? Tan and Rue had been caught; what would happen to them next? Dam told himself, "I will admit all the shortcomings. I must get to my comrades' place!" Then he headed in the direction of Vo Nhai-Trang Xa with determination, and slipped through the forest without stopping to rest.

The news reached us, so we sent people out to search for these comrades everywhere.

Dam came from Thai Binh province. He was big and strong, and normally looked very muscular and healthy. However, after close to ten days of hiding in the forest and escaping the encirclement of the Thai and Dao gang, he looked haggard. His clothes were torn to shreds, and the wound on his shoulder had stopped bleeding and dried up. His eyes were sunken in their sockets, because of lack of sleep and because of worry and sorrow, and his cheekbones protruded. When he spotted me, he hugged me, grabbed my shoulders and said in a gasp, "Now that I've seen you, I know I'm not going to die. It's only at this moment that I know I'm going to live!"

Dam told me about all the things that had taken place at the Mo Re cave. Then he added in a voice full of sorrow, "Duong Thuc has been captured!"

Tears streamed down his face when he said this. Tears welled up in my eyes. I clasped his shoulder and said, "Go and lie down! We'll take care of things later on!"

But Dam went on with his story, and was convinced that comrade Thuc had been captured. He knew that once you fell into the enemy hands, it would be either jail or death. He said, "The security agents were interrogating him and calling his name 'Thuc! Thuc!' so they must have got him!"

But actually Duong Van Thuc had not been caught. He returned to Trang Xa with comrade Quang Long a few days after Dam. So, four men from the third squad who survived had managed to come here from three different directions.

Now, Nguyen Cao Dam was one of three comrades appointed by the Central Committee to the Command Staff of the AFNS Second Platoon.

The second man on the staff was Le Duc Ton.[5] He was ten years younger than I. He was a somewhat cold person, but he had a profound hatred for the foreign occupiers of the country. He rarely smiled and was quiet, but worked very hard.

In my case, the enemy had taken my father away and burned down the house where I had grown up. They were also terrorizing relatives on both sides of my family. To me, then, my unit was my home, the AFNS comrades were my brothers, and the people in the places where the AFNS built their huts to live were my family.

Standing in front of the red flag with the yellow star, we remembered with sadness the comrades who had sacrificed their lives. After the minute of silence in memory of the dead, the initiation ceremony for new Party members began. These were comrades who had met the recent challenges--such as comrades Phuong Cuong, Chu Phong, Ha Manh, Ha Ky, Hong Thai, etc. The whole unit seemed infused with a new vigor and enthusiasm. Hoang Quoc Viet's voice resounded: "In the name of the Central Committee, I recognize the Second Platoon of the AFNS! The Vietnamese Army for National Salvation has the task of maintaining firm our bases and our infrastructure, and carrying on our armed struggle to encourage the movement in the whole country as well as to make a small

---

5. Le Duc Ton is now Vice Chairman of the Viet Bac's Administrative Committee, and a standing member of the Viet Bac Region Party Committee. (Trans.)

but concrete contribution to the Soviet Red Army's fight against the fascist invaders!"

Hoang Quoc Viet stopped. In the sunlight, his eyes shone in an extraordinary manner, as though burned by the intense ardor of his words. The old forest around us still reverberated with the words "maintaining firm our bases and structure, and carrying on our armed struggle . . . make a small but concrete contribution to the Soviet Red Army's fight. . . ."

The task of the AFNS Second Platoon had been clearly pointed out by the Central Committee. Hoang Quoc Viet handed the red flag with the yellow star to the platoon. All the comrades would do their best to implement all the orders of their Command Staff.

The pledge of allegiance ceremony of the AFNS Second Platoon began. The five oaths of the AFNS were read aloud solemnly:

"We will not betray the Party!

"We pledge absolute loyalty to the Party!

"We are determined to fight and revenge the comrades who had sacrificed their lives.

"We will not surrender to the enemy!

"We will not harm the people!"

The sounds of "I swear! I swear!" reverberated. When old Mr. Manh finished his oath, Duong Thi An--the only woman in the AFNS--stepped forward from the ranks. She looked up at the red flag with the five-cornered yellow star and said clearly and precisely, "The twenty million people in our country are groaning in their miseries and sufferings. I am a girl from the ethnic minorities. I swear, under the national flag, to sacrifice everything for the Party and for the people. I'm determined to carry out fully my task as a member of the AFNS. I hereby swear to this!"

As she shouted "I swear!" she raised her fist to her shoulder and saluted the flag.

The young and old Yao women looked at An intently and nodded their heads as though to say, "This girl is doing the right thing! If she can do it, so can we."

After the ceremony, everyone left. The men and women talked about the ceremony with approval as they walked away and reminded each other to maintain secrecy.

* * *

On the way back to our camp, Hoang Quoc Viet and I walked alongside each other. He was a sentimental man, and had lived at my house in the past. Besides Hoang Van Thu, he had been assigned to give direct assistance to the AFNS and the movement in Bac Son-Vo Nhai-Thai Nguyen.

The first time Viet came to my house, he was wearing a black tunic, white pants and slippers, and he carried an umbrella.[6] This scholarly Vietnamese from the lowlands soon became assimilated with our Tay and Nung ethnic minorities.

"What do you think of the ceremony?" Hoang Quoc Viet said, suddenly breaking the silence.

I was jolted from my reminiscences about him, and asked, "What did you say?"

He repeated, "What did you think of the ceremony?"

"It was very good," I said. "They were moved, and understood everything.

He clasped my hand tightly, as though he wanted to communicate to me all his faith and affection, and confided as we walked, "The Central Committee has asked me to go back right away. The critical thing here now is to maintain the movement firmly. You've seen the experience in Bac Son, so don't be overconfident. I have to go. Most of the brothers are new. In everything you do, you should solicit the opinion of the collectivity, and motivate the brothers to act in concert with you. In order to maintain the movement, you must maintain secrecy. You should remind the brothers constantly of the problem of maintaining secrecy."

It seemed as though he wanted to transmit to me all the ideas and experiences he had earned at the risk of his life in the struggle against the colonial administration and their cruel and devious schemes. He emphasized, "You should pay attention to the task of proselytizing enemy soldiers. If we could motivate them not to fight us or to avoid clashes with us, then we could avoid unnecessary bloodshed. With the exception of the security agents and those who deliberately followed the enemy to kill and harm the people, these soldiers are all poor peasants whom the enemy had forced to take up arms and fight the Revolution. Pay particular attention to this, and train the brothers to perform this task well. We don't have many cadres here. When I return to the delta, I will propose that the Central Committee Standing Committee send some cadres up here to reinforce you. I will remain in frequent contact with the movement here. Cam will go with me."

I interrupted him. "Will comrade Cam be going with you?"

My question was really a hint, suggesting that he leave comrade Cam with us. Cam was a cadre who had done a great deal to help the movement. He was considered Hoang Quoc Viet's right-hand man. He was then about 30 years old, tall, muscular and very strong. He was originally a very poor peasant and became a cadre when he understood the purpose of the Revolution. Usually he served as a liaison agent and went on mission with Hoang Quoc Viet.

Hoang Quoc Viet went on, "Cam will accompany me. In the future, if it becomes necessary to send someone up here, Cam knows the way and won't need liaison agents to take him here."

---

6. Traditional costume for Vietnamese men. (Trans.)

When we returned to the hut, the brothers were conducting a meeting.

* * *

In this period, we had withdrawn into the forest and built huts to live in. Our food supplies were insufficient. Our weapons were few and primitive--they consisted of some rifles and muskets used by the Yao people, homemade hand grenades, knives and poisoned arrows. We lived in very difficult conditions, but the local population was extremely loyal to the Revolution, and frequently helped us. Not only did they supply us with food, meat and salt, they also gave us medical supplies. The enemy had destroyed or burned all edible roots and plants in the forest. But at harvest time, the people did not cut the rice in the fields lying near the forest and far from their settlements, leaving the rice to supply the AFNS. In this way, even though we were tightly surrounded on all sides, we continued to obtain food supplies to keep on fighting.

In order to eradicate the guerrillas, the enemy sealed off the three villages of Trang Xa, Phu Thuong, and Lang Muoi--the area where we had chosen to set up our base. There was not one village or settlement, not one section of the forest that the enemy did not search.

The enemy tried all sorts of ways to cut off contact between the people and the AFNS. They gathered the villagers from isolated settlements into a concentration area to facilitate their control. The people were only let out of the camp at eight o'clock in the morning to work in the fields, and had to return at four o'clock in the afternoon, and they were forbidden to go beyond a kilometer from the camp perimeter. Soldiers accompanied them every time they went to the market or to the fields, in order to control them. In the market place, the villagers from each locality were restricted to a separate section, and were forbidden to go to another section. The soldiers forbade the people from various localities to contact each other and exchange information. They restricted the sale of salt and matches, for fear the people would give these products to the AFNS.

While he was in the Vo Nhai war zone, and before he returned to the delta, Hoang Quoc Viet had paid particular attention to the political education of the AFNS in order to bolster their ideological stand. Right after the formation of the Second Platoon, the brothers were very enthusiastic and eager. But later on, as difficulties and hardships increased, some of them showed signs of hesitation. Hoang Quoc Viet had helped us organize a collective life for the AFNS. He suggested that we divide the unit into five squads which would take turns standing guard, fighting and studying. He directly guided us to study the Party policy and the behavior befitting a revolutionary. And as he had pointed out, we saw that it was necessary to establish rules for the brothers' everyday life. No matter how difficult the situation was, we must have discipline and order. Usually, we built our huts near a stream. As soon as we finished cooking, we poured water over the fire to wash away all traces. At first, we carefully made huts with roofs of palm leaves, but our life was so unsettled--we had to move and fight constantly--that we just cut banana leaves and used them to roof our huts. Sometimes we had to move before the banana leaves had time to dry.

In addition, the enemy was throwing many spies into the forest to obtain information. If they suspected guerrillas were operating in some area, they gathered their forces and went in on operation. Sometimes we had just moved to a new area when we got news that the spies were coming, and--like birds fluttering in the forest--we had to move elsewhere immediately. If it rained while we were on the move, then we all got drenched from head to toe. Right after we reached a new camp site, we had to cut down trees and gather banana leaves to build a few temporary huts as shelters against the rain, even if it was dark at night and raining. Some of us went looking for forewood, some cut down bamboo trees, while others gathered leaves and twigs to spread on the damp ground so we could lie down. We piled up the firewood and bamboo and started a fire to dry our clothes and our bags. Our clothes were never put in the sun to dry. After we washed them, we dried them by the fire, and when they were dry we put them in our cloth bags. This way, we were always ready--if there was an alarm, we could leave right away. This was why our clothes always smelled of smoke.

After we built the huts, we built our beds. We cut a few logs and put them at the foot of our beds. In the evening, we drew water from the stream in a bucket, poured the water over our feet [as we stood on the logs] and then stepped on our beds. (At that time, we all went around barefoot--we did not have rubber sandals made from automobile tires like we have now.)

Many military training classes were conducted right in the forest. In addition to theory, the brothers studied basic movements such as carrying the rifles in the hands or over the shoulders, crawling on all fours, crawling on one's belly, rolling, marching, reconnaissance, concealment, practicing ambushes, etc.

The immense and impenetrable forest was a good cover for our troops. Before the enemy could come close to us we had moved to another area. When we came to a new camp site, even if we could only stay for a few days, we carried on our normal activities and our training.

One day at the end of September 1941.

Hoang Quoc Viet set out to return to the delta. After meeting with the Platoon Command Staff, he spent the whole day meeting and talking with the brothers in the unit. He frequently told me, "There are many new brothers in the unit, but they are all good men. They are dedicated to the revolution, and they all hate the imperialists and exploiters. This is the basic reason why they are loyal to the mission of the Party and of the people. You should pay attention and guide them, leading all of them to make progress."

The evening meal included the pork and chicken the people had supplied us. At dusk, I saw Hoang Quoc Viet off. He clasped my hands tightly. He did not say a word, but communicated all his feelings to me in that handshake. We sent a cell composed of comrades Tai, Cham, and Lai to take him and Cam to Khe Mo and then to the main road linking Dinh Ca with Thai Nguyen. Cam will take over as guide from there to the delta.

CHAPTER V

After they ran out of targets in Bac Son, the enemy kept up their frenzied terrorism and gradually shifted their sweep operations toward Vo Nhai. They carried out operations to search for revolutionary organs, encircling and searching each area with ferocity, and doing their best to uncover and destroy our armed forces. At the same time they herded the people in fascist concentration camps in Na Pheo, Dinh Ca, Lang Giua, and Dong En to implement their scheme of "draining the water to catch the fish."

In this period, each villager only had one or two sets of thin, torn and mended clothes left. Their children suffered from malnutrition and looked pale and sickly. Bamboo trees withered for lack of care. Of the houses on stilts, nothing was left but their earth platform and a few charred columns. The houses of comrades Le Duc Ton, Chu Quoc Hung, Hoang Thuong and Hoang Xuan were in ruins. Their bamboo drainpipes were split in two, their rice polishers were smashed, their looms were slashed, their clothes, blankets and mosquito nets were torn to shreds. Anything of value had been seized. Banana, orange, prune and peach trees--big and small--had been cut down. Their gardens were desolate, not one row of cabbage or onion had been left intact. One could no longer hear the barking of dogs, the grunting of pigs, the crowing of roosters, and the clanking of wooden bells around the necks of water buffaloes.

Day and night, the Japanese and French spread their spies to gather information. Their soldiers set up ambushes to attack cadres going on mission. Each area was divided into small square grids and searched. The soldiers even penetrated into the caves and searched the huts in the forest. They tied the blades of grass on the trails into knots, so that if we walked through the knots would untie and they could follow this trail to pursue us. The local spies had many tricks and were familiar with all the roads and paths. They spread ashes in front of cave entrances to detect our footprints.

Following the program already set forth, we split up and went to talk with the ethnic minorities on the task of fighting the French and Japanese, and on the Viet Minh Program. The Tay, Nung, Cao Lan and even the Yao who lived high up in the tall mountains, all loved the AFNS and treated us like members of their own families. We arranged for the people to disperse and hide their belongings, and then to return to their villages and settlements to carry on the struggle. At the same time they would supply us with food and gather information on our behalf.

The armed struggle of the guerrillas resumed and began with the elimination of traitors and spies, and progressed into surprise attacks on French troops, and ambushes.

Usually, in their ambushes the AFNS only aimed their shots at the most reactionary officers and soldiers, the dangerous local officials and spies who guided the enemy.

Along with the fighting, we concentrated our efforts to push ahead the task of proselytizing enemy soldiers. We told the men and women in the villages and even those in jail, who had frequent contacts with the enemy, to remind them of the fact that they had had to leave their homes and families to come here, the land of green forests and red hills, where they would fall prey to malaria and get killed. These men and women also handed the soldiers leaflets calling on them not to attack the people and burn their houses and fields.

One time Trinh, the Assistant to the District Chief, found one of our leaflets on his desk when he came over to sit down. He went green with fear, and wondered how--with high walls around the house, the gates tightly shut, and sentries standing guard day and night--the "Commies" had managed to smuggle this dangerous object in there. If his superiors knew about this, his head would roll. He did not dare make a big thing out of the incident, and not seeing anyone around he hurriedly read the leaflet and then locked it in his desk drawer. Another time, when he plunged his hand in his pants pocket to take out a handkerchief to blow his nose, he pulled out a "Communist" leaflet. His hair stood on end. He broke out in a heavy sweat, and began to tremble with fear, because if the Communists could sneak into his house to do this, they could cut off his head if they wanted to. From then on, he became cautious and did not dare to do anything excessive. Besides, whenever he was about to lead his soldiers to surround, search or sweep an area, his concubine intervened and told him not to do it, so he lost his zeal. In actuality, the "Commies" did not possess the supernatural power the Assistant to the District Chief ascribed to them. It was just that the AFNS was very clever in proselytizing the people. In fact, the concubine of the District Chief's Assistant came from a revolutionary family. Whenever she went home to visit her family, we sent someone to meet her, indoctrinate her, give her leaflets and tell her what to do.

In other cases, we used the families with children or relatives serving in the enemy armed forces, and sympathizers to gather information for us in the various prison camps. Each time the enemy planned to conduct an operation somewhere, they tipped us in advance so that we could avoid the operation, or if we were strong enough we would ambush the enemy.

As for the leaflets and banners calling on the enemy soldiers not to go on sweep operations and not to oppress the people, we disseminated them and posted them in public places.

One night, a cell from the AFNS went to the gate of an enemy outpost, fired a few shots to disturb the soldiers, planted a Viet Minh flag, hung posters and disseminated leaflets. The soldiers did not dare to come out of the post or to return the fire. They only dared to venture outside when morning came. A company was dispatched to pursue the AFNS. The officer shouted to the soldiers, "A lot of Communists came here! Look at their footprints! Look at all the leaves they plucked and put on the ground to sit on! Make an effort, and the big mandarin will award you medals!" It was true that along the way footprints were all over, and judging by the amount of leaves used to sit on, the unit must have been of platoon size. They did not realize that after we completed our mission, we deliberately walked back and forth to leave a lot of footprints, and plucked a lot of leaves to deceive them. The soldiers came from the delta and were unfamiliar with the forest. Besides they were afraid there were too many of us and they were too tired to walk further, so they balked at their commander's orders and refused to go on.

Another day, about two platoons of province troops went on mission in Ngoc My hamlet.

The rice stalks were then about 3 inches tall. At that moment, Ha Cham and Hong Hai went to take up their sentry posts on a hill. Hong Hai, of the Yao ethnic minority, was tall and big. He sat on a log in the fields to keep watch but was lost deep in thoughts. From where he was he could look toward the command headquarters on the next hill, about half a kilometer away. Ha Cham who was looking toward his house which had been burned by the enemy, suddenly cried out, "Soldiers are coming! Look at that yellow mass!"[1]

Seeing that Hong Hai was about to stand to take a look, Ha Cham went on, "Don't stand up!"

But Hong Hai poked out his head anyway, and asked, "Where? Where?"

The soldiers were then gathered on the platform of the house and were looking for footprints left by the "Commies." One of them looked up, saw Hong Hai, and yelled, "There's a big guy over there!"

They shouted to each other to rush up the hill. But Ha Cham and Hong Hai dashed into the forest. The soldiers ran after them. They rushed into the clearing and ran into a squad of our own men. Some were cooking, others were bathing. Surprised, those who were cooking poured away the rice and ran off, carrying the pots with them. Some burned their hands because the pots were too hot. Those who were roasting a dog grabbed the dog and threw it in a bush. Those who were bathing dashed into the forest behind the others. The soldiers fired after them. I was then at the headquarters, about 100 meters from there. I had just finished saying, "Something's happened to the comrades on guard duty," when Ha Cham arrived to report. I told him, "Let's fight!"

We pulled to the Dong Bu River and selected a spot for our ambush. I had figured that the soldiers would certainly pass through here. The eight or nine brothers who were in the forest looked down and saw us. They shouted to each other, "The others have gone out to set an ambush! Let's run down there to join them and fight!"

I asked them, "Did anyone get killed?"

A comrade answered, "No."

"What about the soldiers?" I asked quickly.

"My word, they were yelling, 'there, there, catch them!' but they didn't hit anyone when they fired."

I discussed with Ha Cham and a number of brothers about this group of soldiers. Ha Cham said, "It looks like this group has received our leaflets."

The others nodded their heads in assent. I told them, "Let's call off the ambush. These soldiers are alright."

---

1. The enemy soldiers wore yellow uniforms. (Footnote in text.)

We had had similar experiences before. Our proselytizing effort had had a deep impact on the soldiers. These soldiers had come very close to our men, and it must have been easy for them to hit their targets had they wanted to, but instead they just aimed their shots high while yelling noisily to prove to their commander that they were really chasing and fighting the Communists.

The group of soldiers crossed the forest and then followed a trail to the river. A cell of the AFNS was lying in ambush there. The brothers had been ordered to annihilate the enemy only if they opened fire. Otherwise they should save their ammunition to administer reeling blows to the French troops.

The soldiers rushed to the river to wash their faces. Some scrubbed their hands and feet, others dusted their clothes or picked out thistles. They were talking noisily (the brothers who were lying in ambush nearby could hear everything):

"We were lucky, otherwise we would have been killed today!"

"The Communists killed a dog to 'placate the ghosts,' but neither they nor the ghosts got a bite to eat, and we ended up eating the dog!"

"The Communists were kind-hearted. They didn't want to shoot us. They were behind tree trunks, and we were walking on the trail exposed like water buffaloes in the fields. If they had aimed their rifles at any of us, they could have killed him instantly."

"Anyone who steps out of bounds would get killed. [The best thing to do is to imitate] the style of attack in Nac village. The soldiers fired into the trees to let them run away."

Some were laughing, others were talking, and the stream was noisy with their bantering. The brothers who were lying in ambush had loaded their rifles, but when they heard what the soldiers said they exchanged glances. They knew very well about the event in Nac village. The security police wanted to show their zeal to their French masters, so they took the soldiers on a sweep operation in Nac village. The soldiers, however, had read the appeals in Viet Minh leaflets, so they pushed the security police in the middle of the column and told them, "You walk in the middle, and we'll protect you, otherwise you'll be hit because the Communists are sharp shooters!" Then, wherever they went the soldiers made a lot of noise to warn our men to avoid contact.

One of the soldiers thought his friends were talking too loudly and said, "Don't talk so much! If the others are hiding nearby we'd be finished!"

Suddenly, a voice came from the bush on the edge of the trail, as though to answer him, "You're right! We're right here! If we shoot, you'll die!"

The soldier shook with fright. The adjutant panicked and told the soldiers, "Curse you all! Let's go back and don't talk so much. If the French found out, we'd be dead. It was lucky the French post commander didn't come with us today; if he did, we would have had to fight and waste our lives."

Thereupon he gathered the soldiers and they left the stream bank. When they reached the main road, the soldiers told each other, "See, I was right. They answered us with words. If they had answered us with their rifles we would have all been killed."

Other men in our unit were hiding in that area, rifles at the ready. They could not help saying, "You're right! We're here too! If we want to kill you it wouldn't be too difficult!"

The soldiers hastily and sheepishly retreated to their post.

* * *

November 1941.

Comrade Cam took Hoang Quoc Viet back to the delta at the end of September, and then returned to the Trang Xa War Zone. He was accompanied by a member of the North Vietnam Region Party Committee.

The Command Staff of the AFNS assigned to this comrade, who had been sent up here as reinforcement, the task of proselytizing enemy soldiers.

From then on, we produced all types of leaflets and banners, each type geared to a different kind of soldier: soldiers from the delta, soldiers from the mountain areas, militiamen, and French soldiers. The soldiers from the delta were further divided into groups according to their province of origin: Nam Dinh, Ninh Binh, Thai Binh, Mong Cai, etc. Then there were also soldiers from the provinces of Central Vietnam, and those from the Highlands in South Vietnam. When the villagers informed us which group of soldiers were coming, we had the appropriate type of leaflets ready, which we then spread on the route they were taking, or had mysterious hands place in their pants pockets or handed to them directly by someone. The contents of the leaflets explained clearly to the soldiers: "We are not bandits. We oppose the French imperialists and the Japanese fascists, in order to liberate our country, so that everyone would have enough food to eat and enough clothes to wear, and so that no one would be oppressed and exploited." We pointed out clearly to them: "The Japanese are the ones who have forced your families to pull up rice plants and grow jute for them instead.[2] As a result, your parents, your wives and children had to go hungry. Turn your rifles around and shoot your commanders if conditions permit. If this cannot be done, and you are forced to open fire, then shoot in the air. Let us not shoot one another." The leaflets also reminded them of their native villages: "If you go around burning and looting the people's houses here, and oppressing the peopel, back in your villages, won't your families find themselves in a similar situation? If you sow hatred you'll reap hatred. Please think carefully about this."

If the soldiers from Nam Dinh became "Communized" after they were brought up here, and lost their zeal for killing, then the commanders transferred them elsewhere and soldiers from another area were brought in. Immediately, leaflets arrived with the appeal: "You had better follow the example of the brothers from Nam Dinh. Don't oppress the people. Let's not shoot one another!" In this way the AFNS fought

---

2. This was done to meet Japanese war needs. This, coupled with excessive Japanese rice requisitions and flooding in the Tonkin delta caused a disastrous famine in 1944-1945 which killed 2 million people. (Trans.)

and made propaganda at the same time, motivating and persuading enemy soldiers.

* * *

On a road in Mo Mung, a small valley, on a Winter morning. A squad of the AFNS consisting of Ha Cham, Ha Manh Tai, Son, Hoa, Cuong, etc., and led by Cham and Hoa, was on their way to proselytize the villagers; afterwards they would split into cells to collect rice for the whole unit. The people living near the Na Leng Post had lost a water buffalo, and they had looked for it for two days without finding it. The security police spread the rumor that "the Communists had stolen the buffalo and slaughtered it!" in order to give the AFNS a bad reputation and sow division between the Revolution and the people.

When the cell of Ha Manh and Hoa heard about this, they decided to go and look for the buffalo. Nearing a lime pit, they heard a few weak "meuahs." They went over to take a look and saw a buffalo which had fallen into the pit. The two of them could not pull it out. There was no one around, and they could not go into the village in the daytime because there was a camp of militiamen, security police and province troops nearby. They talked it over and then wrote a few lines on a piece of paper which they stuck to a stick near Na Leng: "Somebody's buffalo has fallen into the lime pit. Come and pull it out." Then they went on their way to perform their mission.

In that period, the enemy was conducting frequent patrols on the Trang Xa-Huong Ba road. Something must have happened, and this was why they had increased the number of soldiers on patrol, and the frequency of these patrols.

The squad from the AFNS returning from their mission had just gone past the main road when they ran smack into an enemy company. The soldiers opened fire. Even though they were caught in an unfavorable terrain and were outnumbered, the brothers quickly returned the fire and tried to retreat from this dangerous spot. Ha Manh aimed carefully at each soldier and said between clenched teeth, "I won't stop until you fellows have 'eaten' all these bullets!"

The shots rang out firmly. Each time he pulled the trigger, a soldier collapsed. This impetuous but hard-working 23-year-old youth was well liked by the brothers in the squad. Manh's intention was to shoot and cover the other brothers so they could withdraw safely. With a Dop 5 rifle and 50 bullets in his pockets, he managed to pin down one whole company. They panicked when they saw over ten of their own men hit either in the head or in the chest. Blood was all over the road. They wanted to rush out and capture this "dangerous bandit," but anyone who popped up was immediately dispatched by Manh. Unable to cope with him, the survivors fired a burst and then fled, carrying their wounded with them.

Ha Cham's squad was dispersed then, but each man headed in the general direction of the headquarters, and they all made it back safely that evening, except Manh. The brothers guessed that Manh had gone to the assembly point agreed upon in advance when they set out on mission in the morning. We told each other, "It's only about five or six kilometers from here to there. It's impossible that Manh hasn't been able to find his way back here in all this time. He must have stopped somewhere." We spread out to look for him. We went to the Mo Mung road and searched the spot where the surprise engagement had taken place, but there was no trace of him. We went back and forth three or four times, but still couldn't find our comrade-in-arms. The brothers went to the settlement where Manh had promised to meet them to go on mission, but there was no sign of him.

Five or six days later, the villagers sent us the news that they had found a dead youth in the forest. He had a rifle slung on his shoulders and clung to two sticks of wood clamped under his arms. The people had buried him properly.

We figured that Manh was seriously wounded, and after the fighting he slung the rifle on his shoulders, broke two twigs to use as crutches, and dragged himself deep into the forest to avoid a new enemy encirclement and to find his way back to the unit. But he lost too much blood.

During the five or six days this impetuous and hard-working youth was gone we had wept a great deal. Now when we got the news, tears streamed down our faces again. Some sobbed loudly. We all felt we must avenge his death.

* * *

After the surprise engagement between the enemy company and the AFNS Second Platoon on the Mo Mung road, the enemy set up a post in Na Leng and appointed Doi Beo ("the fat sergeant")--a native of Cao Bang province--as the post commander. He was a security agent as well as the leader of a province troop platoon, and was notorious for his inhuman beatings and torture.

To cut off all contact between the people and the AFNS, and to prevent the people from passing along information to each other, Doi Beo had devised a very cruel plan. He assembled the villagers from isolated settlements in Na Leng, where he put them either in concentration camps or in prison camps. He said, "This way you won't be able to support the Communists." The fields in Na Leng were then afflicted by a drought, but he could not care less. He wanted the population to starve so that they would not have any food left to supply the AFNS. He forbade small and isolated markets to convene, and allowed only the Dinh Ca market to open.

On market days, he gathered the villagers who wanted to go to the market at 8:00 A.M., at the foot of the Na Leng post, in Dong En. The soldiers accompanied the villagers to the market, marching in front, in the middle, and at the back of the column, their rifles fully loaded, at the ready. The people and Doi Beo walked in the middle. The road from Na Leng to the Dinh Ca market was over 10 kilometers long. On the way, no one could go off anywhere. The whole group went straight to the market. Any villager who rushed out of the column and ran away would be shot immediately.

Once in the market, the soldiers roped off a section of the market place and the villagers did their buying and selling inside this section. The villagers from Trang Xa could only buy and sell in their own roped-off section, while the villagers from Lau Thuong bought and sold in their own separate corner. The Phu Thuong villagers also had their own separate area. People in one section could not wander into another section, and were not even allowed to exchange greetings. The soldiers and Doi Beo, and the security police gang leaders watched each step and each action of the villagers with their eyes full of hatred, their rifles at the ready. The villagers who knew each other were forbidden to talk to each other. If they did, they would be suspected of passing along information or messages.

At 9:00 A.M. or a little later, they took the villagers back. It was the same lineup: the soldiers in front and at the back of the column, Doi Beo and the villagers in the middle. The soldiers tended to be more lax on the way back, because they had eaten and drunk their fill at the market, flirted with the girls, and also because they were tired. Their rifles were still at the ready, but they were not as menacing as when they started out for the market.

All the villagers in the concentration camp wanted to kill the Fat Sergeant. The brothers in the prison camps also sent out a message saying, "We must eliminate the Fat Sergeant. Don't let him get away!" In view of the urgent request of the people, the Command Staff of the Trang Xa War Zone decided to eliminate this dangerous security police gang leader.

This task was given to a squad of eleven comrades--eleven men pitched against a whole platoon of province troops. Besides the Fat Sergeant was as cunning as the devil himself. He was very tricky, and took stringent precautions.

Among the brothers going on this mission were Ky and Son, younger brothers of Ha Manh, the comrade who had sacrificed his life in the previous engagement. Ha Ky was only 22 years old, he was small, slender, but resilient, calm and courageous. He was also a sharpshooter. He asked for the assignment in order to avenge his brother's death, and the War Zone Command Staff agreed.

We formed four cells. One would keep watch and come in as reinforcement, one would shoot the Fat Sergeant and seize his weapon, one would attack the flank of the column and control the road that the Trang Xa post would use to send in reinforcements, another comrade and I would block the road from Dinh Ca to Trang Xa.

A cell under the leadership of comrade Ha Ky was sent out on a reconnaissance mission the previous market day. Ha Ky would choose the site of attack. We were not scheduled to show the stuff we were made of until the following market day. The people, on this market day, would buy oil, shrimp paste, pens and paper, and matches for the AFNS. We also planned to have Miss A and Miss B walk close to the Far Sergeant and flirt with him to put him off his guard. Suoi Bun creek was chosen as the ambush site. It was called Suoi Bun (Muddy Stream) because water was dammed up here, and garbage from all over pilled up here before being carried to the Song Dao River. Besides weapons and ammunition, we took with us enough proselytizing leaflets for the soldiers. After we completed our mission we would disseminate the leaflets right on the battlefield. The brothers stuffed the rolled-up leaflets in sections of bamboo, and sprinkled a little bit of salt on top as a disguise, or they rolled the leaflets up tightly and stuffed them in match boxes.

Market day--the day to avenge the villagers and brothers in the prison camps who had been tortured by the Fat Sergeant, and the death of comrade Ha Manh--arrived. We gathered early in the morning at the ambush site. We stopped about a kilometer from the Muddy Stream, and lay down right next to the road. Then we sent someone out to reconnoiter one more time.

It was a sunny day. On the road the soldiers were taking the people to the market. It was the same scene as on the previous market days: the soldiers accompanied the people, rifles at the ready. The only difference was that today they had a submachine gun positioned in the middle of the column. We were ready, and waited for the Fat Sergeant's gang to return. The minutes of waiting were very tense.

We became more anxious as the sun rose higher and higher in the sky. But there, the soldiers were coming back from the Dinh Ca market, their ranks in disarray!

The avenging muzzle of Ha Ky's rifle pointed at the Fat Sergeant's enormous chest, and moved to keep the sergeant in line of the bullet's trajectory as the sergeant approached from the distance. The task assigned to each cell was clear. Ha Ky's shot would be the signal for the attack.

When the column reached a spot on the road, Mrs. A--one of our sympathizers--asked for permission to go take a leak. Mrs. B asked for permission to go into the bushes. Taking advantage of these moments, these women concealed white sheets for printing leaflets, match boxes and packages of salt for the AFNS, and then rejoined the column. As for Miss A and Miss B, when the column neared the Muddy Stream, they detached themselves and walked at a distance from the Fat Sergeant.

The Fat Sergeant was right within range of Ha Ky's Dop 5 rifle. Ha Ky closed one of his eyes and pulled the trigger, firing in one burst all five bullets, four of which pierced the chest of the dangerous province troop sergeant. He collapsed without uttering a sound. His Dop rifle was flung aside. Ha Son ran over and picked it up, and fired at the soldiers who were trying to sneak away or hide. The soldiers were like a snake with its head cut off and rushed to the stream. They fired noisily in order to alert the two posts at Na Leng and Dinh Ca, and to get reinforcements. The villagers knew that the brothers were attacking when they heard the shots. But not knowing how to avoid the fighting, some of them followed the soldiers and ran to the stream.

"Lie down wherever you are!" I yelled loudly, trying to be heard over the din of shots, "we're the AFNS and we only fight the gang of the Fat Sergeant. Please, don't run back and forth in disorder!"

Suddenly, one of the soldiers plunged to the stream bank, trying to slip through. The AFNS opened fire and he collapsed on the spot. A closer look revealed that he was a local secret police agent notorious for his cruelty.

After getting rid of these two gang leaders, we withdrew, leaving on the battlefield only the "salt containers" and the "match boxes" containing leaflets which the soldiers could put in their pants pockets and take home with them, plus other leaflets which we spread on the ground.

The attack was neatly executed. We had achieved a complete victory, and none of us had received even a scratch.

The attack at the Muddy Stream had a serious impact on the soldiers. They told each other, "See, the Communists only shot at the secret policemen!"

A number of secret police agents who had been very aggressive before became frightened. They changed their clothes and wore uniforms to blend in with the soldiers, but did not escape death either. Later on they stopped walking in front to lead the way, and walked in the midst of the soldiers. The soldiers informed us of this. The secret policemen reported to their superiors and the soldiers were transferred elsewhere.

* * *

Khuon Da was a range of non-rocky hills that separated Nho Village from Nac Village. On the hills, interspersed with bamboo plants, grew huge trees which reared up to the sky--each with a trunk large enough for a man to wrap his arms around. This was the kingdom of the bears, stags, deer, monkeys and wild boars. Once in a while a tiger appeared, leaving behind footprints each as big as a bowl.

We had had to move our camp a dozen times. Enemy patrols had been on the increase. Militiamen and soldiers kept the streams and paths under surveillance.

Enemy leaflets trying to induce the AFNS to surrender were spread everywhere. Large announcements were posted at street corners and at the market place, calling on the people to cut off the heads of the cadres and deliver them to the mandarins in return for rewards. To cope with this new situation, the AFNS withdrew gradually to the foot of the Cai Kinh mountain range.

Units of regular and province troops had been moved here to replace the local troops. Our task of proselytizing enemy soldiers ran into difficulties because the newly arrived soldiers were from minority tribes in Central Vietnam and they spoke neither the Kinh language nor the Nung dialect.

Khuon Da, as its name indicates, was a small and meandering settlement. We stationed two organizations there. One of these, a "cumbersome group," was composed of women, children and old people, and put under the leadership of comrades Nhi Phung, Phuc Lam, Hoang Tai, and Ha Cham--generally speaking, this group consisted of people not fit for combat. Old Mr. Ha Cham was in charge of this group. About ten kilometers from this "heavy" group, was the light [mobile] organization, which provided leadership and command for both groups.

Sympathizers in the surrounding areas had given us a good deal of information about the enemy's intensified activities. Informed, we posted more guards and were constantly on the lookout. Even though the enemy outnumbered us, all we had to do was to remain alert and act cleverly, and they could do nothing to us.

Remembering Hoang Quoc Viet's instructions before he returned to the delta, we held study sessions and discussions every night. During these sessions and discussions, each fighter reported his own activities and those of his cell that day, and each of them expressed his pride at being a National Salvation soldier. When we repeated the sentence, "The struggle of the AFNS will encourage the movement in the whole country and make a small but concrete contribution to the Soviet Red Army's fight against the fascist invaders," to be frank, at that moment I did not fully understand how the shots from our primitive rifles in the Viet Bac mountains and forest, in the midst of the enemy's unbroken rings of encirclement, could echo across our borders to support the Soviet Red Army's struggle against fascism all over the world.

At the time, we only knew we had to deal with the enemy soldiers and secret police who outnumbered us, and whose fire power was vastly superior to ours. However, we had the hearts and minds of the people, and the mountains and forests were on our side. The shots from the AFNS's rifles and muskets continued to resound.

One night, a group of six or seven of us went to Nho Village and waited till the next day to collect rice. The next morning, the people went to the fields to harvest their rice. The soldiers stood guard on a hill next to the fields. When the sun came up, the people spread out the paddy they had harvested and threshed on the spot. The people would reserve this paddy for the AFNS. When it was time to go and the soldiers had blown their whistles five or six times to hurry everyone, the villagers only scooped up the paddy in the wood and bamboo threshers. We had a cell watching the soldiers and another one scooping up the rice that the villagers had deliberately left for the AFNS.

Some of us found a hiding place near the fields but far from the watching eyes of the soldiers in order to talk with the people. One woman told us, "That fellow Sang climbed on a tree and reported that there was a lot of smoke in the forest, and said that the Communists must have their camp there."

An old woman said, "My sons and nephews, that good-for-nothing guy Sang has sided with the French. He is very cruel. You must be careful!"

Before we could say much, the sun was high in the sky and it was noon. Whistles blew. The old woman told me, "The soldiers are forcing us to leave. I'm leaving this pile of paddy I'm drying here for you, as well as the other pile over there!"

The yells of the soldiers reached us. "Let's go! Carry it all back! Anyone who leaves his paddy behind for the Communists will have his head cut off!" And, "You old crones, hurry up! Vite![3] We're very hungry!"

The fields became deserted. The last soldier had turned around, his back toward us, to urge the villagers lagging behind with their loads to hurry up. We went to the places where the people had hidden paddy for us. We were full of respect and admiration for these sisters and mothers, and at the same time we felt sad that we had not been able to do anything to alleviate their sufferings. What the villagers told us indicated that the soldiers had detected our presence, and it was possible that they would launch a surprise attack any time. We held a meeting, and unanimously agreed that Khanh Phuong, Phan, Pho and I should go at once to warn the heavy group and help them move immediately to a different location.

---

3. French word for "faster." (Trans.)

We walked around the mountain slope to reach this group. On the ground, footprints of wild boars, deer and antelopes dashing off at the approach of someone were still visible. Pho said right away, "Some people must have passed through here a short while ago!"

I thought that was a correct observation, and inspected everything more closely as we moved on. When we reached the stream that flowed out of Nac village, we saw enemy soldiers converging from three directions: one group coming up from the stream, one coming from the path leading out of Nac village to Khuon Da, and the third one coming from Dau and Vang villages and following the mountain slope into the pass. I thought, "Alright, let us fight it out! Even though we're outnumbered, we'll take them on!" There were only four of us, and we were armed with two muskets and two rifles.

We hid ourselves to observe the enemy's deployment in order to devise a plan of action. If the soldiers followed the stream they would run into the camp of the heavy section, but this route was difficult and there were many steep slopes and waterfalls along the way. The soldiers veered to the right. We must reach this section full of women, children and old people, no matter what!

At the top of the Khuon Da pass, we saw that footprints from nailed boots had stomped out a new trail.

I signalled to the other brothers to remain quiet. Then the four of us split into two groups. We hid part of the rice we had collected away in order to facilitate our movement in combat.

Perhaps the soldiers had gathered their forces and arrived in Khuon Da settlement. We went to the trail and could hear them urge each other on and curse each other.

"Phan, go ahead and be our point man." I assigned a different task to each man. "Khanh Phuong will be second and I'll be third in line. Pho will take up the rear."

Phan accelerated and was about twenty or thirty meters ahead of us. When he was halfway down a slope leading to a clearing, an enemy platoon appeared at the top of a slope on the other side. He jerked his hand as a signal for us and then rushed down to the clearing to hide and get ready to fight. Khanh Phuong ran down after him. I was following behind, and seeing them do that, I rushed down the slope. The soldiers fired a few shots after us, but missed. The bullets hit the ground and flung up red dust which stained our clothes. Pho was about to rush down the slope and join us in the clearing, but the enemy fire was so intense that he had to turn into the forest.

When we reached the clearing, we lay down, each man about two or three arms' length from the other. We crawled closer to each other, and hid behind a fallen tree.

I jerked my chin and asked Khanh Phuong, "Where's Pho?"

"He knows what to do, don't worry," Khanh Phuong answered.

The soldiers were coming down the slope. They saw me wear a blanket, but could not see my rifle which I grasped between my thighs. Two soldiers fought with each other:

"You shoot first or I shoot first? Look, he's wearing a bright red blanket!"

"Let's get this guy, we can hit him easily!"

Emboldened by the fact that they outnumbered us and were better armed, the soldiers ran down the slope, yelling like mad. The corporal shouted, "A l'assaut!"[4]

I could not figure out what he had said, and asked Khanh Phuong, "What did he yell?"

Khanh Phuong was puzzled, and clucked his tongue. "He must have told them to rush down here!"

I smiled and told Khanh Phuong and Phan, "Stay calm! Aim at one soldier at a time, and open fire. Each shot should hit its mark."

"Have confidence in us," Khanh Phuong said. "I can fell a tiger even with my musket."

Khanh Phuong was usually very proud of his musket. I looked toward the soldiers. They were egging each other on:

"What the hell are you afraid of?"

"Let's go!"

Four aggressive soldiers rushed down to the clearing first. We could hear them loading their rifles and the sound of their nailed boots. I turned to Phan and said softly, "Wait till they are within range."

Phan nodded. He moved the long barrel of his ten-bullet rifle[5] to keep it trained on the soldiers. Suddenly, bang! Phan's rifle fired a ringing shot. A soldier in yellow uniform collapsed like a felled tree and rolled on the ground. Phan pulled the trigger a second time but the bullets jammed as they crowded each other into the barrel.

Khanh Phuong's musket suddenly became temperamental this evening! He pulled the trigger three times, but each time we only heard a hollow "click" sound.

Seeing this, the corporal knelt down and aimed. He moved his rifle and trained it on Khanh Phuong. Khanh Phuong compressed his lips and pulled the trigger a fourth time. His rifle rang out before the corporal could pull his trigger; he fell down and flung his rifle away. The soldiers rushed down in disorder. Khanh Phuong could not load his musket any more. It was only then that I used my rifle, and each of my shots was a sure hit. We kept watch on all three sides as we fired. The soldiers were yelling and making a terrible din:

"They're in the middle of the clearing. Feu!"

---

4. French for "forward, attack!" (Trans.)

5. A submachine gun, also called a "Pac hooc." (Footnote in text.)

The soldiers fired a burst, and a shower of leaves fell. Suddenly, a voice yelled, "They're at the rotten tree trunk near the stream. Fire!"

Each time one of them discovered a target, they all poured their fire in that direction. They did not even realize that I had changed my position. Another voice, perhaps the voice of a corporal: "They're loading their rifles, I can hear the click click sounds!"

The soldiers mistakenly believed that our group in the clearing was rather large. They had just lost a few more dead and wounded, so they hesitated and did not dare to advance forward. They did not realize that the "click, click" sound was made by Phan as he desperately tried to dislodge the bullet stuck in the barrel of his rifle with a musket priming rod. My hiding place was very shallow and half of my body stuck out. But we were all good shots and the soldiers were scared. Some of the soldiers saw us and argued loudly with each other in their hiding place:

"He's just popped his head out!"

"How could you have missed such an easy target!"

"You're all good for nothing!"

A couple of them went around and fired madly at us from below. I turned around and aimed at those who were popping in and out behind the trees. I aimed at a militiamen and opened fire. The hat on his head was knocked away. If he had raised his head a little higher, he would have been hit in the brain. I could see the others behind the trees shake so much with fright they could not shoot.

"Throw down grenades!"

The soldiers up on the slope screamed, "Fire!"

"You mother . . . , if you see them, why don't you fire yourself!"

Because we managed to keep ourselves well hidden, the soldiers kept missing us even though they were firing like crazy. All they did was to cut down branches and scratch the rocks.

We waited for a long time, but no grenades were thrown. So, the soldiers were only trying to scare us. They had lost six or seven dead, but none of us had been hit.

Almost an hour had gone by. The light was fading. Khanh Phuong who could not load his musket said softly, "There's one. Go ahead and shoot. He's poking his head out!"

I wanted to hand him my rifle to shoot, because he could see the soldier. But it was slung over my shoulder, underneath the blanket, and I got all tangled up as I tried to pull it out, and couldn't pass it to him.

At that moment, reinforcements came for the soldiers and they began to fire their grenade launchers toward us. Judging from the fact that it was getting dark, and from the way the soldiers were fighting, I knew they were not going to stay here for long. Perhaps this was the sign they were going to withdraw. The sounds of explosions reverberated in the mountains and forests. If we stayed in one place, it would be difficult for us to continue the attack. We must maneuver to deceive the enemy and circle around. I threw a stone as a signal to Phan and signalled to Khanh Phuong to withdraw. They understood and nodded. I aimed at the confused soldiers and fired two shots. They flung themselves down, with their faces to the ground to avoid the bullets. The three of us rushed across a tree as large as a table which had fallen across the stream. We ran up the clearing, into the forest, in the direction of the heavy organization. We ran at that speed for half an hour.

The camp was deserted.

It rained heavily as darkness fell. We could not light a fire and cook. We cut banana leaves to cover ourselves from the rain and slept in the Khuon Da camp.

In the morning we went to the spot where the engagement had taken place the previous day and searched all around there, moving further and further away, without finding anyone. We wondered whether this group of women, children and old people was hiding some place, or whether they had been scattered and gotten lost. We saw no sign of Pho either, and we wondered what he was doing during the mad exchange of fire between the enemy and us, since we did not hear him fire any shots during the whole attack. However, our deepest concern was for the heavy organization. We even went to positions 1 and 2, which we had chosen in advance as withdrawal points for them in case there was an alert--but we did not find any traces of them either.

We spent the whole day searching for this group. We examined the marks on the trails leading to their camp, but nothing indicated that enemy soldiers had been here. We figured they had moved away, but could not tell in which direction they had gone.

* * *

What in fact did happen to the group led by old Mr. Ha Cham? When he heard gunfire echoing in the mountains, he told his people, "They're fighting over there, right above our camp. Let's go! We'll go to Ngoc My first."

He did not actually know that our mobile organization was stationed in Ngoc My, but his common sense and his knowledge of the terrain in this part of the forest told him it would be best to move there.

So the people left--the women with small children carried the babies on their backs and led the older ones by the hand, while the others carried pots and pans, bags of clothing, rice and corn. They took everything with them, and did not leave anything which could indicate to the enemy that they had camped there.

They walked all night, led and encouraged an an old man, Mr. Ha Cham.

The next morning, while we were anxiously searching for them in the two positions of retreat agreed to in advance, the old man led the people to Ngoc My forest, right to the spot where the mobile organization was stationed. Pho and the brothers who had gone with us to Nho village to collect rice had returned, and needless to say, they were happy to see this group come in. They carried the children into the huts and put them in bed; they supported the women to sit down, gave everyone water to drink and prepared rice. Old Mr. Ha Cham drew on his water pipe and related the story of his group's journey. But since the three of us--Khanh Phuong, Phan, and myself--had not come back, everyone was agitated, as though he was sitting on fire, and could not concentrate hard enough to hear his story from beginning to end.

That whole day, they all looked out into the forest and waited.

At night, we still had not returned, and some people began to weep.

At dawn the next day, we returned to the headquarters. Hearing us coming in, everyone leaped out of bed, and wept and laughed with joy.

* * *

Later on, the people in Dau and Van villages, and the brothers jailed in the Trang Xa prison camp sent a message to the AFNS saying that "the soldiers had carried nine dead back. Among those killed was the corporal."

* * *

The enemy scheme of separating the people from the AFNS was really cruel, and caused the AFNS a lot of difficulties. Our food supplies were running low, and we had had to begin supplementing our rice rations with roots.

Previously, the villagers had tried by every means to supply us with food; for example, they left their threshed paddy in the ricefields or in the crop patches in the forest. They left salt, matches, paper and food concealed in tree hollows or rock cracks, or near the water mills. In order to feed for an extended period of time a unit composed at times of up to seventy men unable to farm, as well as a number of AFNS fighters' families who had to flee enemy repression and follow their men into the forest, the sparsely populated villages in the Vo Nhai area had to cut down on their own food consumption. They had to tighten their belts and sacrificed themselves to a high degree. But now their ability to supply us had decreased enormously. We were worried that we would not have anything to eat during the period when the grains from the previous harvest ran out and the next harvest had not arrived, because most of the population had been concentrated in camps. The monsoon rains were also approaching. If the AFNS did not come up quickly with a solution to cope with this situation, they would find themselves in a very dangerous position.

Finally, we ran into another difficulty: we were completely cut off from the Central Committee. We had gone many times to the liaison stations located in Tam Thai (about 6 kilometers from Thai Nguyen town), in Long Giang (near the foot of the Deo Khe Pass), and Khe Mo, but there was no news of the Central Committee--there was no letter, and no one showed up.

The situation became even more critical and urgent. The enemy surrounded us on four sides and their encirclement covered Vo Nhai-Bac Son, Dong Hy, Yen The and Huu Lung. We continued to operate right in the midst of this blockade. The Central Committee had instructed us that our basic task was still to persevere and keep up our guerrilla warfare, and resist terrorism. We reviewed these instructions together to see how much we had accomplished and what we had been unable to achieve.

Having a firm grasp of the spirit of the Central Committee's instructions relayed by Hoang Quoc Viet before he returned to the delta, the AFNS Command Staff decided that we should take the initiative to solve our problems, set forth our own plan of action, boldly develop the innovative spirit of the collective, and act immediately with determination. If we clung to our war zone to cope with the enemy, the people and the revolutionary forces could not avoid suffering losses.

Because enemy repression was getting fierce, because the revolutionary movement in the whole country had not been strongly propelled forward, and because we had been unable to decisively mobilize the people in Bac Son-Vo Nhai in order to combine political struggle with armed struggle, after months of combat, the AFNS saw that it was necessary for them to withdraw in many directions and break out of the enemy's encirclement.

However, the AFNS must not withdraw all of its forces. When the enemy concentrated their forces in Trang Xa to "drain the water to catch the fish" they must have left a gap in Bac Son. The day Hoang Quoc Viet left for the delta, he suggested that we send cadres there to reconsolidate Bac Son and restore the movement in that area. Unless Bac Son was restored, we would not have safe corridors to move through in the future. So, now the AFNS Command Staff decided to send cadres to the Phu Thuong and Bac Son region. (Since the people in this region were devoted to the Revolution, it was not long before Phu Thuong-Bac Son became a reliable political corridor.)

A section of the AFNS was scattered among the people to carry out armed propaganda and set up infrastructure among the masses. On November 28, 1941--that is to say the 10th day of the 10th lunar month in the year Tan Ty--comrades Nguyen Cao Dam, Nhi Phung, Phuong Cuong, Mong Phuc Quyen, Hoang Thi Mon, Hoang Thi Ngoan, and Duong Thi An slipped through the enemy encirclement and went to Dai Tu to contact comrade Duong Nhat Quy[6] who was operating there, in order to expand the movement to the areas of Dai Tu, Son Duong, Yen Son, and Dinh Hoa. A second cell consisting of comrades Hoang Van Thai, Dinh Che, Tai, Hoa, and Phan went to Phu Luong and Dong Hy. A third cell composed of comrades Phan Van Thai, Phan Van Lai, and Quang Hien went to Huu Lung and Yen The. (It was these sections, dispersed among the people, who succeeded in building up a large infrastructure in the provinces of Thai Nguyen and Tuyen Quang, and helped create the favorable conditions which made the future insurrection possible.)

The main body of the AFNS, composed of 40 people, continued to confuse the enemy with maneuvers, carry out ambushes, disseminate leaflets, and attack the enemy by every means.

While going around to proselytize the people, we met many villagers who urged us to withdraw temporarily elsewhere as they handed us food supplies.

---

6. Duong Nhat Quy, a Nung, was from Dai Tu district, Thai Nguyen province, and joined the Party in 1933. He took part in the Bac Son uprising. (Trans.)

We discussed this among the Command Staff and talked it over many times in the unit. Many questions, many problems were raised: should we go or should we stay? If we left, where could we go? If we stayed, where should we set up camp? Should we attack strongly or let the situation remain the way it was? Someone said, "It would be best for us to move to Yen The. That was the territory of De Tham[7] and was famous for its courageous resistance to the French in the old days." But another man answered right away, "The enemy has also concentrated the people in camps in Yen The. The soldiers are surrounding every area there. The situation there is the same as here in Vo Nhai and Dinh Ca." A comrade asked, "If we stay here, the way things are, how are we going to expand?" There was a bold opinion: "Let's cross over into China, the French won't be able to do a thing, and will have to give up."

The Command Staff raised a few alternatives so the brothers could discuss them. With the exception of the brothers on guard duty, all those who stayed at home took part in the discussion. The 7th Central Committee Resolution had said clearly: "We must preserve and expand the Bac Son armed forces in order to transform it into the military core for the future insurrection." We all remembered this very well. The existence or loss of the base area also depended on us. The brothers reached a unanimous conclusion: conditions did not permit us to attack the enemy, we could not move to Tuyen Quang because we had not been able to establish contact with our organization there, we could not move to Yen The because the enemy was encamped there. We must leave, definitely.

But where should we go? The Command Staff had carefully studied the area where the AFNS Second Platoon could move. That area was one where the revolution had maintained an infrastructure for a long time, where the beneficial influence of the period of revolutionary high tides led by the Chinese Communist Party--such as the Red Lungchou and Red Kwangchow period of 1927[8]--still lingered on unchanged among the local people, and where many comrades who had taken part in the movement during these periods were still active.

This was also an area where many Vietnamese revolutionaries had been passing through, back and forth, for over a decade. The local people had understood and helped our revolution with a high spirit of friendship and disinterest. Many families had protected, fed and housed cadres. Comrade Nguyen Ai Quoc had operated in this area. And comrade Hoang Van Thu himself was well loved by the people there. To them he was like a member of their own families and a local cadre. Whenever he was away, they talked about him often, and whenever he came back, everyone--from the old people to the children--greeted him and received him warmly, and invited him home. They did their best to protect him and take care of him.

Also, many AFNS brothers were familiar with the road leading to this area. It went through mountains and forests, and so it would be easy for us to conceal our movement. All along the length of this route--from Bac Son to Binh Gia, to Van Mich--we had a network of

---

7. See footnote 3, p. 66. (Trans.)

8. This refers to the Canton Commune of 1927 and the Left River Soviet set up by the Chinese Communist Party in the Lungchou area of Kwangsi province in 1929-30. (Trans.)

sympathizers. That Khe was the native place of comrades Phan, Pho and Lam. The Nung minority had lived in this area along the China-Vietnam border for generations, and on both sides of the frontier they had relatives, acquaintances and friends. In their souls and hearts, they did not pay any attention to the border markers or the lines that delineated the two countries on maps.

All we would have to do would be to cross the border into China and go for one or two kilometers, and we would reach villages where many of us had relatives. For example, comrades Duong Van Tu and Duong Van Thuc had relatives in Kheo Meo. Mine were in Ban Trang. Comrades Hua Dinh Khanh and Ha Cham also had relatives in this area. Comrade Nhi Phung's family who used to live in Bang Tuong had also moved there. The families of a few other comrades had fled there to avoid enemy repression.

Once there, we would escape from the control and repression of the French and Japanese. If we could meet the diplomatic organ of the Viet Minh there,[9] it would be easy for us to operate. If not, we could count on the support of the local sympathizers and on our relatives to live and deal with the Chinese Kuomintang and the bandits.

This area would also constitute a convenient springboard from which we could easily cross back into Vietnam to operate and build up our infrastructure among the people.

For us ethnic minorities people, to have to leave our villages and families was something which weighed heavily on our minds and hearts. I said, "If our Viet Minh diplomatic delegation is still there, everything will be favorable. If it's no longer there, we might be persecuted by Chiang Kai Shek, and we might be arrested and thrown in jail. But even if they put us in jail, they would eventually have to release us. We should not complain about hardships and difficulties. My family originally came from Ban Trang, and I still have relatives there. Other brothers also have relatives over there. Although we live on different sides of the frontier, our family ties are deep and strong. This is a factor which should work to our advantage. However, we won't rely entirely on them. Once there, we'll rely mainly on our own resources and strength to study, train and create conditions for our return to our country to operate."

I stopped. I was quiet by nature and never talked much--or to be more exact, I did not know how to talk on and on for a long time. But that day I felt that I had talked very long and that I had poured out to the brothers the deepest feelings in my heart. I remembered what old Mr. Thu Son had told me once: "The Party member--whenever he is living among the workers or the peasants, in the mountain areas or in the lowlands, in our country or abroad, should constantly engage in revolutionary activities, and expand the Party infrastructure and the mass bases. We are fighting not only for our Fatherland's independence and freedom, and for our people's happiness, but also to contribute to

---

9. The Viet Minh did not have direct relations with the KMT government in this period, and was dealing with it through their front organization, the "Vietnam Branch of the International Anti-Aggression Association," set up by Ho Chi Minh in early 1942. The Chinese KMT was planning to enter Indochina to attack Japanese supply lines and maintained cordial relations with this association in the hope of obtaining its assistance when their troops entered Vietnam. (Trans.)

the liberation of the proletariat and the oppressed nations in the world. Wherever there is oppression, there is struggle. Wherever he is, the Party member should earnestly take part in this struggle."

I thought, "If we could hold Tuyen Quang and Bac Son, and add to it a border area, then we would have a solid base of operation until we could return to Pac Bo--and this would be a great advantage for us." Once in Pac Bo, I would solicit instructions from the Old Man. I was anxious to find out whether he had run into any difficulties. The more I thought about what he had taught us in those days, the more profound I found his teachings to be. In this situation, they were like a compass guiding us on our way.

I continued, "The people in the area we're going to are suffering as much as our own people. Since they share our sufferings, they will love us and help us. But we are revolutionaries, and we cannot rely entirely on the people there. We'll have to do a lot ourselves, with our own two hands. We can only operate if we can assure our own livelihood."

"Right! What comrade Cu[10] has said is true," a number of comrades agreed immediately.

A comrade analyzed, "In the previous meeting, someone raised the question of pretending to surrender to the enemy. But to do this would mean we're afraid of hardships and difficulties. Besides, the enemy won't allow us to live in peace, and they will try to induce and pressure us to do as they ask, and we'll end up betraying our fatherland."

Le Duc Ton, who had remained quiet, suddenly said, his face clouded with anger, "If we pretended to surrender to the enemy, we would have to put our weapons aside. This is out of the question. The Central Committee has told us to keep up the armed struggle. We should not act in an irresponsible manner."

"The more critical the situation becomes, the more the enemy spread bad rumors," Nong Thai Long added. "They said for example that one of our brothers died of starvation and when they opened his belly, they found only undigested leaves. They took villagers as hostages and said, 'If the Communists kill one of our men, we'll shoot three hostages in return!' They spread counter-propaganda among the people, saying, 'The Communists are finished. They've been badly defeated by the Great French Government, and are fleeing into hiding!' They want to demoralize and discourage us."

I added, "If we want the Revolution to succeed, we must persevere and be skillful in our struggle. We cannot be pessimistic and desperate. Neither can we be reckless and adventurous in the fashion of 'even if we don't succeed, we'll be mature men.' The AFNS is the military organization of the Party, and has been assigned a clear-cut task by the Central Committee. We cannot, because of temporary difficulties, take it upon ourselves to dissolve the AFNS or change its mission. Therefore, we must be determined to preserve it, we must not allow the enemy to destroy it, and we must not dissolve it ourselves by one action or another."

---

10. Chu Van Tan's alias. (Trans.)

Everyone raised his fist and expressed unanimous agreement. An atmosphere of enthusiasm and confidence enveloped us.

* * *

During the time we lived close to the Central Committee comrades--and later on through the news that they sent us from the delta before contact was cut off--we learned to assess the revolutionary movement in the country, as well as to deepen our understanding of the situation prevailing in the world at the time. Once in a while, we asked sympathizers to bring us back a few newspapers from Thai Nguyen--such as the *Dong Phap*, *Trung Bac* and *Tan Van*. This understanding helped the AFNS to work out its policy of temporary withdrawal.

On December 7, 1941, the Japanese fascists suddenly attacked the American naval base at Pearl Harbor. After that, the German-Italian-Japanese axis declared war on the United States. It was only then that the Chinese Kuomintang declared war on Japan. However, they continued to concentrate the main body of their forces to attack the Red Army--which was fighting the Japanese--in the rear. The Japanese troops attacked and occupied many colonies belonging to Great Britain, the United States, France and Holland--such as Hong Kong, Malaya, Singapore, Burma, the Philippines, Indonesia and New Guinea. They met with no significant resistance from the Allied forces. In addition, the Italian and German troops were putting intense pressure on the British forces in Egypt.

Although the Soviet Red Army had lifted the seige of Moscow and achieved some initial success in Leningrad, the German fascist forces were still formidable. The Chinese Communist Revolution, on its part, was going through its most critical phase. Their liberated zones had shrunk, and they were running into many economic difficulties because of the Japanese and Kuomintang blockade.

On December 13, 1941, the Japanese militarists forced the Decoux[11] gang to sign another agreement giving them complete power to act in Indochina. The Chiang Kai Shek troops attacked the North Vietnam border region, and the question of "China's entry into Indochina" was raised.

The Party Central Committee's policy was to let the Viet Minh Front negotiate an alliance with the Chungking government to fight the French and Japanese on the basis of equality and mutual support. At the same time, the Central Committee assessed that the situation in the country in general did not permit us as yet to carry out a direct revolution. The conditions for an insurrection did not obtain, but we should urgently prepare our forces to cope with a sudden and unexpected turn in the situation.

In this situation, the AFNS would break through French encirclement, and withdraw temporarily to preserve their forces. The AFNS would temporarily avoid a confrontation with a much stronger enemy force, and then fight and clear a route back into the country in the future. Once the AFNS had withdrawn, the enemy forces would withdraw sooner or later. The sections of the AFNS who stayed behind to remain

---

11. The Governor General of Indochina. The French Vichy government in Indochina was collaborating with the Japanese. (Trans.)

in close contact with the infrastructure would--along with the people--take advantage of this opportunity to reinforce and reconsolidate their forces.

After we had unanimously approved of this line of action, each AFNS fighter would tell the villagers whenever they met them, "We're withdrawing in order to create conditions for our return. We are not going to cross over into China to lead a life of ease and leisure."

All communication routes from the war zone to the outside had been cut. The villagers had gone through eight months of brutal repression. The enemy's encirclement around the Vo Nhai-Trang Xa area was tightened further and further with each passing day. We had no news whatsoever of the AFNS sections that had been sent to Dai Tu, Dinh Hoa, Son Duong, Phu Luong, Dong Hy, Huu Lung and Yen The to operate. Their task of expanding the movement was not an easy one, because the mass organizations in those areas still had few members and were not firm. In a word, it was not possible for us to move there.

We would break through the enemy siege. Along the way to the frontier, there would still be many dangers, and many unforeseen things could happen to us. No matter how thoroughly and how carefully we planned everything, it was impossible for us to prepare for all eventualities. But to make revolution, we must remain resilient and calm to overcome one obstacle after another. We must gather each victory, no matter how small, and be determined to struggle until final victory is achieved. It was only in moments like this that we could see clearly how accurate the Old Man's words had been.

* * *

Our contact with the Central Committee in the delta was cut off, and this worried us. In the first lunar month of the year (February 1942) we sent an agent to the delta to report our situation to the Central Committee and to ask for instructions. Unfortunately, he was caught when he arrived in Phuong Lien (Thai Nguyen province). This bad news reached brother Quoc Hung in Dinh Ca. He immediately sent a liaison agent to go in all urgency to Trang Xa to inform us. Knowing from past experience [that the enemy would carry out a raid] we immediately moved our camp. At the same time, we resolutely continued to prepare for our long journey.

CHAPTER VI

It took us one month to prepare for our journey. We polished rice, roasted glutinous rice to use as dry food supplies, wove baskets, made shoulder poles to carry our baggage in order to make it less heavy and less tiring to lug around. We figured that at the beginning each of us would have to carry a load of 40 kilograms, consisting of blankets, mosquito nettings, clothes, food supplies and weapons. We planned to replenish our food supplies in Dinh Ca, and then go on straight from there without resupplying.

We assigned the task of reconnoitering our route to a squad in Phu Thuong and a squad in Bac Son.

The Phu Thuong squad sent Mr. Quay all the way to Van Mich two or three times to check on the situation there and to gather information about the route from Van Mich to That Khe. He also carefully checked the guard posts and the patrols carried out by soldiers blockading the Vo Nhai-Bac Son region, in order to find out their patterns of operation.

The AFNS cells further south were ordered to intensify their activities in order to divert enemy forces. The unit in Cay Thi (in Dong Hy, at the junction of the three districts of Dong Hy, Yen The and Vo Nhai) deliberately walked in muddy places and left a mass of footprints pointing toward Huu Lung in order to deceive the enemy into pursuing in that direction. Along the way, they also plucked a lot of leaves and put them on the ground to sit on--each man using two or three leaves to make the enemy believe that the main body of our unit had withdrawn to Phu Binh and Yen The.

During this month of preparation, we held up to three or four meetings. All our camps were raided by the enemy. The soldiers planted booby traps in the forest--grenades tied to strings stretched across the trails. Once Quoc Hung's section had to move and Quoc Hung led the way. On the way, he found a string and, suspecting that the trail had been booby trapped, he had to turn around and follow another route.

In addition to the posts scattered here and there and a force encircling our area, the enemy also despatched a main force of a few hundred men to pursue us in the direction of Yen The. But at that very moment, the main body of the AFNS was moving north.

* * *

We travelled during the daytime after we left Bu Cu-Da Trang. In the early morning, we had our breakfast as normal, eating till we were full, and then set off. The reconnaissance unit walked in front. There were thirty of us; the oldest man in the group was Mr. A (Mr. Nhi's alias) who was close to 50 years old, and the youngest was Hong Long[1]

---

1. He is now a cadre in Vo Nhai District. (Footnote in text.)

who was 14-15 years of age. Each man carried a musket. There were only two rifles for the whole group. I carried a submachine gun.

It took us one day, going across the forest, to reach Lau Thuong village. We waited till very late at night and then moved down to the fields of this village. We circled around the guard posts and arrived in the Con Gau (Bear) Mountain (in Dong Trong hamlet, Phu Thuong village) when it was almost daylight. The other AFNS section, composed of comrades Quoc Hung, Thai Long, Binh and Quoc Vinh had arrived from Bac Son earlier; they welcomed us with joy and our happiness was beyond words.

The villagers here had been concentrated in Na Pheo by the enemy. Under the leadership of a few comrades who had succeeded in keeping their cover and who had been assigned to maintain the local movement--such as brother Luc Van Du (alias Phu), Mrs. Sang, sister Pinh, Miss Thu, Miss Sam, etc.--the villagers protested and forced the enemy to allow them to go out and farm their fields.

A short time after daybreak, the women--carrying machetes to clear vegetation to plant crops--brought us cooked glutinous rice and a couple of cans full of rice.

We stayed here for a day. The next day we met with the women in the infrastructure to talk some more about their mission. We agreed on secret signals and meeting places to be used in the future whenever the AFNS wanted to contact the local infrastructure--such as special knife marks on tree trunks, and "letter boxes" hidden in rock cracks and tree hollows. We told the comrades staying behind that after the AFNS withdrew, the enemy would lose the immediate target for their searches and their soldiers would be worn out, so if these comrades took advantage of this situation to intensify their proselytizing of enemy soldiers, then perhaps the troops would all be withdrawn. If this happened, the first thing for them to do would be to organize the villagers to clear land for cultivation in order to avoid hunger. Too much land had been left uncultivated, and without rice the revolution could not last very long. Finally, the comrades should motivate the families with relatives jailed in the Dinh Ca and Cho Chu posts to send petitions--either written separately by each family, or by groups of families--to these posts to demand the release of their relatives. We also told the comrades staying behind to make a special effort to re-establish contact with the cells operating in Dai Tu, Son Duong, Dinh Hoa, Yen The and Huu Lung.

The villagers came to see us in a constant stream in the morning and in the afternoon. Quite a large number of them came, and each brought a gift. We told them we would not be able to come back until the end of the monsoon season--at the end of the 8th lunar month and the beginning of the 9th. We told the comrades in the local infrastructure, "To make revolution one must persevere. From now until final success is achieved, we'll have to go through many more difficulties. So, you must at all costs maintain the revolutionary spirit of the people by continuously organizing struggles against easy as well as difficult targets."

In the early morning of March 8, 1942, the AFNS fighters set out again. We had taken along enough food to last us until we reached the border, and we would not have to resupply ourselves along the way. The women had brought us cooked and uncooked glutinous rice, flat cakes and cones made with glutinous rice and wrapped in leaves.[2] Before going out to clear land, many of them came to send us off.

On behalf of the brothers, I said, "Making revolution means resisting the imperialists. It is only natural that the imperialists are terrorizing us like this. But don't let this terrorism worry you or frighten you to the point that you accept defeat and no longer dare to struggle. Bad elements are always trying to demoralize us, buy us off and entice us. We must unmask them! We should unite with one another into one bloc and we must love one another. After we--your sons and brothers--are gone, you--our mothers and sisters--must remember to contact the people in the Dinh Ca jail. You must keep your eyes open and try to contact Trang Xa. You shouldn't all come out into the open to operate."

The people understood our feelings and these ardent words. When we said goodbye, many of them could not hold back their tears, the tears of love and trust.

We followed each other and climbed to the towering mountain peaks by Phat village. The feelings of attachment to their homeland and the thoughts about the difficult road ahead must have weighed more heavily on each fighter than the baggage and weapons he carried.

Rifle shots echoed from an enemy post. We walked in the direction of Bac Son, crossing steep slopes and deep gorges. When it was almost evening, we arrived in the Khuoi Noi clearing. After a short rest, we again cut through the forest, crossed the Nga Hai stream and Van Ha, and arrived in Ban Loong settlement. This used to be a liaison station linking Vo Nhai and Bac Son, but now it was completely deserted. Ricefields were left uncultivated and the ground was covered with moss. There was not a soul passing through. We walked on for a while, and when the night was very advanced, we stopped at the foot of the Ban Loong mountain.

The crop patches in the forest had not been completely overgrown with weeds, so we spread leaves on the ground and slept there. Jungle leeches, sensing human odor, aggressively crawled around--some even crawled into our ears, inside our clothes, and on our necks. We started to bleed all over from their bites. The night mist was chilly.

In the morning of March 19, we resumed our journey, going through the forest in order to reach Bo Tat (Vu Lang). Bo Tat was far from any settlements or roads. The old crop patches had become overgrown and reclaimed by the jungle. There was a deep cave with a pool of water in the middle of the forest, familiar to all of us. We stopped here.

During our stop, we divided up various tasks: some went to reconnoiter the route, some stood guard, and some cooked. The others rested.

Though we had gone through many difficulties and dangers in the first few days of our trip, everyone was talking and laughing happily. Many brothers sang revolutionary songs, and a feeling of optimism and enthusiasm welled up in our hearts, in contrast to the day we left our native villages to make the journey.

---

2. Unsalted glutinous rice cakes made by the Nung and Tay people, wrapped in the shape of a funnel. (Footnote in text.)

Comrade Thai Long thought up an idea to improve our diet. He bent paper pins into fishing hooks, found some bait, and dropped his line in the pool.

Our meal that day included a few fish that Thai Long had caught, in addition to the usual fare of salt and shrimp paste. But no one wanted to eat the fish, each wanting to save it for the others. They said:

"Let old Pho eat it because he has to carry a heavy load!"

"Thai Long caught the fish, so let him eat it!"

"Save it for the brothers who have malaria. It will cure their illness right away."

In the end, each man ate a little, and saved most of the fish for those comrades who were weak or who had to carry heavy loads.

After we finished eating, we hastily got ready to move on.

We tried to pass quickly through the valleys while it was still light, and waited till dark before we resumed our march through the trails.

The fog became colder as the night advanced. Our group silently moved on, passing Bo Tat, Na Tou, Cau Hin, and then the Na Yeu area. We reached Lung Pan at daybreak. We stopped. A desolate sight greeted us: wrecked and burned trees and houses--all that was left were a few charred poles. Not a soul anywhere.

Comrades Vinh, Thai Long and I walked over to the platform of the house that used to belong to old Mr. Van. Ever since the outbreak of the Bac Son uprising, his house had been a stopping point for the revolutionary cadres who passed through. When the French came here, sowing terror, they took his whole family away and threw old Mr. Van in jail. Hatred for the French bandits burned more intensely in the heart of each AFNS fighter.

The sun rose. The fog dissipated slowly. Our unit hurriedly withdrew into the forest to rest. We split into cells, bivouacked close together, and kept very quiet in order to maintain our presence secret in case spies were searching in this area. In the old days, they used to go through here frequently, and at night they used to set up ambushes or conduct patrols to look for signs of our cadres' activities. The brothers--with the exception of those who had to go on reconnaissance or stand guard--read books or documents, or cleaned their rifles.

Quoc Hung, Duc Ton and I took this opportunity to review the leadership of the march in the past few days, and discussed our forthcoming tasks. Soon, we would have to cross a dangerous area: the vast fields of Huu Vinh and Trang Lang villages, where the enemy had assembled many soldiers and secret policemen. Guard posts were everywhere, and we would not be able to go for a kilometer without bumping into a post.

Darkness had just fallen. Instead of following the trail, we made our way through the tortuous gaps between the boulders, overgrown with thickets. The Lung Pan pass led to the Can Cuom pass which was usually guarded by the militia and the secret police. In the midst of this enemy encirclement, if we just made a noise different from the usual sounds, the guard post nearby would immediately sound the alarm by hitting on hollow pieces of wood, and banging their drums and cymbals. And within minutes, the soldiers from the posts and the canton and village militia chiefs would surround us tightly, and it would not be easy for us to get away unscathed.

But we calmly continued our journey. We edged our way through the only trail that led out of the Canh Cuom pass, and reached the main road going from Dinh Ca to Bac Son. There was no way for us to tell where the enemy had and where they had not posted guards on this stretch of the road, which ran through a mountain pass. (Much later on I found out that it was on this stretch of the road that we were seen by a militiaman who told the village militia chief, "Look at that black mass of men moving down there, what shall we do?" The village militia chief brushed him aside, "Let them pass!" and then led the militia away to allow us to go through. After we were gone, this village militia chief was arrested by the French who asked him, "You were standing guard there, how come you did not know they were going through?" The village militia chief shook his head, "I really did not see them." The French threw him in the Ba Van prison camp. He was released when the Revolution succeeded, and told me this story himself when we met again.)

After we had gone through a few passes and valleys on the way from Long Dong, the cocks began to crow. Suddenly we heard noises; thudding footsteps, sounds of branches cracking underfoot, and rustling of leaves. It was a flock of antelopes which were out looking for food in the darkness and, running into us, bolted away. Some comrades did not want to let such fine game escape and would like to shoot them--especially Quoc Vinh who was sorry not to have been able to add antelope meat to our diet of shrimp paste. But to fire a shot here would land us in an enemy encirclement, so although we were sorry to have missed such a chance, we told each other to remain quiet and to proceed through the pass.

It was almost daylight when we passed Lung Luong. The villages and settlements began to stir. Our unit quickly crossed into Tam Canh. So, we had succeeded in slipping through the thick encirclement that the imperialists had thrown in the area from Bac Son to Vo Nhai. From the Tam Canh mountain chain, looking toward Keo Ai, we could see clearly the Binh Gia fields and the French representative's post looming in the distance before our eyes. I signalled to the brothers to move quickly into a dense spot well shaded by trees. I talked with Quoc Hung and Duc Ton, and we admitted that this mountain area was extremely dangerous. Ahead of us was the post of the French representative in Binh Gia, and behind us was an area teeming with the imperialists' soldiers and secret police. This rocky mountain chain was relatively well covered by trees and vegetation, but it was like a pocket. If the enemy blocked the way up and down the mountain, then we would not be able to escape. However, we had no other solution, so we led the unit up the mountain to rest. We stopped when we were halfway up.

We spent that whole day lying in rocky crevices halfway up the mountain--each man lying in a separate crack. How long the day seemed to us! It is true that a day of worry lasts as long as a year of leisure.

The sun was about to go down. Light faded gradually. We ate our dinner, and then slowly moved down to the main road.

We walked in the middle of the Binh Gia fields--on one side were mountains, and on the other side were located the posts, district seat, the towns and villages. At that precise moment it turned very windy and rained heavily. The night was as black as Chinese ink. In just a short time the water in the fields overflowed the embankments. Our clothes were soaked. We walked on, because we figured the enemy would not dare to go out on patrol on such a dark and rainy night.

It rained harder and harder as the night wore on. Quoc Hung and I discussed taking the unit into the Lung Noi mountain chain, and sending two comrades into the village to contact acquaintances. The next day-- the 6th day of the 2nd lunar month (1942)--would be a market day, and in the afternoon we would send a number of AFNS fighters to meet sympathizers from Pa Niem, Lung Noi and Hang Cau, and ask them to check on the situation of the route from Van Mich to Binh Gia.

We pulled into the Lung Noi mountain. Vegetation was not dense here, but it had just rained and the ground was damp and wet, so although it was still nighttime, we could not lie down to sleep, and just sat there.

Comrades Hong Thai and Hoa were sent to meet Lau, a Nung in Lung Noi. He came out to see us. We talked with him for a long time. After we finished our discussion, he asked, "What can I do to help the AFNS right now?" We asked him to cook some food for us, to buy two kilograms of fish paste and two flashlights, and to check the situation. He accepted with eagerness.

So, on their way to break out of the enemy's encirclement, the AFNS had succeeded in implanting a political nucleus [by recruiting Lau] in an area only two kilometers as the crow flies from the Binh Gia post. This success made us very happy.

Our unit climbed halfway up the mountain and broke up into cells to disperse and hide behind jutting rocks and a few scattered trees. When it was broad daylight, we could see about a kilometer of the road which was thronged with villagers going to the market. A little later, a few hundred well-armed soldiers arrogantly moved toward Lang Son. Lau had told us that the soldiers routinely conduct this patrol, so we were certain we had not been detected.

A comrade playfully poked his rifle through the rock crack and pointed it toward the soldiers, saying, "If I open fire now, which one will fall?" But he was just joking, for who would dare to fire? The brothers even made an effort not to bump into small trees, for fear that the trees would shake and attract the eyes of the suspicious enemy.

The market began to break up. The hour for our rendezvous with the villagers drew near. The reconnaissance cells came back and reported that down in the middle of the Lung Noi fields there were many people walking around to check their ricefields and then making a detour into the mountain toward the spot where the unit was stationed.

The group of villagers approached. When we could see them clearly we realized that we knew all of them. There were old people and children, and young men and women.

Our meeting was very moving and happy, we grasped each other's hands and our faces shone with joy. An old man from Pa Niem said, "We haven't seen you for years, but now heavens have allowed us to meet again!"

It was almost noon then. It turned out the villagers had come up here right after they finished ploughing. I said, "Don't come in a group like this, the enemy will see you and they can guess what you're up to. Come separately, by one or two, just as though you're going up here to gather firewood."

One man nodded his head in approval. "You're right! We've done a silly thing!"

Mrs. Ba--Lau's sister-in-law--was also present. She gave me all the things we had asked him to buy for us, and said, "We didn't hear anything. The soldiers have all left."

Seeing an old man wearing many layers of clothing and perspiring heavily--his face and neck were covered with sweat--I asked, "Do you have malaria? I have some quinine pills right here."

He unbuttoned his shirt, pulled it open, and answered, "I thought you had come by yourself, alone. I didn't know there were so many of your until I got here. I heard that you brothers had been living in the forest for the last seven and eight months and that your clothes had become torn, so I brought along a few extra shirts for you to wear and share among yourselves for the time being."

An old man standing next to him pulled out a pair of scissors and said, "A lui! I was told you had been living in the forest for eight months and that your hair had grown very long and that you looked as unkempt as a bear, so I took along these scissors for you to trim your hair!"

Then, some women took a few cakes out of their bags and said, "We were worried you might not be able to survive on the diet of leaves you've been eating in the forest where you've been forced to live day and night. When we heard you'd come back, we bought a few cakes for you to eat."

It turned out that, without telling each other, when they heard the news that we had come back, the villagers went to the market--some bought a few cakes, while others went to the noodle shops to buy a couple of chicken and duck feet to take to us. The villagers did not understand fully either the activities or the life of the AFNS. This showed how poisonous the [propaganda] of the imperialists and reactionaries was. Their intention was to destroy the revolutionary armed forces and at the same time to demoralize the people and make them lose their confidence in the revolution.

We explained clearly to the people the current situation and the mission of the AFNS and of the ethnic minorities in this historic period. While talking with the people, the brothers also showed them revolutionary books and newspapers, and gave them leaflets and copies of the Viet Minh Program as souvenirs.

We explained clearly to them that we did not lack clothes, blankets and mosquito nets badly, and that although we did not have a lot of weapons we had enough for our use.

"Now I know. I thought the French and the soldiers from the posts had burned all the houses," the oldest man in the group said with sorrow and pity in his voice, "and I was wondering where you could find shelter? I wondered whether you had to live like the bears in the forests." His face streaked with tears. "When I heard the secret police gang say this, I thought you had all perished."

We explained to the villagers how to set up an infrastructure. They told us, "Come back when the rain slackens. Come in small groups of a few men and we'll conceal you in the cave. Come back and teach us how to make revolution."

They said goodbye to us. They could not say much, and tears fell down their faces.

At dusk, we went with Lau to the home of Phung, the village militia chief, to have dinner and take this opportunity to talk with him about the revolution. Phung had sent someone he trusted to check the roads for us. From Binh Gia to Pac Nang, only the Van Mich post deployed sentries on guard duties.

After dinner, we got ready to leave. Both Lau and Phung--his nephew--took us to a shortcut leading to the main road near Binh Gia, to go to Pac Nang.

At Pac Nang, the main road ran between high mountains. There, we met the brothers who had gone on ahead to reconnoiter the route and were waiting for us. They reported that "the situation was quiet." We said goodbye to Lau and Phung. I took Lau's hand and gave him some additional advice, "When you go back, if they find out and ask you, just say, 'I don't know.' Even if they beat you, you must bear it and refuse to give them information which can harm the revolution. To make revolution, you must not be afraid of difficulties, and you must firmly believe in the final victory. When conditions permit, we'll send cadres down here to help you."

Lau looked at me and nodded his head.

* * *

Our unit headed straight down the main road leading from Binh Gia to Van Mich. The road was large, but we managed to maintain complete secrecy when we passed by the villages scattered along the road. Any of us who made a noise--no matter how small--by displacing the pebbles received stern and reproaching glances from the rest of the group.

About five kilometers from Van Mich, there was a path which veered to the right. We all turned into this path which ran through a hill. After covering a short distance, we followed the course of a small rivulet. The bed was very narrow--large enough for us to put one foot down at a time. On one side were high mountains, and on the other side was a short drop--if we slipped we would fall about twenty or thirty feet. As we walked, we had to make sure not to knock down the banks in order not to leave any traces of our passage. It took us a long time to cover this stretch.

After we left the rivulet we came to terraced ricefields belonging to a few small settlements. We groped our way down toward the direction of the Hat Quang waterfall. This was the second time we crossed this waterfall.

Dawn began to break. From the Hat Quang waterfall, looking to the left, we saw the bright white mass of the Van Mich post, only about 800 meters away. In front of us was an unbroken line of towering mountains. We urged each other to walk faster, because we were near the post, and if we were detected it would be very dangerous. (There were hundreds of soldiers and militiamen stationed in the Van Mich post.) We crossed the waterfall, encouraged each other to make good time and climbed straight into the mountains in front of us.

The fog banks flowed by one after the other and stung our eyes. There were many moments when the man walking behind could not see the one in front. Then the clouds lifted gradually and the sun came up. The Command Staff decided to look for a resting place, because if we kept on walking, we could very easily be spotted. The fog had not lifted completely at that moment, and we could not see clearly around us. We talked it over and decided to go up the hill to rest. But when we were on the hill we discovered that it was covered by elephant grass reaching up to our chests, and that the hill was in a rather poor strategic position. The fog dissipated. The merciless sun seemed to pour fire on our heads and backs. All of us burrowed under the elephant grass and used the blankets to shield ourselves from the sun.

I was extremely worried. Crouched here, we must be clearly visible from the road--anyone coming out of the village, anyone grazing buffaloes, or anyone ploughing on the next hill could see us clearly.

At around ten o'clock, the sun became fiercer, and the water we had brought along ran out. Everyone was thirsty and tired. Thai Long, Thanh, and Hong Thai crossed the trail and went to the stream to draw water. They ran into the village militia chief who asked for their identity cards. Thai Long who had presence of mind answered, "We're on our way to buy water buffaloes. There are a few more men coming up behind us. I gave my identity card to one of them to keep. He's coming with the bags. He'll be here and he'll show you our identity cards."

The village militia chief and his gang found the whole incident rather strange, and turned around and went back.

The brothers hastily drew some water and ran back to where we were to relate what had happened.

The Command Staff held a meeting to discuss ways to deal with all eventualities. Meanwhile, the village militia chief and his men had gone back to the village to change clothes in order to go to Van Mich. Some of them turned their heads as they passed our hiding place and looked up toward us. Some even stopped and inspected the place. Their actions could not escape the eyes of the comrade on guard duty and of the villagers around them.

We all thought, "It's one hundred percent certain we have been detected." Some comrades suggested that we withdraw into the forest to escape. But we were unfamiliar with the terrain here.

"Let's move on ahead to set an ambush and fight them!" one comrade said, stressing each word.

Another one questioned him, "And where will we go after the fight?"

I said slowly, "There is no village from Van Mich to That Khe. Since they've seen a large group of men, it is their responsibility to go and report. They'll have to go for five or six kilometers and cross a river before they can reach the Van Mich post. This will take them over an hour. After they've reported to the post, it will take the soldiers at least another two hours to get ready to cross the river. So, even if they pursue us, they won't be able to catch up with us--especially since it will be almost dark by then. This will be an obstacle for them. They'll be afraid to get too close to us. But if they are adamant, we'll ambush them and destroy part of their forces and then crash our way through their line. It's now almost noon, if we leave now we'll be able to pass That Khe at eleven o'clock tonight. Once we've gone past That Khe, we'll be relatively safe."

Many brothers nodded their heads in approval. After a short discussion, we decided to "pass through That Khe at eleven o'clock that night." Hoang Thinh and another comrade were ordered to put on their Nung clothes and carry their submachine guns to go out on reconnaissance.

The two of them hurriedly left.

* * *

Khau Tap Pang was a high, steep and tortuous hill. When we were halfway up the slope, it was three or four o'clock in the afternoon. The reconnaissance cell disguised [as Nung villagers] and walking ahead of us on the crest of the hill signalled to us that "a group of men--about a company strong--were pursuing us."

I thought, "It's almost dark. I doubt that they would dare to attack when they see how large our group is."

An order immediately went out to the unit: "Walk in line, in rows of two!"

The unit moved from the far side of the path over to the side on the left of the mountain chain, and lined up in rows of two. Our aim was to show off our strength to the enemy.

The soldiers walking at the head of their column saw us moving in a long line, and stopped to look. Quoc Hung understood the psychology of the enemy, and calmly told the brothers, "Take your time, walk slowly."

Our troops marched on calmly, as though nothing was going on. Five or six minutes later, the brothers keeping watch on the crest of the hill reported that the soldiers were regrouping and heading back toward Van Mich. Just as we had guessed, they were only pursuing us for appearance's sake, and since they were afraid to get killed they had to turn back.

We were encouraged and continued with our journey, crossing one mountain pass after another. We arrived in Po Co[3] at eight o'clock in the evening. At exactly eleven o'clock we passed That Khe. We passed

---

3. Po = hill; Co = walnut trees. Po Co was located in That Khe District. (Footnote in text.)

near the Pac Cam post at dawn, and we could see clearly the three-story-high building with many embrasures. When we were close to the post, we turned into the villagers' orchards. We pulled up the bamboo stakes in the fences to pass through, and then carefully put them back in place.

In the morning of March 24, our unit arrived in Na Cai hamlet, in Dai Dong village. We walked on for another kilometer, and then turned into the forest to sleep. This was a very old forest full of precious wood trees, such as the *Van Tam*, walnut, and especially the *Cay Khao*--even the small ones were as big around as a house support column and up to twenty meters tall. The unit rested for one whole day there.

Comrades Pho and Dam were designated to go down and contact the family of old Mr. Phu Ngan. This family was a nucleus that Hoang Van Thu had recruited as far back as 1934. When the Central Committee comrades passed through here on their way to attend the 8th Central Committee Plenum, they had stopped and spent the night at his house. Pho came from this village, so he knew the way. He took Mr. Phu Ngan's son to see us. We asked him about the Pac Cam post.

He said, "The village militia chiefs have gone to the French representative's post in That Khe for military training. There's nothing for you to worry about. They haven't returned from their training yet."

Afterward, he bought two roosters for us and fixed us lunch. Pho carried the rice into the forest for the unit to eat.

Mr. Phu Ngan's son had met me when I came through the previous time. We were of the same age, so we immediately became very close. At dusk that day, he insisted that we all come to his house. He wanted to invite me to drink a cup of wine before we left. I firmly refused. So he promised that he and I would "booze it up" when I returned.

This time, our guide was a very poor farmer. He was over 30 years old, of average height. He was agile and had made frequent trips into the forest to collect forest products for sale. When he found out that we were revolutionaries, he was overjoyed, and volunteered to drop his work and take us to the border. Since we had a trustworthy guide and since we were only a few kilometers from the border, we were sure nothing further could happen to us.

Ploughed fields completely devoid of vegetation stretched in front of us as we walked from Mr. Phu Ngan's house to the turning point. We moved on unhurriedly. At the intersection leading to Pac Cam, Kim Ly and to the border, half of the group were on the trail leading to the border and half were walking on the ricefields bundings. Suddenly we heard the sounds of many rifles being loaded.

Pho and two other comrades were ordered to stop and hide behind the bundings. [They were told], "If these are militiamen and they are decent, reason with them. If they are soldiers, shoot two or three, and then leave. After twenty or thirty minutes, if nothing happens, catch up with us."

We walked on for another kilometer without hearing any rifle shots. The three-man cell which had laid in ambush caught up with us in Kim Ly.

There was a very reliable infrastructure in Kim Ly. In 1941, Hoang Van Thu had taken us there to rest. The very poor farmer who was guiding us pointed to the houses of a few villagers and told me, "Go in there to rest."

"There are too many of us. We'll go on." Then I took his hands. "Thank you very much for having guided us. From here on, many of us know the way. Why don't you go into the village to sleep. Go back to your village tomorrow. Tonight the enemy might ambush the route you take to go home."

"I'm not afraid," he said, shaking his head. "I'm going back to Na Cai."

I told him once more not to do it, and many brothers in the unit also joined me in urging him not to go back, but he had made up his mind: "I'm very familiar with the terrain here. There's nothing to worry about, really."

When he reached the spot where we had heard noises earlier, the canton and village militia chiefs and their men who were lying in ambush rushed out and captured him. No matter how badly they beat him and tortured him, he refused to divulge any information. They shot him on the spot. (It was only much later that the local brothers reported this to us. The local movement wanted to kill these wretches. They talked it over, back and forth, and then decided not to go ahead, because they were afraid the enemy would terrorize the villagers and destroy the infrastructure. This was why these wretches survived until March 9, 1945, when the movement reached its high peak and they had to pay for their crimes.)

We crossed Kim Ly and Na Khau, and reached Na Ke, the last settlement on Vietnamese territory. We climbed the hills covered with elephant grass and headed toward the hill crests that marked the border. The higher up we got on the hills, the clearer we could hear the noise of dogs barking--echoing from the distance. It seemed as though someone was pursuing us, and the barking of dogs was spreading from one hamlet to the next behind us.

Here was the hill crest separating the two countries! It was around 10:00 P.M. We talked it over and decided to sleep on the hill top, and not to go down to the Chinese village on the other side, because it was already late at night and the people there might take us for bandits. We reinforced the number of sentries and posted guards on both sides in case the enemy was pursuing us.

In the dead quiet of the night, suddenly we heard a guard asking someone for the password, and rifles being loaded, followed by the voice of a man--floating up to us from below--answering in Nung dialect, "This is Nhac[4] returning from mission!"

It was the voice of someone I knew--the stammering of Nhac. I hurriedly ran out.

Nhac was comrade Mac Van Hai, who had been operating in China for a long time. Recently, he returned to Vietnam to contact our organiza-

---

4. The last name "Mac" is pronounced "Nhac" in Nung dialect. In the border region, people usually refer to each other by their last names, rarely by their first names. (Footnote in text.)

tion and to set up grassroot bases in a few Vietnamese settlements along the border. Mac Van Hai was full of joy and grabbed my hand: "Are all of you OK? Is anyone missing? I was in Na Cai on mission and went to Mr. Phu Ngan's house. His son told me that you had just passed through. I immediately left, running at full speed. . . ."

I understood then why the dogs were barking behind us. I asked him, "Why were you in such a hurry to catch up with us?"

The brothers had come and surrounded Nhac. He told us that the situation on the other side of the border had become tense. The Chinese Kuomintang had started to make an about-face. There was news that they were persecuting the Viet Minh Diplomatic Delegation. The Vietnamese Kuomintang and the Vietnam Revolutionary League (Viet-Nam Cach Menh Dong Minh Hoi)[5] must have been behind all this. Brother Ly Quang Hoa (that is to say, comrade Hoang Van Hoan[6]) had to go back to Cao Bang.

Nhac was full of worry, and he stammered even more: "You . . . you've come in such a large group. . . . I'm a . . . afraid we won't be able to accommodate you all."

Under the pale moonlight, the cells discussed this news in whispers:

"We've avoided the tigers only to run into the wolves!"

"We're armed, we can just set up a war zone right here on the border to operate."

One comrade interrupted them in a rather harsh tone of voice, "Let the Command Staff discuss things first. There must be a way to deal with the situation."

Mac Van Hai said softly, "The villagers are afraid of reprisals."

I asked, "How many brothers are left here?"

"There is only Khai Lac and me," Hai answered.

"Which Khai Lac?"

"Khai Lac from Bac Son."

When I heard him mention Khai Lac, I felt very moved. Khai Lac was with the AFNS group that marched to Cao Bang with Phung Chi Kien

---

5. These two exiled Vietnamese political groups were sponsored by the Chinese KMT. They were the rivals of the Viet Minh and tried to sabotage it. (Trans.)

6. Hoang Van Hoan was then the head of the Front Organization of the Viet Minh in China. He went to China in 1926 and was a graduate of the Whampoa Military Academy. Before, during and after the Second Sino-Japanese War, he was active in Canton, Nanming, Kunming, Liuchou, and Chinghsi, where he was a self-employed tailor and a Viet Minh revolutionary. He was one of the founders of the Viet Minh in 1941. He is now a member of the Politburo of the Vietnamese Lao Dong Party, Vice-Chairman of the Standing Committee of the DRV National Assembly, and represents Nghe An province in the National Assembly. (Trans.)

and Luong Huu Chi. I had not had any news from them since then. I told myself, "When everything's arranged, I must ask him what happened. It's not a good time to ask now...." I talked with Quoc Hung and Le Duc Ton. The AFNS's activities would run into many difficulties. However, my Chu clan had about a hundred families here, and the Duong clan inhabited a few settlements in this area. The population here was large, and the villagers were good people. If we relied on the people and worked hard we would be able to solve all problems, no matter how difficult they could be. And this would also give us the opportunity to assist our Chinese friends' revolutionary movement at a time when they were going through many difficulties.

Then I turned around to tell Mac Van Hai--but also to tell the AFNS brothers indirectly, "You've given us some timely information. That's good. Before we came here, we figured we might run into this type of situation, so we devised a plan to deal with it in advance. All that has to be done now is for the brothers to keep calm, maintain discipline and secrecy, and to rely on the people. You and comrades Pinh Chi and Khai Lac will come and fetch us early tomorrow morning halfway up the hill behind the village."

After Mac Van Hai left, Le Duc Ton, Chu Quoc Hung, Nong Thai Long and I met to discuss the situation and ways to cope with all eventualities.

It was late and very quiet. The moon had set a long time ago. Our shoulders were damp with mist. The cold air here on the border seemed more biting and more chilling to the bones than the cold back in our home villages. None of us could go to sleep. Thoughts and worries about the future and about our revolutionary mission troubled our minds.

A flock of egrets which had been looking for food all night cried out to call each other and to return to their nests. A rooster suddenly crowed, and its cry was taken up by many others. A fire leaped to life in a house on a hillside which had been just moments before plunged in complete darkness.

I was exhausted and yet I could not plunge into a deep and restful sleep. I lay awake, thinking of the things I would discuss with Pinh Chi and Khai Lac the next day. Pinh Chi was Chinese and came from Ban Khiec, the village we were going to the next day. He was a very close friend of Hoang Van Thu's. Previously, Pinh Chi had donated to us a pac-hooc submachine gun which could fire 10 bullets, and it was given to Phung Chi Kien to keep.

Dawn broke. A pink cloud floated above a distant mountain peak. The rolling forest was a deep green mass. The mist was damp and wet. Then the sun lit up the hills covered with burnished gold elephant grass. Partridges called out to each other from one grassy hill to the next. Their cry sounded to us like "Our homeland!" and "How we miss our homeland!" In the valley, along the stream, the blanket of fog looked like fluffy white cotton balls. A civet-cat ran across in a flash and plunged into a melastome bush on the hillside. The monotonous sound of a water mill echoed in the valley. Flocks of birds flew out of the forest and landed in the crop patches, twittering.

Ban Khiec appeared in front of us, with its twenty or so houses on stilts perched precariously on the mountain side--up and down, in an uneven and broken line--with its winding paths and its rows of luxuriant fruit trees. Each house had its own fence and its own yard for drying paddy. Cooking smoke began to rise from the weathered thatched and tiled roofs. In front of the village were terraced fields--each one a small plot--circling and hugging the mountain and covered with rows of yams, peas and peanuts.

We parted the elephant grass and silently followed the wet and slippery path leading down to the village. The man walking in front had to knock the dew off the blades of grass with a stick, so that our clothes would not get wet. From here we could see clearly the two roads leading to Na Slieng and Ban Nac. Another path wound around the hill behind the village and led to Kheo Meo. The view here was not different from the one back in our home area, and it had the same familiar appearance of the Nung minority's life-style. Again, we felt enthusiastic and confident in our ability to proselytize the people and in our revolutionary experience. We were certain we could stay here for the time being.

From afar we could see comrades Pinh Chi and Khai Lac coming up to fetch us. They both looked worried, in contrast to the atmosphere of joy I encountered when I took the Central Committee members to the Pac Bo conference the previous year. When Khai Lac saw how large our group was, he too seemed very worried.

I pulled Pinh Chi and Khai Lac aside, and asked softly, "Have the villagers found out yet?"

They both said, "Nhac has been whispering about your presence, so the villagers know about it."

We talked it over and decided we should first take the unit to the village, because it was not a good thing to leave them exposed on the hill during the day. We would continue to discuss all the problems and try to find ways to solve them later on.

On the way to the village, I asked Khai Lac, "What is the attitude of the people?"

He replied, "They're happy to hear that you brothers have arrived, but they also worry that if the Kuomintang finds out, they will be persecuted. The villagers have always been kind to me; their attitude hasn't changed. They talk about our comrades all the time, especially brother Hoang Van Thu."

I explained further to Pinh Chi, "The French are repressing the Vo Nhai movement so fiercely that we've had to move here to your territory for a while; then we'll figure out a way to go back to our own area to operate."

Pinh Chi answered eagerly, "We're friends, so just make yourselves at home here, just act as though you're still in Trang Xa. If you need anything, let us know."

When we reached the village, we saw that every family had come out and stood at the door of their houses to welcome us; their eyes showed both joy and worry. As directed by Pinh Chi, the AFNS split into cells and each cell went to stay with a different family. The brothers immediately plunged into work, helping the host families with their chores, all the while talking with them. The villagers had heard of the AFNS for a long time, so although it was our first meeting, these generous and hospitable frontier people quickly became close to us, men who shared their purposes and feelings. Seeing that Nong Thai Long had a bamboo flute, the youths and children surrounded him and with eyes wide open with eagerness they urged him to play the "Flowing Water" tune to enliven the atmosphere. This carefree and spontaneous attitude of the young dispelled the worries of some of the comrades. All that the AFNS would have to do was to know how to propagandize the people, maintain secrecy, and resolutely help the villagers in their work, then we would certainly be able to remain here for a while to operate, and even to give some help to the local movement.

* * *

In this Bo Cuc area, the revolutionary movement under the leadership of the Chinese Communist Party continued to exist through the clandestine activities of a nucleus of men such as Pinh Chi in Ban Khiec, Phan Sen Chan in Na Slieng, Nong Ky Chan (i.e., Tai Thau) in Na Trao, Khim Di and Quai Dinh in Ban Trang, and Hen May, Lao Giam, etc.

Comrade Hen May was blind, but he had great prestige among the people. At that time, there were a great variety of political factions in the border region, and each one of them wanted to build up their influence among the population. When they came to the Bo Cuc area to propagandize, however, the people only asked them one question; "Does Hen May support you?" "No, Hen May supports the Communists!" "Then we won't support you. We support whoever Hen May supports." Their answer was unequivocal. Hen May did not earn this prestige overnight. The people knew that Hen May had taken part in the Red Lungchou movement, and that for over ten years--even though he had become blind--he had protected the rights of the villagers in a steadfast and clearsighted manner.[7]

Later on, we held a meeting for all the cadres in the unit. Our Chinese friends--for example, comrades Pinh Chi, Hen May, Lao Giam and Phan Sen Chan--also came to attend the meeting. Le Duc Ton talked about our struggle in the last eight months. Khai Lac talked briefly about a few of our exiled revolutionaries in China whom he had just found out about. The Chinese comrades explained the local situation to us--about the revolutionary spirit of the people, the policies and lines of the KMT, the work and life-style of the people, as well as their religious beliefs and customs.

Thanks to a good rice harvest, the villagers were leading a relatively comfortable life. But they must grow other additional crops in order to have enough to eat till the following harvest at the end of the year. Chiang Kai Shek's security police and French intelligence

---

7. After the August Revolution succeeded, Hen May came to Vietnam. In his long struggle, there had been times when he had to withdraw to our country to fight the Chinese KMT and join us in our fight against the French. In 1949, Hen May and his comrades, along with the local people rose up to seize power and to fight Chiang Kai Shek in the Lungchou-P'inghsiang area. Then, all of China was liberated under the leadership of the Chinese Communist Party and of the beloved and respected comrade Mao-tse-Tung. When the French Expeditionary Force withdrew from our country's border region, Hen May and a few other comrades came and stayed on the Vietnamese side of the border for a while, and then returned to Ban Khiec. He fell ill and died there. (Footnote in text.)

agents came here occasionally. Banditry had not fallen off, even
though the resist-Japan propaganda had improved lately.

   The meeting assessed that although we came from two different
countries, all the villagers here were ready and willing to feed, support and protect the AFNS, because of their affection for people of
their own ethnic background who spoke their dialect, were related to
them, and in particular came from the same social class and shared
their revolutionary goals. However, since the KMT regime was strong
and since their policy toward the Vietnamese revolution was treacherous
and cunning--one moment, they allied themselves with the Vietnamese
revolution, and the next moment they turned around and destroyed it--
the villagers were somewhat apprehensive that they would be terrorized
and repressed as a result.

   The villagers were worried. The Chinese comrades promised to
join forces with the AFNS to explain the situation to the people and
strengthen their spirit of struggle. We promised to brave all difficulties and dangers, accept all responsibility, to do everything possible to avoid implicating the villagers, and to do our best to contribute to the consolidation and expansion of the local revolutionary
movement. The meeting decided to adopt a concrete plan of action which
included proposals on how to deal with the enemy, how to motivate the
people, how to settle the material and living problems of the unit, how
to maintain discipline and secrecy, how to guard against spies, and how
to proselytize the people.

   After the meeting which pointed out the direction of our new mission and set forth a clear program of action, all the brothers felt encouraged and set to work with confidence. The AFNS was divided into
small cells of Party members and non-Party members to mingle with the
villagers. Each cell was capable of taking independent action to carry
out its mission and to fight.

   A number of brothers whose relatives were serving as hamlet chiefs
managed to obtain passes, and went openly to Lungchou and P'inghsiang
to operate.

   One section of the AFNS--about a squad--built huts in the forest
in the mountains right next to the border to live. They were equipped
with weapons and ammunition, pots and pans, and other supplies which
they stored in the forest. During the day, they worked in the forest,
grazing oxen and buffaloes for the villagers, or clearing crop patches.
At night they came down to the village to eat, and then returned to
their huts in the forest to sleep.

   On the third day of our arrival, it was possible for the AFNS to
split into cells of three or more men each and for each cell to move
into a settlement to live, after we had checked the situation in each
settlement and discussed the move with the local Chinese comrades.
First, the cells moved to the settlements where conditions were favorable while the others waited for the situation to clear in the other
settlements before moving in. We were dispersed, but our presence remained secret. Only the people in the settlements where the cells were
staying knew of their presence. Settlements such as Ban Khiec, Ban
Trang, Kheo Meo, Na Slieng, Ban Nac, Ho To, Ai Keng, Na Trao and Ha
Dong, all housed AFNS cells. Later on, one of our cells even moved to
a settlement located as far away as Doong Hinh, near Lungchou.

The brothers helped the villagers cut down trees, gather firewood, pick mushrooms, or clear crop patches, prune crop plants, and graze oxen and buffaloes. Back at home in the evening, they helped the families in their household chores--cooking, sweeping the floor, weaving baskets, and repairing agricultural tools. In many things, the brothers turned out to be more skillful than the villagers themselves. They talked as they worked. They exchanged farming and hunting experience, and told stories about their families and villages, and about their revolutionary struggle. The old people, the children, the youths and the women--everyone loved to listen to their stories. On these occasions, the brothers tactfully made propaganda about the revolution, heightened the villagers' awareness of their ethnic and class background, talked about international friendship, and told the people how to guard against spies and maintain secrecy. The brothers strictly observed and respected the local customs.

With their basic willingness to support the revolution and their admiration for the AFNS, all the villagers grew to love and trust the brothers, when they saw with their own eyes that the AFNS fighters were well behaved, worked hard and skillfully, knew how to maintain secrecy and were devoted to helping the people. Within a week--with the exception of the brothers in charge of guarding the storehouse who had to return to their huts in the forest to sleep after eating supper in the village--all the brothers had moved in with relatives or other villagers to live and work. Very soon all the households and settlements lost their fear of enemy repression and competed with each other to invite the brothers to come and stay with them, and looked upon the AFNS as members of their own families. The youths, in particular, followed the brothers everywhere.

The AFNS had assimilated with the people and adopted their clothing, their style of speech, their pattern of work and living. They were so much like the local people that a stranger coming in from afar could not tell them apart from the villagers. Once they had established a foothold in a family, in a settlement, and were supported and protected by the people, the brothers immediately expanded the grass-root base, spread it to every household in the settlement and then to the whole canton, thus creating a firm base of support for the whole unit.

Bo Cuc canton, bordering on the two Vietnamese districts of Dong Khe and That Khe, had a population which numbered in the tens of thousands, and was remote and isolated. It had many forests and mountains, and vast fields--such as those in Tong Phou and Ai Keng. There were about 200 households in Ban Trang. The people here were all Nung. They understood the revolution rather well, and the revolution had set up an infrastructure here as far back as 1930. Most of our revolutionary cadres going abroad had all stopped and stayed here. The majority of the people were good, but a small number of them were bad and became bandits.

The canton chief of Bo Cuc was a nephew of mine. Seeing that the people trusted and protected the AFNS, he had a great respect for us. One day I went to see him and asked to test him, "Now that I'm here, do you think you can guarantee my safety?"

He boasted, "Uncle, there's nothing for you to worry about here. If you want to go to Lungchou I'll issue you a pass right away!"

Afterward, he issued passes to Chu Quoc Hung and me, which allowed us to move freely and openly in the entire area of Hsiatung, Lungchou and P'inghsiang.

Like fish thrown into water, the AFNS began to roam and operate. This marked the beginning of the phase during which we gathered the revolutionary forces, and prepared to build grassroot bases to clear our way back to Vietnam.

* * *

One day, while Khai Lac and I were talking about all the things that had happened, I asked him about the journey the AFNS undertook to Cao Bang. It was then that I learned of the heroic deeds of Phung Chi Kien and Luong Huu Chi.

Ha Khai Lac was very familiar with the cross forest and cross mountain route that led from the Khuoi Noi forest to the border. Before joining the Revolution he had prospected for gold in Kim Hy, in Na Ri district, Bac Can province. Phung Chi Kien gave him the task of guiding the unit. He led the brothers toward Khau Pi.[8] This was a remote mountain chain unfrequented by anyone but the smugglers and jungle animals. The brothers would go to Khau Pi and then go across the forest to Ngan Son. Unfortunately, when they were near Khau Phi, they fell into an ambush set by a group of militiamen led by Phuong, a canton chief from Na Ri district.

Phung Chi Kien tried to persuade this fellow by talking to him about the just cause of the revolution. But the canton chief was too blinded by the generous cash award and the medal which the "Great French Government" would give him, to listen. He shouted to the militiamen to tie up Phung Chi Kien. However, Kien remained calm, and looked the militiamen who were surrounding him straight in the eyes. Bravely and kindly, he reasoned with them, using logical and sentimental arguments. He appealed to them not to open fire on the revolutionaries and to turn their weapons around to shoot the French and their lackeys. The militiamen did not dare touch him, some of them glanced fearfully at Canton Chief Phuong. Seeing that this young man standing in front of him could immobilize the soldiers under his command with arguments, Canton Chief Phuong roared, "Catch him! The guy who lets him escape will have his head chopped off!"

Seeing that the situation--instead of cooling down--had become tense because of the violent attitude of the canton chief, some brothers suggested "killing a few soldiers and breaking through." Unfortunately, besides these militiamen, a group of secret policemen who had been following the brothers' footprints came on the scene. While the brothers were off guard, they opened fire on Phung Chi Kien. Rifle shots rang out. The militiamen were thrown into confusion. Kien collapsed, his pac-hooc submachine gun fell on the ground. The AFNS immediately returned the fire. Comrade Lam pulled out his rifle and aimed accurately at the canton chief who collapsed, his face on the ground. Lam rushed forward to save Kien, but the enemy was firing without letup. They outnumbered the AFNS and were firing a relentless spray of bullets. They tightened their encirclement. Luong Huu Chi had no choice but to order the brothers to clear a path of blood and break out.

---

8. Khau = mountain; Pi = banana flower. (Footnote in text.)

The enemy in the surrounding areas were alerted. Pontique (?), the Militia Inspector in the Bac Can Post, cabled all areas of the province to have all the roads blocked. The Ngan Son post commander and the Ngan Son district chief dispatched province troops and militiamen to block all routes leading into Cao Bang province.

Phung Chi Kien was seriously wounded and remained behind. The secret police rushed in, beat him almost to death and then carried him to the Bang Duc post (in Ngan Son district) to get their rewards.

Partly because Kien was seriously wounded and lost a lot of blood, and partly because he was left lying in the rain in the yard of the post all night, partly because he was cruelly tortured by Vi Van Bao,[9] the District Chief's Assistant, Kien breathed his last.

Meanwhile, Luong Huu Chi gathered the brothers and led them on to their destination. Unfortunately, he fell ill on the way. He tried to go on, however, and constantly encouraged the unit to reach their destination. When he no longer could go on, he assembled the brothers and said, "Brother Phung Chi Kien is dead. Do not let the unit be destroyed because of me. You comrades go on and leave me here. I'll join you later."

During the years he operated in China Luong Huu Chi had served as a Battalion Commander. He spoke the Mandarin dialect very well. He chose this solution because he was concerned about the unit. The brothers disagreed, but he said, "I'm your commander. You must obey my order. Go on ahead to the Cao Bang War Zone. When I recover from my illness I'll join you. I know the terrain here, so you don't have to worry about me."

Seeing that the brothers were hesitating and could not make up their minds, he said, "I've already told you I'm your commander here, and you must obey your commander's order. Well, go on. You must steel yourselves. I can speak Mandarin and I'll know how to deal with things."

After he finished saying this, he went to a tile kiln and lay down. The brothers brushed their tears and said goodbye to their beloved comrade and commander.

All the brothers made it to Cao Bang. Afterward "fat" Ma (i.e., Ma Thanh Kinh), Lam, Hai Tam and Ha Khai Lac crossed into China.

Luong Huu Chi fell into a delirious fever and was captured by the enemy who threw him in the Cao Bang jail. His illness worsened and he died. (Later, comrade La[10]--a member of the Cao Bang Province Party Committee--told me about Luong Huu Chi and said, "We were planning to organize a jail break for him. However, three days before he was scheduled to escape, he came down will a terrible bout of malaria and died. What a shame!")

When I heard this story, my heart was heavy with sorrow and pain. I mourned the death of Kien and Chi, two talented military commanders

---

9. Vi Van Bao had to pay for his crime in 1954. (Footnote in text.)

10. Hoang Duc Thac alias La was the Secretary of the Cao-Bac Lang Inter-province Party Committee in 1943. He died on June 25, 1959. (Trans.)

well loved by all of Bac Son. I felt in the deepest reaches of my soul a powerful hatred for the French colonialists and their lackeys who had murdered them.

The more I thought about the heroic death of Phung Chi Kien and the selfless attitude of Luong Huu Chi who had sacrificed himself for his comrades, his Party and the Revolution, the heavier I felt my responsibility to be. We were not going to remain here in China forever to eat well and lead a life of leisure. We must return to our country. But would our return be as safe as our departure? Who could tell in advance? From now to that day--the day when we again set foot on our native soil and fight the enemy on our own territory--if I let anything unfortunate happen to the unit, then I would have committed a great crime toward those who had sacrificed their lives, as well as toward the comrades who were still living.

I said to Khai Lac, with all the affection I had for him, my own comrade, "It's thanks to the leadership of the Central Committee and of the Old Man, and to the people's wholehearted support and protection that the AFNS has survived to this day. The moment the situation in our country calms down a bit, we'll go back. We owe such a heavy debt to our people that till we die we still won't have repaid all of it."

Khai Lac nodded his head and said, "Of course we'll go back. Whenever you need me, just say the word and I'll leave at once."

* * *

Besides continuing to live and work with the Chinese people in the settlements in Bo Cuc canton, making frequent propaganda about the Chinese and Vietnamese revolutions led by the Communist Party of China and Vietnam respectively, and educating the people about the spirit of international proletarianism and about friendship between nations in order to consolidate the new AFNS base, our Command Staff set forth as our first task the necessity for assembling the Vietnamese revolutionaries scattered all along this border. We saw that we must quickly unify leadership and coordinate our activities, in accordance with the spirit of the resolutions and directives of the Party Central Committee and of the Viet Minh General Headquarters, which had been communicated to us when we were still back in our own country. If this could be accomplished, then it would help to propel our revolution forward and reinforce the ranks of the AFNS.

The Vietnamese revolutionaries in the China-Vietnam border region at that time were not unified. There were many reliable and committed revolutionaries who had been recruited almost a decade ago by Old Mr. Thu Son, brothers Hoang Van Hoan (alias Ly Quang Hoa), Phung Chi Kien, Hoang Van Thu, etc. There were also the comrades who had operated back home but had had to come here because of enemy repression. Among them, some continued to be active, others were confused and lost, and were waiting to make contact with revolutionary organizations. A few-- either they wanted to lead a quiet life or because they had no other means of earning their living--went to work for the Chinese KMT. There were also the patriots who had originally followed a wrong political path but now, enlightened, wanted to join our Party. There were even convicted criminals who had fled to China. When they saw that the Revolution had a just cause they reformed themselves and wanted to take part in revolutionary activities. This did not include the small number of traitors and opportunists who disguised themselves as revolutionaries.

Ha Khai Lac and I obtained passes to go and contact revolutionaries in various places. The other commanders--Chu Quoc Hung, Le Duc Ton and Nong Thai Long--remained in Ban Trang, Ban Khiec and Na Slieng to keep in contact with the AFNS, maintain their pattern of activities, preserve discipline, push the task of proselytizing the people ahead, consolidate the existing infrastructure and build up new ones, and enlarge the base area. These comrades also took turns going on mission in outlying areas.

When we passed through Lungchou in 1941, Mr. Bui Ngoc Thanh, a veteran revolutionary who had lived in exile for a long time and who knew about the situation among the Vietnamese revolutionaries, came to see us and tell us about the situation in each area. This was how we learned that there were many revolutionaries scattered around who had not been brought under a unified leadership.

In April 1942, I met Mr. Bui Ngoc Thanh again for the second time. In addition, I also met Messrs. Ho Duc Thanh, Lam Phu Thinh, Nong Nhi Co, Au Duong Tat and Dung Pin Sin. These men had been introduced to me by Hoang Van Thu, and I had known them since last year.

After the meeting with the above Party and non-Party members, we learned that the situation was as follows. In general, the revolutionaries here did not have a clear and correct direction for their activities. Each lived in a different place and acted independently on his own. Liaison was haphazard and inadequate. They had not banded together to form a definite organization with routine meetings and discussions, and with a central leadership. All along the stretch from Hsiatung, to Lungchou, to P'inghsiang on the China side of the border, and from Trang Dinh to Thoat Lang, to Van Uyen, on our side of the border, each revolutionary just stuck to his own corner.

A few groups and cells, such as those in Na Hinh and Na Sam, maintained close contact with each other, but they too performed whatever task cropped up; they did not have a long-term plan, and did not learn from their own experience. As a result, they remained what they were-- a few isolated men working on their own--and did not succeed in building up a strong and extensive movement.

Faced with such a situation, the AFNS met to set forth a plan. We must quickly unify all these scattered forces, expand our grassroot bases among the people, and establish contact with our organization in Vietnam. We must begin to create safe corridors so we could clear a route back to the Bac Son-Vo Nhai War Zone, and link up with the units in Dai Tu, Son Duong, Dinh Hoa, Phu Binh, Yen The and Huu Lung.

Comrade Le Duc Ton was sent back to That Khe to prepare the grassroot bases there with the local comrades. Brother Quoc Hung went to Thuy Khau, Na Lan, and Dong Khe, and kept in touch with Mr. Bui Ngoc Thanh. Ha Khai Lac and I went to P'inghsiang to meet Lao Chuong and Ly Mung Sung and then to Lungyiu to meet Ma Khanh Phuong in order to propel the local movement ahead; finally we went to Ban Quyen and Keo Ai (China) to meet Be Chan Hung,[11] Voong Tai (e.g., Hoang Kieu),[12] Voong

---

11. Be Chan Hung is now the Deputy Secretary of the Lao Dong Party Committee of Lang Son province, and Chairman of the Lang Son Province Administrative Committee. (Trans.)

12. Hoang Kieu is now an alternate member of the Party Central Committee, the Secre-

Nhi, Mung and To.

This was only the first step we took to build up the infrastructure. Afterward, comrades Le Duc Ton, Chu Quoc Hung and Ha Khai Lac, and many other AFNS brothers and I took turns visiting these areas many more times.

Comrade Be Chan Hung came from Na Hinh, located right on the border. Comrades Voong Tai, Voong Nhi, Mung and To came from Hoi Hoan (Thoat Lang district, Lang Son province). After the Command Staff talked it over, Voong Tai and his brother were assigned to return to Hoi Hoan to operate. "Doors" had been opened, and the "bridge" leading back to our country had been established. Comrade Be Chan Hung, for his part, returned to Na Hinh. I also went there to stake it out. I would stay there with Be Chan Hung to operate, make propaganda about the revolution, start Viet Minh training classes, and set up AFNS organizations. Na Hinh was 30 kilometers from Hoi Hoan, so if these two infrastructures could link up, it would be very helpful. These comrades operated with a great deal of zeal, and within a short time, Voong Tai and a number of AFNS brothers--such as Chu Phong and Hong Thai--managed to set up firm grassroot bases thrusting deep into the interior of Vietnam. We now had a safe springboard, and it would be easy for the AFNS to march forward.

Wherever we went, we were warmly welcomed by the majority of the revolutionaries who agreed with our policy of assembling all forces, unifying command, and pushing all activities strongly ahead. These were the aspirations that they themselves had nurtured for a long time, but had not had the conditions to carry out. They all agreed that in order to make revolution, they could not afford to sit passively and wait, and that instead they should create the opportunity and conditions to continuously expand their activities. Internal unity became stronger. They organized the study of the Viet Minh General Headquarters' documents and program of action. They studied the experience of the eight-month-long struggle in the Trang Xa area, and exchanged experience on how to proselytize the people. The brothers who had been operating in an isolated manner along the border were assembled. The AFNS ranks were enlarged and strengthened as a result. All the infrastructures were consolidated, and began to take common and unified action.

The work of consolidating the mass bases on both sides of the border was proceeding favorably. After the initial contact to make propaganda, comrade Le Duc Ton handed over the task of consolidating and training the infrastructure in That Khe to the local comrades and returned to Hsiatung to meet the Command Staff to reassess the situation and set forth a new program of action. In June 1942, he went again to Ban San to check the progress of the movement in That Khe and Trang Dinh, and then returned to Lungchou to participate in diplomatic negotiations with the Chiang Kai Shek government.

Ha Khai Lac and I also made frequent trips to propagandize, train and enlighten the people in order to help out the infrastructure in the areas of Na Pung and Tau Ai (China) and Na Hinh, Phieng Phan, Na Ngoa and Ban Tai (Vietnam).

---

tary of the Tay Bac Zone Party Committee, and the Secretary of the Tay Bac Military Zone Party Committee. (Trans.)

Comrades Voong Tai, Voong Nhi, Be Chan Hung, Mung, To, Ha Cham and Thai Long were also very active in the areas of Hoi Hoan and Thoat Lang. A few other cells also made frequent trips to areas on both sides of the border.

* * *

The life of the cadres working to build up the infrastructure [on the Vietnam side of the border] was full of hardships then. The canton militia chiefs and the village officials had a list of wanted cadres to be tracked down. The crooks and traitors were waiting for the cadres to let down their guard to cut off their heads and obtain rewards of rice, salt and cash.

However, at night from our hideouts in the forest we continued to cross the border into Vietnam and to come down to the settlements. At first, we rendezvoused with our contacts at the edge of the forest or of the village. However, sometimes they did not show up, and we had to go back without accomplishing anything. Sometimes we did not know our way and got lost. Sometimes we ran into militia patrols. Not to mention the inclement weather, the beasts, the hunger and diseases that we came up against constantly. Gradually the villagers invited us inside their houses, and we sat in a corner of the room talking about their poverty and suffering. Once a cadre "sank roots" in a family, within a short time he would get to know everyone in the settlement. But he would still have to be on guard against the watching eyes of the secret police and informers.

Very early every morning we mingled with the villagers and followed them to the fields or the crop patches in the mountains, depending on the season, to plough or transplant rice, or to weed, or to build bundings, or to harvest crops. Before we could propagandize and enlighten the people, we had to work in order to produce enough food to eat. In the afternoon, the people returned to the village while we went to sit in a watch tower which had been abandoned by the militia. If there were no alarming signs, the villagers brought us lunch after they finished eating. If there were suspicious signs that the enemy was watching, we would have to go hungry. Usually lunch was brought to us quite late, and by the time we finished eating it was already one or two o'clock in the afternoon. Then it was time for the villagers to resume their work in the fields or in the forest. We followed them and worked till evening when we returned with them to the village. We walked in the middle, protected by the villagers. After dinner, it was pitch dark, we split up to hold group meetings with the people.

During the day, while working with the villagers the cadres usually took the occasion to enlighten them. However, the night meetings were the opportunity when the cadres really propagandized the people in depth. The night meetings were always well attended and happy. The villagers were very eager to learn and to know things. The cadres pointed out the crimes of the imperialists and feudalists, the underlying causes of the poverty and sufferings of the people, and the need to make revolution. Then they talked about the Viet Minh Front, the rules and regulations of the Viet Minh Associations, their program of struggle, their organization and operation, about the propaganda task and the maintenance of secrecy, etc.

Many meetings were very lively and the discussion lasted till midnight--and could even go on much longer. We had to summon all our knowledge to satisfy the demand of the people. We ourselves learned a great deal from the villagers in many fields. We learned from their patriotism, their spirit of sacrifice for the sake of the revolution, and from their way of working and living. The more the AFNS mingled with the people and worked among them, the more their capacity to act independently increased. Compared to the Vo Nhai period, they had made a lot of progress.

After these publicly held discussion sessions, I usually went to the militia watch tower on the hillside near the border to sleep, in order not to implicate the villagers. Many nights I was by myself, and I tossed and turned without being able to go to sleep. The forest mosquitoes were numerous and noisy, and plunged down incessantly to suck my blood. The moss and moldy leaves covering the roof exuded a dank smell. Owls hooted in cadences. I was besieged with all kinds of thoughts. The route back to our country had been opened, but from now until we could go back, there were still so many things to do. The work of consolidating the infrastructures was going too slowly, and the work of expanding them was not going very fast either. Some of our brothers were growing impatient and reluctant to bear hardships. The moment they heard that the enemy had withdrawn from Vo Nhai, they wanted to move the unit back. Up till now we had not figured out a way to contact the Central Committee. Half a year had gone by, but we had not heard from them and they had not received any news from us. We had no idea how the revolution was progressing in the whole country.

One night the weather was unbearably hot. Dark clouds rose and covered the horizon. Then chilly winds started to blow. Rain came pouring down and splashed onto the floor of the watch tower. I sat in the tower, with the legs of my trousers rolled up to my knees, and got wet and cold. I wondered how much of their houses and fields the people back home had managed to rebuild. Mrs. Sang and brother Du had just sent word that we could send cadres back to Trang Xa and Phu Thuong. I must immediately talk with the Command Staff about having someone ready to send back.

Then the rain stopped. There was a noise behind the tower, as though someone was moving back there. I turned and pulled myself up, flattened myself in the darkness and grabbed my pac-hooc submachine gun. But no one was there! Perhaps it was an antelope out looking for food which had bolted away when startled by some noise. I remembered one time Khai Lac, Nhac and I went to Pingyi on mission. The moment we stepped in the canton chief's house, we saw pasted on the wall a list of wanted Vietnamese cadres who were being tracked down by the Chinese KMT. My name was on the list. When he saw guests coming in, the host went to boil water and prepare food. He then brought out the food, poured wine in our cups and invited us to drink. After he asked Khai Lac what his name was, he looked at me and asked, "What is your precious name? How old are you? And where are you from?"

I answered, "I'm Chu Huu Quang, 33 years old, from Ban Trang."

He downed his wine, and laughed, "I'm honored! honored! It turns out I'm older than you, Mr. Chu. Let's become brothers. Allow me to wish you ten thousand profitable things!"

The four of us ate, drank, and talked in a very intimate fashion.

When we were out of the house, Khai Lac scolded me, "Are you still so attached to the Chu name?"

I answered, laughing, "There are so many people bearing the name Chu. They want the head of Chu Van Tan from Vietnam; I'm Chu Huu Quang from Ban Trang, so what is there to be afraid of?"

At this late hour of night, sitting here by myself with my rifle, I was deep in thought. I wondered what had happened to all the brothers who were operating back in our country?

Dawn came. The roosters were crowing noisily in the settlement down below. A sleepless night had passed. The red-pink clouds presaged a sunny day ahead. The road of the revolution was still long, but if we persevered and patiently moved on, we would certainly reach our goal. On both sides of this border, there still existed a mass of laboring peasants who supported and helped the cadres, and protected the revolution with devotion. If this huge force became enlightened, the skies and earth would be transformed, and the sufferings of the poor would end.

Clanking noise of wooden buffalo bells. The villagers were streaming to the fields. I ran down, and mingled with the crowd. Another day of production labor and absorbing revolutionary work began. The road leading back to our country was shortened by another day.

CHAPTER VII

It had been two months since the AFNS left Vietnam. What had happened in Vo Nhai during this time? Was the enemy still blockading and terrorizing the area? Had the movement survived? Who was still active and who was dead? What had happened to the AFNS comrades who had had to move to Dai Tu, Son Duong, and Yen The? All these questions were raised. Day and night, we were anxious to find out about the situation back in our country, but no news reached us.

Who was capable of re-establishing contact for us? Any AFNS comrade who went back would easily be uncovered and arrested right away. The person whom we would send on this mission should be someone we could trust, someone who knew the roads and the people back home well, someone whom we could be certain would not be arrested. It was not easy to find someone with all these qualifications.

Quoc Hung suggested, "Why don't we go and ask Aunt Sao to help us out?"

I thought about this and realized that no one else but she could do it. "It would be difficult to get her to accept. But let's try anyway. If by chance she agrees then it will be great."

Mrs. Sao was my father's cousin. A few years ago she made one or two trips to Vo Nhai to visit her older sister who had married Mr. Sang Khi--I called him my uncle-in-law--a merchant in Phu Thuong. We thought we would ask her to use the excuse of visiting her relatives in order to gather information. Chu Quoc Hung and I went to visit her all the way in Lung Sluong (Bo Cuc canton).

When she saw us step into her yard, she said, "So you two are back; come in!"

Chu Quoc Hung answered for me as well, "We've been back for a long time. Today, we've come to visit you and uncle."

We went into the house. My uncle dropped whatever he was tinkering with and went to boil water to make tea. After he poured us some tea, he said, "Well, if I had met you two by chance in the street, I wouldn't have been able to recognize you."

Since she had not seen us for a long time, my aunt asked meticulously about all the things that had happened back home. I told her in detail about the enemy's repression, about the destruction of our village, and the dispersal of our relatives. The more I talked the more painful I felt about the loss of our country and the destruction of our families. Hatred and resentment rose within me and choked me. Mrs. Sao wept, full of sorrow and pity for her own blood relatives. My uncle was also very moved, and averted his face. Our common suffering and hatred tightened our family bonds and drew us closer together.

Seeing how badly affected my aunt was--she was weeping and sobbing --I tried to comfort her and said, "You and uncle feel sorry for my family, but it won't do any good for you to weep and grieve now. When we left to make revolution we had figured that we would certainly have to bear such losses. My father himself--although he is old and loves his sons and nephews very much--knows that unless we carry out a revolution, we will die of cold and hunger, and we will always be slaves. This is why he encourages us to act with resoluteness, and he is not afraid of tortures and imprisonment."

Mrs. Sao asked, "But you only have a few dozen men, and you're badly armed, so how can you fight them?"

I answered, "We're few in numbers and we don't have enough weapons now, but we'll become stronger. Right now, in China as well as in Vietnam, poor people everywhere are rising up, determined to overthrow the enemy. Haven't you noticed that our relatives and the people in this area are helping us to the utmost of their ability? You and uncle can help us also."

She said, "We're poor and old, so what can we do to help you?"

I said, "To help the revolution, you don't have to have a lot of money. Actually, the rich have never done anything for the revolution. In fact all they've done is to harm the revolution. If you're old you can do things that don't require too much effort. All we need is your commitment. I've come here today because there's something I'd like to ask you, my aunt, to do for me."

My uncle asked, "What is it? Go ahead and tell us. Will it be alright if I do it for you?"

My aunt hesitated, "Everything you do is dangerous, and I'm only afraid that I might make a mess of it, because I'm not used to doing such things. And if I get arrested, it will be very bad."

I said, "What I'll ask you to do is just physically tiring. If you act cleverly, it won't be too dangerous. We want you to go to Vo Nhai to gather information and to see whether the enemy's repression is still continuing, and whether the people have returned to their settlements to live and work as before. The only thing is, if you do this, uncle, it won't be very convenient. Auntie can do this more easily, because she already knows the roads and the people back home, and especially she won't attract the attention of the enemy and they won't be watching her the way they would if it was a man going back."

My aunt thought about this and then asked, "What about the family of Uncle Sang Khi, what's happened to them?"

"When we left they were in good health and their work was going well because the enemy wasn't terrorizing them. You can say you're going there to visit them, this will be a perfect excuse."

My uncle told her, "That's alright, you can go. I'll take care of the work here at home. It will be alright even if you have to be away for a couple of days or half a month. But you, my nephew, must tell her exactly what things she is supposed to look out for."

Finally, Mrs. Sao cheerfully accepted our request. We discussed a plan for her journey. As a disguise, she would continue to wear her Chinese Nung costume, but she should not wear her hair in a bun--instead she should wrap her hair in a coil on her head, and tie a scarf over her head in the style of the women on the Vietnam side of the border. On the way, if anybody asked her, she should say that she came from Hang Cau, That Khe district, close to the border with China, and that she was going to visit her relatives in Na Pai and Phu Thuong. She should only carry a bag containing two changes of clothes, and she would not need any papers. Once she arrived at destination, she should not try to gather information, instead she should make the rounds, going to visit relatives and acquaintances and inquiring after their health in a normal fashion, and naturally her relatives and acquaintances would tell her what they knew in the course of the conversation. At first, she would only need to find out about the situation in general, and check whether the enemy's repression was still continuing. She should find out where the enemy posted sentries, where they conducted patrols, who among the villagers had died, who were still alive, who had been arrested, who had been released, in what state were the houses and fields--whatever she heard she should try to remember. Gradually, when it was most convenient for her to do so, she should contact Luc Van Du (the man who had stayed behind to maintain the grassroot base in Vo Nhai) and ask him to stop by Mr. Sang Khi's house. Then she could gather more information in detail from him.

Mrs. Sao left.

We anxiously waited for her return day and night. We wondered whether she had managed to slip through safely. She could not speak Vietnamese, and if she ran into complications, we wondered how she would react. We worried about her going on such a journey by herself, far from her homeland. Even though we were dogged by these worries, we kept up with our normal activities. We continued to visit different base areas, and wherever we went we performed manual labor tasks with the local people and made propaganda about the Vietnamese revolution.

Two weeks later we got word that Mrs. Sao had come back. We heaved a sigh of relief, as though we had just gotten rid of a heavy burden. Quoc Hung and I hurriedly went over to see her. My aunt and we were happy that her mission had been carried out successfully, without hitches.

Mrs. Sao told us that a few days after the AFNS withdrew, the Foreign Legionnaires and the regular troops also withdrew, leaving behind mostly province troops and militiamen. They announced in their propaganda that the AFNS had dissolved and fled to the mountains where they were living like savages. The enemy had now set up a few isolated posts, and their sweep operations had decreased in frequency. The people were concentrated only in Na Pheo, but they too had begun to return to their old villages to produce. Even the families who had been jailed because they were suspected of being Viet Minh, or because their relatives had left to join the revolution, had been allowed to return to their old villages to farm. However, they still had to return to the concentration camp in the evening. The comrades who stayed behind secretly led the people to carry out a struggle. The people went to the district capital and to the post to protest and request that these families be allowed to move back to their old houses to farm before the planting season was ended. The enemy had to accede to this request. Even Mrs. Kham, my older sister and Quoc Hung's wife, had been allowed to return to the village. Although the secret police continued to probe and search, and the rich bullies and the village officials kept up their sabotage, the situation had become less tense and a lot calmer.

My father had died at the prison camp in Cho Chu. The work of re-establishing contact with the AFNS comrades operating in Dai Tu, Son Duong, Phu Binh and Huu Lung had just begun.

The news that my father had died at the prison camp was very painful for me, and brought back memories. I recalled my childhood days. I was the youngest child in the family, and so my father loved me very much. After I left, he was arrested by the Post Commander who tortured him and beat him, and tried to force him to call me home. My father cursed him. Whenever he met someone he could confide in, he would say, "Tell my son that his father is not afraid. My only worry is that my children out there are not doing a good job. I don't worry about myself at all. I only worry about my children and about the revolution."

The more I thought about my father's words, the more I felt how numerous and serious the imperialists' crimes were. "They will have to pay for their crimes." It could not be otherwise.

Finally, Mrs. Sao said, "Brother Du, Miss Thu and Mrs. Sang wanted me to tell you that you can start sending a few cadres back. You must wait till the end of the monsoon rains before sending them back. There won't be anything to eat till the early harvest comes."

Listening to Mrs. Sao, our enthusiasm and our confidence in the revolutionary forces intensified.

We relayed to the AFNS brothers the news concerning the situation back home. Everyone was happy and wished he could grow wings in order to fly home right away. But from now until it became possible for us to go back, we would have to make an all-out effort to solve many problems. We should not be impatient and impulsive.

* * *

At that time, the struggle of the Vietnamese revolutionary cadres against the Chinese KMT was rather complicated. The policy of Chiang Kai Shek and his gang toward the Vietnamese revolution was treacherous. Sometimes they ruthlessly repressed and terrorized the Vietnamese revolution--at times they even allied with the French in order to sabotage it. Sometimes they allied themselves with it and supported it, hoping to buy it off or to pull it over to their side in order to carry out their dark schemes.

Basically speaking, the KMT government had only one desire and this was to destroy the revolution and the Communist movement. But the existing situation forced them to adopt more discreet and cunning tricks, and prevented them from being too brazen about it. Under popular pressure, the ChungKing government finally had to declare war on Japan, and so they had no choice but to accede to our Party's correct appeal for an "alliance between Vietnam and China in order to overthrow the French and Japanese." Besides, the Vietnamese revolution had become a sizable and significant force, and could not be ignored.

Contacts between the people living on both sides of the border were considered both illegal and normal. The border was a line delineating the territory of China and Vietnam. To the regimes in both countries, it was illegal for the people to cross back and forth, and they forbade the people to do so. However, to the people themselves, it was extremely natural and normal for them to go back and forth because they had relatives, friends and acquaintances on the other side, or because their children had married into families living across the frontier. The mountains in the border region were linked in an unbroken line. Sometimes relatives were only separated by a hill--a man could hear his brother calling him on the other side of the border.

After the AFNS crossed into China, they were helped by the Chinese cadres. The AFNS performed well their civilian population proselytizing task by helping the villagers to build houses, to plough, to transplant rice seedlings, carry manure to the fields, etc. The AFNS did all these things skillfully, and thereby earned the love and affection of the Chinese people. The villagers discussed the Vietnamese Revolution, the Chiang Kai Shek regime and the Chinese Revolution. Once the people understood what the AFNS was doing, their sympathy for the AFNS intensified, and their confidence in the Chinese Revolution became more solid. It would not be easy for the enemy to try and displace our influence. However, the KMT still held to the hope that by allying themselves with us, they could attract our cadres into their ranks and detach the population from our Party. They wanted us to lead them in the end into Vietnam[1] so they could replace the French and the Japanese as masters of Indochina, as the Vietnamese Kuomintang, the Vietnamese Revolutionary League and the Vietnamese Restoration Party had done before. However, the concrete measures they applied to achieve these aims varied from area to area, from moment to moment, from official to official--sometimes the measures taken contradicted each other, and the actions of the upper and lower levels conflicted with one another. Therefore, our strategy was to do our best to obtain their support--as far as was possible--and in certain situations if we were clever and knew how to exploit the contradictions within their ranks, we could do many things that were of advantage to the Vietnamese revolution.

One of the tricks that the KMT used with our cadres at the time was to make it difficult for them to earn their living, so that in desperation they would go and work for them. With the exception of our military cadets who had been sent to Nanning to study and who had a relatively secure life--though their living standard was very low--all the scattered cadres who operated along the border had enormous economic difficulties. Those who were energetic and had operational experience continued to stick with the movement. They worked for their living, and at the same time they propagandized and organized the people. In the end, it was precisely these grassroot bases which they had set up which helped them to earn their living with ease. However, there were a few cadres who, either because they were not capable of operating independently on their own, or because they wanted to lead a quiet life, went to work for the KMT regime. But those who did so to betray the revolution were very few in numbers. The majority did it in order to earn their living, while waiting for the opportunity to resume their activities, or they continued to operate but in a lukewarm and deliberate fashion while waiting for the right opportunity to arise.

Around the end of May 1942, Khoa and Han Sinh suddenly came to Bo Cuc to see us.

Han Sinh came from the border region and had been active for a long time. Khoa was a member of the AFNS First Platoon and had par-

---

1. The Chinese KMT was then planning to enter Vietnam to attack the Japanese and establish their political control. They were using exiled Vietnamese political groups in China to further their plans. (Trans.)

ticipated in the Bac Son uprising, and had followed Cap's and An's squad to P'inghsiang in July 1941 during the enemy's wave of repression in Bac Son. Ha Khai Lac told me that both of them were working for the KMT regime in Chinghsi, and that they were doing so for the time being probably because they had to earn their living somehow, and not because they had any intention of betraying the revolution. However, I had not seen them for a long time, and who knows, maybe they had changed in the meantime. What was their aim in coming here to see the AFNS? We consulted with each other beforehand to decide how to deal with them.

The news that Khoa and Han Sinh were coming to see us made me suddenly remember a story that Ha Khai Lac had told me. This happened almost a year ago. After the first group--led by Phung Chi Kien and Luong Huu Chi had left--the second group led by comrade Dang Van Cap also began their journey.

According to the assignment of the Bac Son War Zone Command Staff, comrade Cap (who was then 48 years old) would take a number of comrades abroad to study. This group included An (Hoang Van Thai),[2] Minh (i.e., Binh),[3] Khoa, Lang (Hoang Nhu Y) and X (who, forced to join the province troops in That Khe district, had left to join the revolution). They planned to go to Lungyiu, Muc Nam Quan,[4] and Lungchou where they would wait for a number of other students to be sent from Vietnam to study in China.[5] With the exception of X and Lang who were new in the movement, the rest were veteran cadres from the Bac Son uprising.

Binh knew the way, and led the brothers through the forest. For over ten days and nights of climbing hills and crossing passes, each man only had a pouch of dried food to eat. It rained without letup day and night. Their clothes and food got wet. One night, around nine or ten o'clock, they crossed into Diem He district. They wanted to sneak through the Khanh Khe bridge, but unfortunately halfway across the bridge, they ran into a group of opium smugglers who yelled noisily. Afraid that they would be detected, they turned around and ran, not daring to cross the bridge. But the river blocked their way and they had to cross it in order to proceed toward their destination. They wandered around for a long time and finally found a place where the villagers had dammed up the river to catch fish with traps. They crossed the river at this spot, alternately wading and swimming to the other side. That night, drenched and tired, they went to the house of one of Binh's acquaintances. This family used to trade in opium. They served them a meal consisting of nothing but rice and pickled papaya, but the brothers were so hungry and tired that they ate with a ferocious appetite. After they finished eating, they went to a hill in the forest to sleep. They did not dare to sleep in the house, even though it was the house of an acquaintance. At that time, pictures and names of Communists were posted everywhere. They were being tracked by the province and regular troops and by the militia, and even the opium

---

2. Hoang Van Thai is now a Lieutenant General and the Deputy Chief of the Joint General Staff of the People's Army of the DRV. (Trans.)

3. He is now the Secretary of the Bac Son District Party Committee. (Trans.)

4. China's Gateway, near Lang Son. (Trans.)

5. As part of their plan for entering Indochina, the Chinese KMT was providing military training to Vietnamese revolutionaries. (Trans.)

smugglers joined hands with the soldiers to track them down when necessary. Leaving their cradle--the grassroot and mass organizations--the brothers felt very lost and exposed.

The next night, they went to Dong Dang. When they were near it, they were pursued by soldiers. They fled into the forest and split into two groups. One composed of comrades Dang Van Cap, Lang and X, had a musket and an Italian grenade; the other had only a couple of knives as weapons. Cap's group reached Lungyiu first. The others did not arrive until the next night.

Afterward, a number of them went to the military academy in Tientung, while the rest remained in Chinghsi to study attacks on fortifications with explosives. What happened to Khoa later, how he ended up working for the KMT--I did not know. Han Sinh was someone we had met before. Believing that these two brothers were basically decent men, the Command Staff talked it over and decided that we must try to persuade them, rekindle the revolutionary flame in their hearts, and convince them to serve the AFNS again. We still lacked cadres, and if we could add just one more man to our ranks, it would be worth the effort. We had already investigated each of the men operating along the border. If in this meeting these two turned out to be rotten elements, then we would have no choice but to detain them. The AFNS by that time had already established itself firmly in the area, and if need be, we could resort to force to deal with our enemies.

I went out to meet Han Sinh and Khoa. They seemed embarrassed, and ill at ease. Khoa, in particular, was reserved and quiet. I cheerfully asked about their health and their families. When we recounted our happy and sad experiences during the period of intense and decisive struggle in Bac Son, the atmosphere became more intimate. I talked about the eight months of armed struggle in Vo Nhai. They listened, looking reflective and moved. I said, "Although the enemy's savagely terrorized the people in Bac Son and Vo Nhai, the movement won't be stamped out. On the contrary, the cadres as well as the people have become more experienced and better trained as a result. Naturally, if we act clumsily, and if we fail to understand fully the line and policy of the Party, then the movement might encounter some temporary setbacks. But we should not let ourselves become discouraged just because of a few temporary difficulties."

Khoa said, "My family is still back in Vietnam. To be honest with you, I have never forgotten you brothers, the Fatherland and the revolution. However, one cannot be rigid, and must accommodate oneself to changes. Because I had a hard time earning my living, I had to go and work for the regime here. But up to now I haven't done anything for them really."

It was now possible for us to be frank with each other, so I asked, "I don't know what your purpose is in coming here. It would be best for us to be frank with one another. If you still consider the AFNS as your comrades, then don't hide anything from us. If there are any problems, we'll help each other to solve them."

Han Sinh glanced at Khoa, as though to urge him to speak out. I poured tea and invited them to drink. After a minute of reflection, Khoa looked straight into my eyes and said slowly, "Right after you crossed into this region, the informers and security police kept watch over you and reported to the command organizations of the 4th Front

Army. We heard that even General Chang Fa-k'uei had ordered Ch'en Pao Hsiang (Tran Bao Xuong), the Director of the Military Academy, to personally find our more about your group in order to prepare for their planned entry into Vietnam. They have sent us here mainly to probe the Viet Minh movement, and in particular to gauge your political stand, and get to know your leadership core. In short, we want to know whether you are Communists or not, what your attitude toward the French, the Japanese, as well as the Chinese Army, is. Then, on the basis of data they have gathered, they will devise a concrete line of action to deal with you."

I thought, this means that the Ch'en Pao Hsiang group had only managed to gather a few general facts about us. They must still have some doubts about us, and this was why they had sent Khoa--a former member of the AFNS who knew and understood us--here to investigate further. Since the KMT was deceitful, the more we kept our strength and all other things about ourselves secret, the better it would be for us.

In response to Khoa's frank words, I answered in an attitude of trust, "You were active in the movement for a long time, and have fought in combat. Now you've acquired some experience in dealing with the KMT. In your opinion, how should we deal with this investigation of theirs?"

Perhaps partly because he was jolted when he remembered his responsibility as a revolutionary, and partly because he had never thought about how to deal with the investigation, he replied, "I'll do whatever you comrades ask me to do. That is their intention. I'll leave it up to you to decide. To tell you the truth when Ch'en Pao Hsiang sent me here, I was bewildered and did not know what would be the proper thing for me to do. But now that you comrades have shown you understand my situation, and since your feelings toward me haven't changed, my mind is now at ease and I feel reassured, and I know what I should do. I've come back to the Party, and I leave all decisions up to the Command Staff. I'm prepared to do everything you ask."

Han Sinh also said, "I feel exactly the way Khoa does. On our way here, we told each other that if we met our organization it would be possible for us to resume our activities. So, assign us any task, and we'll carry it out no matter what the difficulties are."

I said, "You're doing the right thing. We brothers can never abandon one another. As to ways to deal with the Ch'en Pao Hsiang group, the Command Staff will meet and discuss it in detail later. I think that you should not report the truth to them, instead you should --depending on how much they know--fill them in a little, selectively. But in cases where they do not know anything, then give them a false report. If they know clearly our policy and position, and our composition and organization, they will certainly not leave us alone. Just emphasize our goal of fighting the French and the Japanese, and our slogan calling for a "Sino-Vietnamese" alliance. As to the name of our organization, you can call us the Viet Minh movement, or you can invent a new name for us--depending on what the situation is."

Khoa interrupted me, "In general, I can take care of the things you've just mentioned. But if we want them to trust and believe us, we must provide them with some concrete evidence of our cooperation."

"Don't worry about that. Just go back and tell them that you've contacted Vietnamese cadres you've known before, and this is why you have managed to recruit a number of Vietnamese cadets who have volunteered to study in Chinese military academies in order to help the Chinese army enter Indochina to fight the Japanese in the future. We'll select a number of brothers and send them to attend training classes, and you pretend you've recruited them yourselves for the KMT. Once they have these 'hostages' in their hands, they will certainly support us, and your work will be facilitated."

Khoa said, "We propose that the Command Staff allow us to rejoin the ranks of the AFNS to operate. Something dangerous might happen to us if we keep on working for the KMT for a long time."

"As for your assignment, we'll discuss it thoroughly later. The Command Staff will do everything it can to arrange for your early return into the ranks of the AFNS. The sooner the better. But for the moment, you must perform well this immediate task. When we need you, we'll ask you to come back right away."

Han Sinh and Khoa went to see a few AFNS brothers they used to know. Everyone greeted them with warmth and joy. After a long period of living in exile in a foreign country, being back with people they knew and were close to filled them with warmth and enthusiasm.

The Command Staff met with Khoa and Han Sinh to discuss a plan of action to deal with the KMT. Six AFNS comrades--Quoc Vinh, Liem, An, Quang, Dong and Bo--were chosen to go to Chinghsi to attend Chiang Kai Shek's military training class. The significance and purpose of their training were explained to them in detail. This was a way to deceive the enemy. Outwardly, we pretended to cooperate with them to prolong our period of operation here so we could create conditions for clearing our way back to our country. In obedience to a Party order, the brothers agreed to go, but deep down none of them wanted to go and receive training in this fashion. This in fact was a very difficult mission which would test their loyalty--as revolutionaries living in the mud, they must not be contaminated.

I told them for the last time, "Study whatever the school teaches you. Study their techniques in order to serve our political goals. Study them in order to understand them thoroughly, so that in the future we'll know how to deal with them. But you should always remember the Fatherland and the Party. You must stay close to each other and help each other. And remember to write us and send back information in a way that would not arouse suspicion. When your training is completed, we'll find a way to get you back."

Chu Quoc Hung was chosen as their representative, and led them on the way. It took them four days to reach Chinghsi, after corssing an area which was sparsely populated but full of impassable mountains and bandits. Wherever they went they only saw malnourished and ragged people, and emaciated and feeble children--a situation not too different from the situation in our own villages and settlements under the foreign yoke back home.

When they reached the Headquarters of General Ch'en Pao Hsiang, they were kept waiting for three days in the guest room. During these three days, security policemen were sent to talk with them and investigate them. Afterward, Ch'en Pao Hsiang saw Hung three times to probe which organization our forces belonged to, what our political inclination was, where he had come from, which route we had taken, etc. Basing his answers on the discussion we had held back in Bo Cuc, Hung gave him information which fit the reports of Khoa and Han Sinh, but which--

though more concise than the reports--was still very general in contents. Ch'en Pao Hsiang also asked about the situation in Vietnam--for example, the conflict between the French and the Japanese, the activities of various political parties, our country's economic resources, grain yields and food supplies, and the attitude of the people toward war. In reply, Hung mainly denounced the repressive and exploitative acts of the French and the Japanese, such as taxes and levies, forced conscription of laborers, the sufferings of the people and their aspiration to drive out the imperialist invaders.

In Chinghsi, Hung met Vi Duc Minh and Duong Cong Binh. These two comrades were in the same situation as Khoa. They had gone to work for the local authority to earn their living temporarily while waiting to re-establish contact with our organization to resume their activities. They helped Hung a lot and showed him how to deal with the KMT.

After accepting our six cadets, Ch'en Pao Hsiang organized a celebration party to which he invited all the Vietnamese cadets studying in the academy. Seizing this favorable opportunity, Chu Quoc Hung stood up and talked about the situation in Vietnam, denounced the crimes of the French and the Japanese, and thanked China for her assistance. Ch'en Pao Hsiang also expressed his views and called for Sino-Vietnamese unity to fight the Japanese.

A few months later, the military training course in Chinghsi was completed, and these six brothers returned safely to Bo Cuc to rejoin our ranks. They had acquired some knowledge of basic military techniques. This proved very useful to us because of our limited knowledge then, and helped us to expand our training of the mass infrastructure which was then lacking cadres.

The day prior to their departure, in his last meeting with Ch'en Pao Hsiang, Hung presented him with the following four requests:

(a) Issue passes to Vietnamese cadres so they could operate without difficulties on Chinese soil and move without hindrance along the border from Chinghsi to Lungchou and P'ing-hsiang.

(b) Help them to openly establish an organization which would serve as a liaison station for internal communication as well as for communication and relation with the Chinese government.

(c) Provide them with weapons to fight the Japanese and the French.

(d) Help set up military and political training classes for our infrastructure along the border.

Ch'en Pao Hsiang agreed to the first request, promised to give an answer to the second later, but tactfully turned down the third and fourth ones. After the meeting, he invited Hung to take a tour of the school and the town, and gave him 500 Chinese Dollars for travel expenses.

* * *

In this isolated border region, the farthermost end of Chinese territory, the people in Bo Cuc led a miserable life under the yoke of the KMT. Hundreds of calamities fell on their heads. We saw these painful scenes with our own eyes, and this reminded us constantly of the life of slavery that our people back home were leading. Since our people and the Chinese people shared the same plight, our resentment of all acts of repression and exploitation--whether they were perpetrated by the French, the Japanese, or Chiang Kai Shek--deepened and we felt that we must unite with the local people to fight our common enemy.

China was then being invaded by Japan. However, the Chiang Kai Shek government was not seriously interested in resisting the Japanese, and this was why they were not at all concerned about improving the life of the peasants in order to strengthen this most powerful and numerous force and unite it to resist the Japanese. The landlords and the rich bullies had free rein in the countryside. In spite of the continuously bad harvests, brought about by various natural calamities, the landlords and the rich bullies continued to collect exorbitant rents with impunity. They also used the resistance movement as an excuse to solicit contributions from the peasants, conscript soldiers and laborers, and levy all sorts of new taxes. Besides these forms of exploitation, there were other brazen acts of robbery which occurred daily--for example, the soldiers bought goods without paying, and the bandits murdered and plundered the villagers. The people's resentment piled up as high as a mountain.

In the Bo Cuc area, the Chiang regime had set up a few outposts to control the border. The soldiers manning these posts were familiar with the terrain here and knew the local situation and villagers. Sometimes, they ranged very far in their patrols. They were like thorns in the back of the AFNS, and it would not be easy for us to remove them. They blocked the roads, and caused us a lot of problems along the length of our communication route to Hsiatung and Lungchou. At that time, only a few of us had obtained passes, and the majority of the brothers had to avoid them whenever they went on mission by slipping through dangerous and difficult mountain paths.

Thanks to the help of some old people, we discovered a secret trail that went from our base in Ban Khiec and Na Slieng to Dong Chiu, Po Muc, Pa Mac, Na Noc, Ban Va, Ban Dan, Na Trao, Ban Seng, and Ta Man, and across the river to Doong Hinh, Sang Kheo, Ban Cang, Na Leng (e.g., Cuc Khau Kheo), all the way to Kieu Tam and Lungchou. This route was full of obstacles and dangers, and was the hideout of the bandits. An old villager once said, "I've lived through three generations here, and never once dared to go through Khau Kheo by myself. And yet the Vietnamese revolutionaries--many times going unarmed--have managed to go back and forth constantly through this area without anything happening to them. They're really very brave!" We could do this, not only because we knew how to obtain the support of the people, but also because the bandits and outlaws in the forest had a "healthy respect" for us.

One day, five or six Chinese youths from Ai Keng, Ban Trang and Na Slieng came to see us. From inside we could hear them talk loudly at the doorway, "Where's brother Quang? Is he home?"

"I'm here! I'm coming!" I answered quickly and ran out of the house.

These youths knew me well, and we used to meet each other at the market place. Their faces still glowering with anger, they said, "You must lend us a hand. Let's fight! Unless we attack and kill them, our anger will not go away."

"They're really too troublesome. Let's hit them hard and show them the stuff the men in this area are made of!"

We invited them to sit down, and asked them to tell us what had happened from beginning to end. It turned out the soldiers in the Tong Phou post had abused the people in these three villages. This was a frontier outpost located in a ricefield which ended abruptly at the foot of the mountains. From there a route led to Vietnam. For a long time now, the soldiers had relied on the fact that they were armed to harass the people and make demands on them. Sometimes they bought chickens at below the market price, sometimes they asked for a bunch of vegetables--putting their request in such a way that the villagers did not dare to refuse--sometimes they cadged a free pipe of opium, sometimes they forcibly borrowed clothes from the villagers, sometimes they deceived the people out of their cash and belongings, sometimes they extorted money from the villagers. They were unhygienic and slept around, and spread diseases. The youths resented most the way they frequently broke into the courting festivals and teased the village girls. On several occasions one or two soldiers went into the village to seek fun and were ambushed by the youths in the forest and beaten to a pulp, but they did not change their bad habits. The youths secretly agreed among themselves that unless these soldiers were given a hard lesson they would not be intimidated.

They told us, "If we wipe out the soldiers in the Tong Phou post our troubles would end and you brothers would be able to move around without difficulties to operate. This time, we must wipe out everyone in the post."

"How can we do it? They are well armed and have fortifications," an AFNS comrade said.

A strapping and muscular youth--perhaps the leader of the group-- rolled up his shirt sleeves and declared loudly, "You don't have to be afraid. We're used to dealing with them. They're well armed, but it's not difficult to fight them. We know the way in and out of the post. It's also easy for us to keep close to them. We've stopped in the post and played cards with them sometimes when we went to the market."

Another youth pulled his arm and said in a more tactful and less belligerent tone, "We want to discuss this with you and then carry out our attack. If we seize any weapons, we'll donate them to the Vietnamese revolution."

If the men here said they would do something, it would be done. They were also familiar with the handling of weapons since they went hunting for wolves or bears practically every day. It was only because they respected and trusted us that they had come to solicit our opinion. But we could not let them resort to such violent action.

I asked, "Have you asked brother Phan about this?"

Brother Phan was comrade Phan Sen Chan, a Chinese cadre. He was about 40 years old, a stocky and muscular man, with a huge head and a pointed chin. He was a very kind and calm person. He was with the Red Army (during the Red Lungchou period) in 1927,[6] and had great prestige

---

6. There was a communist-led peasant movement among the Chuang ethnic minorities of

among the men here. He had also been most helpful to the Vietnamese revolution. Guests came to see him so frequently that he always had a tray of food ready to treat the visitors. He was like an elder brother to me. On his part, he had great trust in the AFNS because we had made an effective contribution to the expansion of the local movement. He and the other Chinese comrades had a great affection for the AFNS. At that time the [Communist Chinese] New 4th Army and the 8th Route Army had not yet succeeded in linking up with the local movement.

"Brother Phan is away and we haven't seen him," one of the youths replied.

I said, "It's true that if we could destroy the Tong Phou post, you would avenge yourselves, and we would pull out this thorn in our side and also obtain over ten rifles. But this could also bring disastrous consequences for us, because the Tong Phou post is not the only one around here--there are many others. Do you intend to attack the other posts as well after you destroy the one in Tong Phou?"

"We are not strong enough to attack so many posts."

"If you can't destroy all the posts around here, soldiers will pour in here and terrorize the people; what will you do then?"

They were silent. One youth was unfazed, "Should we give up then? Let's just wipe out this gang first, and we'll deal with the others later."

I became stern and said, "If brother Phan was home, he wouldn't let you do such a thing."

We patiently explained to them that if we destroyed the Tong Phou post out of momentary anger, we would avenge the people and obtain a few extra weapons for the AFNS, but the Chiang Kai Shek gang would certainly send troops here to terrorize the villagers. Just feeding these troops would be enough to ruin the people. Besides, our forces were still weak and could not fight them back. Our suffering and our humiliation was not caused by these few soldiers in this frontier outpost. These soldiers themselves were living in misery, and were no better off than watch dogs. It was the ringleaders all the way down in Lungchou and in Chungking, the landlords, feudalists and capitalists who were the real culprits responsible for all the people's sufferings. In order to overthrow them, we must carry out a revolution. To kill the weeds, we must pull them up by their roots. But to make revolution, we must not be reckless and adventurous, we must not let ourselves be blinded by a temporary and small gain, and forget about long-term advantages. We advised the youths to repress their anger and nurture their hatred in order to consolidate the revolutionary forces for the day when we could topple the existing regime--from top to bottom.

The youths seemed to understand. Rationally, they accepted our arguments, but emotionally they were still angry and frustrated. Later, we met comrade Phan Sen Chan and discussed with him how to explain it further to them. The young were by nature aggressive, but also impulsive; if they received good guidance, they could achieve great things.

Kwangsi province in 1926-29. The Left and Right River Soviets--which sprang from this movement--were not set up by the Chinese Communist Party until 1929. (Trans.)

* * *

The KMT authorities in Bo Cuc, Lungchou and P'ing-hsiang had gotten wind that the AFNS's activities in China were not necessarily to their advantage. They did not want us to oppose the Japanese and the French so much as for us to submit ourselves to their policy. They did not have any concrete evidence, but they sensed that there was an invisible but strong tie which bound the AFNS to the local population. They wanted to investigate us and keep watch over us, but they constantly stumbled against this invisible wall of protection which the people threw around us.

Their patriotism, their revolutionary spirit, their mass lines, their simple style of living--these virtues of the AFNS were good examples for the local people to emulate, increased their confidence in the revolution and provided them with experience to carry out their struggle. The link and mutual support between us and the Chinese comrades such as Pinh Chi, Phan Sen Chan, Nong Ky Chan, Hen May, Lao Giam and Khim Di became stronger with each passing day. The KMT was aware of this, and felt that they should take countermeasures.

Comrades Thai Long and Thanh were arrested and put in jail because they did not have residence permits and passes. Then came the turn of the comrades in Doong Hinh--such as the two brothers Ha Cham and Ha Ky. Some were jailed for five or six days, others were detained for a month. Hua Dinh Khanh went missing for a month, and we thought he had disappeared until we found out that the KMT had kept him in jail during all this time.

The brothers who had a taste of life in Chiang Kai Shek's jails still shuddered with revulsion whenever they thought about it. The jails were awash with slime, refuse, excrement and urine; flies droned, lice and bedbugs swarmed everywhere. Rice stank of lime, and the rotten fish was full of worms. After only a couple of days in jail, you became covered with sores and boils. The wardens and guards beat the prisoners without restraint with whips and rifle butts, especially when the prisoners did not have money to bribe them. The prisoners came from a bewildering array of backgrounds: political prisoners, peasants in debt, dishonest merchants and swindlers, tax evaders, robbers and thieves, gamblers and prostitutes. The jail was in constant turmoil, as the criminals fought and insulted--and sometimes even murdered--each other. Many prisoners were dying even before their sentence was pronounced. Some were crippled for life by the time they were released. In such prison conditions, it was a real struggle for the revolutionaries to keep their bodies intact so they could resume their activities after their release. It was a struggle which demanded their full energy and for which they had to summon all their wit.

After Chu Quoc Hung returned from Chinghsi with the papers that Ch'en Pao Hsiang had issued, he got a number of brothers out of jail before their prison term was over. Afterward, we motivated our relatives or the hamlet and village chiefs we knew to put up guarantees for the brothers who were still in jail, and consequently these brothers one by one were released. Perhaps in this period the KMT policy toward the Vietnamese revolution had become more flexible and the authorities in Chinghsi had ordered the Lungchou officials to release our men. This was how the Command Staff assessed the situation, and we felt we must grab this opportunity to intensify our diplomatic efforts.

Ch'en Pao Hsiang had agreed with brother Chu Quoc Hung to issue passes to the AFNS so we could move around and operate with ease, and to study the establishment of a permanent National Salvation liaison office to facilitate contacts with the KMT. After we obtained this agreement, we urged the lower level officials in Lungchou to carry it out as soon as possible. Mr. Ho Duc Thanh knew Hai Canh Cuong, the Lungchou Divisional Commander, and obtained without difficulty an appointment for us to see him. Hai Canh Cuong then issued passes to the AFNS, allowing us to go all the way from Chinghsi to Lungchou and P'ing-hsiang.

Around September 1942, Hai Canh Cuong informed us that General Chang Fa-k'uei, the Commander of the 4th Front Army, had agreed to let us open a liaison office in Lungchou, which would represent the Vietnamese Revolution operating in this area.

This was a significant diplomatic victory for us at that time. Leading a revolutionary force to break away from the French encirclement, taking it to a foreign country to operate, and living under the authority of a regime basically opposed to our political line--in doing all this, we had managed to avoid opportunism. By refusing to surrender or to negotiate irresponsibly with our opponents, and also by not following the masses to take reckless and adventurous action, the AFNS had acted with strict accordance to the Party Central Committee 8th Resolution, and had shown that they knew how to rely on the masses, carry out diplomatic negotiations, and retain their political independence. In the end, we forced our opponents to recognize us as an allied force which they could not dismiss as insignificant.

After we were publicly recognized by the KMT regime, the prestige of the AFNS rose even higher. Now that they had official blessing, the village and canton chiefs who had always been sympathetic to us supported us even more earnestly by providing us with information and papers. The security police and the informers slackened their surveillance. The villagers no longer had to hide their action, and felt free to invite us home each time they organized a meeting, or a festival, or a banquet to celebrate the anniversary of their ancestors' death. Many brothers who came from far away automatically came to contact us.

We were very happy and saw that this was a good opportunity for us to intensify our operation, and as a result we became even more enthusiastic and worked intensely in order not to waste a moment. However, we were on our guard against the treachery of the KMT; they could publicly recognize us and still secretly try to sabotage us. The period of open activities for us might not last very long, but if we knew how to profit of this opportunity, by the time the KMT reversed their policy we would already have completed the most necessary work.

We needed money to celebrate the opening of the Liaison Office. Hai Canh Cuong's divisional headquarters in Lungchou gave us 4,000 dollars,[7] but this sum was too small and inadequate. Our students in Nanning sent us a little money when they heard the news. We were in a bind and were trying to raise more money when the people in Bo Cuc urged each other to donate all sorts of things--cigarettes, cakes, candies, sugar and tea--although they themselves were living in privation.

---

7. 4,000 dollars of Chiang Kai Shek currency. At that time, a bowl of noodles already cost 500 dollars! (Footnote in text.)

They even lent us a few presentable sets of clothes so we "diplomats" could temporarily go on "mission"! This really showed that the local Chinese people looked upon each small success of the Vietnamese Revolution as their own. As the saying goes, "One bite when one is hungry is worth a bag of food when one is full." Whenever I recall these days of privation and hardship, I cannot help but feeling moved [at the memory of the people's support].

We carved a large wooden seal with the sentence "League for the Liberation of Vietnam--First Overseas Liaison Office." At that time, the attitude of the KMT toward the Viet Minh League was still unclear, but basically they were more suspicious than sympathetic. We were afraid that if we went ahead and used the name "Viet Minh League" we would run into difficulties. We thought that as a first step we would use this name as a screen, but in the meantime we would continue to use the Viet Minh Program to propagandize and enlighten the masses. We would wait till we could establish contact with the Central Committee and obtain further instructions, and it would not be too late then to change the name if this became necessary. The grassroot bases that we had succeeded in organizing would always remain our own.

The presentation ceremony took place in a KMT administrative office in Lungchou. The hosts included Bui Ngoc Thanh, Ho Duc Thanh, Chu Quoc Hung, Trieu Khanh Phuong, Lam Phu Thinh, Ha Khai Lac and myself. The guests included the representatives of Commander Hai Canh Cuong and over twenty administrative agencies and local organizations. The tea and food served was adequate.

After the hosts and guests had introduced themselves, Chu Quoc Hung, Trieu Khanh Phuong and I took turns giving speeches. We did not discourse on ideological theories, and instead just talked about the miserable life that the Vietnamese people were leading under the domination of the Japanese and the French. We mentioned in detail all their crimes, such as exorbitant taxes and levies, customs fines, fines imposed on villagers who gathered lumber and other forest products, forced conscription of soldiers and laborers, imprisonment of people, causing dikes to burst [through negligence], [condoning] robberies, gambling, prostitution, opium addiction, superstition, diseases, and encouraging frequent litigation by the population. These were all the things that we had seen with our own eyes. The Japanese aggressors who had arrived recently were the equals of the French in their cruelty. They seized land to build barracks, grazed their flocks of mules and horses in ripening ricefields, buried people alive by stuffing them in horses' bellies, and forced the people to destroy their crops to plant jute. This was why we had to make revolution to overthrow them. China was also resisting the Japanese, and so the Vietnamese and Chinese people should form an alliance to defeat their common enemy. Finally, we called on the Chinese people and the KMT government to help us even further, and thanked them.

The guests then took turns expressing their support and wishing the Vietnamese revolution success.

We sent cables to various areas and received congratulatory cables in return. We even sent cables to Chiang Kai Shek, Chang Fa-k'uei and Ch'en Pao Hsiang. Seeing our success, our military cadets in Nanning also planned to campaign for the establishment of a Liaison Office there, but gave up the idea afterward when they saw that this was not yet necessary.

From then on, our relations were carried on in an open and legitimate basis. Contacts were swiftly established with many revolutionaries. People from Chinese agencies and associations visited us frequently to discuss various activities with us. The Viet Minh program was translated into Chinese, printed in large numbers and distributed in the entire region. The influence of the Vietnamese revolution--as a result--spread very quickly and penetrated deeply among the masses.

On the excuse that our office had a large staff who had to travel frequently, and mentioning the slowness with which the KMT authorities took to issue passes valid only for a short period of time, we asked to be allowed to issue the passes ourselves to save the KMT officials a lot of bother. Hai Canh Cuong, the Lungchou Divisional Commander, agreed. From then on, we were free to roam within the boundaries of the two districts of Lungchou and P'ing-hsiang, to make propaganda and organize the revolution. This development--whenever I think back on it--makes me laugh at the KMT. They had no concept of national sovereignty--just because they did not want to be bothered, they granted to us foreigners the right to sign passes which allowed us to move freely on their own soil.

Although we had a permanent headquarters and conditions to operate openly, we tried to keep secret the strength of our forces stationed in Bo Cuc and continued to penetrate deeper into the basic masses and to set up grassroot bases. Only comrade Chu Quoc Hung was chosen to run the Liaison Office along with Mr. Bui Ngoc Thanh and Mr. Ho Duc Thanh. (This office operated for over a year until December 1943 when Ch'en Pao Hsiang--using the excuse that Vietnamese revolutionary forces should be unified--proposed that our Liaison Office in Lungchou be merged with the Liaison Offices of the Vietnam Restoration Party and Revolutionary League of Vietnam in Chinghsi. The KMT wanted to use this opportunity to interfere and take over our organization. But by that time the AFNS had already returned to Vietnam, ending their phase of overseas operations. In March 1944 the KMT again requested the merger of various Liaison Offices and their transfer to Nanning. Mr. Ho Duc Thanh left to attend the meeting on the unification of Vietnamese revolutionary forces, while Chu Quoc Hung immediately returned to Vietnam to operate. Our diplomatic mission was considered completed and ended there.)

* * *

The reason the AFNS was able to maintain a foothold along the border was that it knew how to rely on the people and win the support of the KMT regime. Besides the KMT, there was another group which was ready to sabotage us, and if we had failed to win them over, they would not have left us in peace. Anyone who had operated along the border must have run into them. These were the bandits.

For many generations, the people living along the Vietnam-China border had had to bear this horrible calamity. They lived in fear and worry, and could not earn their living in peace. Their houses might be burned and they might be robbed of their money and belongings at any moment. If the bandits took away their few buffaloes and oxen, this would spell the end of farming for them, and there would be nothing for them to do but to sit and watch their families go hungry. A girl could be kidnapped at any moment, blindfolded and gagged, and sold as a concubine or a slave in faraway places. A human life was only worth a few piastres and was less valued than a chicken or a dog. Sometimes an entire hamlet was burned, or a whole settlement was plundered. Roads were blocked and crops were destroyed. Both the Chiang regime and the French authorities were powerless to deal with the situation. They carried out a few raids but suffered such heavy losses that they left the bandits alone, free to wreak havoc on the people. It was only later, after the revolution succeeded and democratic reforms were carried out that this social ill was eradicated.

The bandits' forces were large and strong. Each group seized a territory and knew all the roads, shortcuts and byways in that area. They were well armed, and it was not easy to annihilate them. If one group dissolved, another one would crop up, because banditry was rooted in the corrupt social system, and was the outcome of the oppression, injustice, poverty and debauchery that the ruling cliques had inflicted on the working class. The bandits were usually criminals who had banded together. Sometimes powerful landlords or rich bullies became the gang leaders. A number of peasants also joined the gangs, either because they were too impoverished or because they had been forced to do so. Many youths who liked to loaf and have a good time, but lacked the money to gamble, visit prostitutes, or keep up with their dissolute friends, also became criminals and bandits.

The most dangerous aspect was that the bandits usually managed to maintain a total domination over the people. Many bandits led a normal life, mingled with the population, and only occasionally banded together to plunder. Because they were afraid of reprisals, or because of complicated ties, the honest villagers often did not dare to oppose them, and on occasion even protected them so they could escape the pursuit of the officials and soldiers. There were bandits who banded together to form permanent groups, such as those operating in the Khau Kheo area. This was a very high mountain covered with a bluish vegetation, enveloped in clouds all year around. The tall mountain was covered with thick forests, and became the stronghold of the bandits. With their careful sentry system and their tight organization, they managed to spread their control over this whole area. Once over 10,000 Chiang troops came here to attack them, but could not penetrate into their stronghold. The transportation of food to supply the troops was enough to exhaust the KMT, and the soldiers had to be withdrawn from Khau Kheo.

The AFNS ran into the bandits all the time. To the bandits, money, girls, drinks and opium were the most important things in life. The AFNS fighters were poor, but the imperialists had placed high prices on their heads, and so the bandits would not hesitate to cut off their heads, cross the border and deliver them to the French representative in That Khe for bounty. Sometimes they would kill you for a trifle--either because they misunderstood you, or were angry at you, or suspected you about something. Some of them had no idea what the revolution was all about, and looked on the AFNS as a different type of bandits whom they could either befriend or kick out to seize more territory for their operations.

The AFNS lived with the help of the people. But since the people's life was unsettled because of the constant plunder, the AFNS had the duty to help them cope with the bandits.

In some areas, the bandits lived among the villagers and kept them in fear. In order to reach the people and become close to them to educate and motivate them, the AFNS could not avoid coming into contact with the bandits through whom they could link up with the people living in the areas under the bandits' domination. Unless the bandits acquiesced, the villagers would be too frightened to come close to the cadres and the cadres themselves would be in danger. But once the people and the cadres became close to one another, the bandits would immediately become isolated.

In order to reduce the plunder and the killing, and in order to avoid unnecessary clashes with the bandits, the AFNS took the initiative to meet with them, reason with them, and restrain them on their criminal and cruel path. This we could do perfectly because we understood their psychological makeup and also a number of their weaknesses. Although they were reckless and violent, they wanted to stay alive and were afraid of death--like owls fearing daylight--because both the French and the Chiang authorities were tracking them down. Besides, there was constant competition for plunder, betrayal and revenge between various bands. Although the villagers were intimidated this did not mean that they were completely resigned. If they had the opportunity, they did not hesitate to strike back at the bandits, and many areas had organized self-defense units.

The bandits lived in fear and worry. They were ignorant, devoid of any guiding principles, and could easily be persuaded. Seeing that the AFNS was also pursued by the French and Japanese imperialists and arrested by the KMT regime, and seeing that the AFNS had never done anything to harm them, the bandits automatically placed us in their own category and considered us as "people in the same boat." They mistakenly believed that they could join hands with us to strike back at the authorities and get us to help them in their "affairs." And who knows--[their reasoning went]--if the revolution was successful, the AFNS fighters would become "big mandarins" and would certainly remember them as "friends in the dark old days." This was why the bandits wanted to rely on us in one way or another. Also, in view of the fact that the AFNS could not be easily intimidated and enjoyed the affection of the villagers besides, the bandits were afraid to cross us. Some of them said, "The heads of the revolutionaries will fetch high rewards but are difficult to 'reach'--before we can touch their heads, ours will be gone!"

There was a very famous bandit chief right in Ban Trang. His underlings were scattered from here to Thuy Khau. He had sat and drunk tea and wine with Nong Thai Long, a few other brothers and me at the villagers' houses. The villagers here had the custom of organizing parties when they built a new house, for example, or on the birthdays of the members of their families. Or they invited people to drink wine when a new planting phase began--ploughing, or rice transplanting, or spreading manure. Since we worked for the people, they always invited us to these parties. This bandit chief owned a house, was married, had children, and was armed. But he was not as rich as May Sen, a bandit in P'ing-hsiang, because May Sen carried out more raids and had more underlings. The bandit chief in Ban Trang had three brothers who were all sorcerers. He was then about 40 years old, very strong, and knew martial arts. He was a sharpshooter, and never missed a shot.

Once when we counselled him to give up his activities, he said, "You fellows have to make revolution because you are dirt poor. I too am poor, and this is why I became a bandit. You want to overthrow the rich. I too plunder the houses of the rich. So, what's the difference?"

We said, "Of course it's different. You plunder and rob people, and you have brought sufferings to a lot of people. Everyone hates and resents you. And in the end, your life is just as miserable as when you started. Only by making revolution to bring happiness to everyone will your happiness be long-lasting."

He was a little tipsy and said, "I haven't seen you guys enjoy any happiness. You joined the Communists, but all year round I haven't seen you manage to have a few cents in your pockets or to buy a bowl of beef soup. Me, I kill people--killing makes me feel good, and besides it gives me money to spend right away."

This was how brazen the bandits' arguments usually were. It would not be easy to reform them overnight. But no matter what, we had to persevere, to reason and restrain them. We showed neither fear nor contempt in dealing with them, and instead explained to them the advantages of making a revolution versus the disadvantages of leading a life of plunder. Then, we also motivated their relatives and the villagers to reason with them and stop them. Gradually they listened to our arguments, and reduced their plunder somewhat. Of course, our success was limited because in order to reform them completely we had to change the conditions that were prevailing in the society at the time.

Besides educating them and reasoning with them, we had to resort to other means to restrain them. Once, the bandit chief assembled his underlings to carry out a raid. The villagers got wind of this and secretly informed comrade Thai Long who immediately went to see him to try and stop him.

At first the bandit chief said, "I'm going to rob people so I can have money to spend. You too need money to spend."

The bandits usually plundered the markets, because in every market there were gambling stalls--mahjong, dice games, and betting games using beans--which paid gambling fees to the Chiang authorities.

Nong Thai Long's jaw jutted out as he rebuked the bandit chief, "We don't need your money. You should not carry out this raid."

The bandit chief got mad, and brushed him aside.

Knowing that it would be useless for him to argue any further, Thai Long said, "Well, where do you plan to carry out your raid this time?"

"In Na Teng."

"You won't get much out of that poor settlement with a few scattered houses. Besides, that settlement is too close to here, if the soldiers come to investigate the raid, we might be in trouble ourselves. Also, I have acquaintances there. You should at least have some consideration for us!"

"Alright, then which area do you think I should raid?"

"You shouldn't carry out any raid anywhere. But if you are determined to plunder, why don't you raid the houses of the Customs and Forestry Service officials, the landlords and the rich. They themselves have robbed the poor."

"It's difficult to rob them because they're armed."

"If you're afraid of them, then you should give up altogether. If you want to get a lot of money, you should go to these places. You shouldn't touch the peasants."

They thought this was a convincing argument, and since the prospect of rich booty whetted their greed, they decided to postpone their raid in order to make preparations to plunder a landlord's house. That raid was successful, and this success encouraged them to follow this pattern. However, in some subsequent raids they were badly beaten by the officials and soldiers. Each time they planned to plunder the people, and we failed to either stop them or steer their raid to targets other than the laboring masses' houses, we secretly informed the people in that village so they could take precautions and raise the alarm to alert everyone in the village. After a few such failures, the bandits became discouraged. Sometimes, we also tactfully arranged for the villagers who had been raided to get their belongings and draught animals back from the bandits for a low fee.

In view of the way we dealt with this situation, the bandits did not dare to bear any grudges against us. Instead, they feared and respected us. Our chivalrous attitude, our correct behavior, and our resolute efforts to pull them out of their criminal path moved a number of bandits who gradually mended their ways. The gang leaders admired us, because we could always predict--based on our military experience-- whether their raids would fail, and our prediction always turned out to be accurate. Some bandit gangs asked us to be their "advisors" because we could draw up plans. Taking advantage of such opportunities, we drew up plans which looked very scientific, but which required a long period of investigation and contained awesome dangers and difficulties to frighten them off and dampen their enthusiasm for plunder.

In the end, we gained some measure of control over their actions, and reduced this calamity for the population. The prestige and fame of the AFNS began to spread among the bandits. This was why we could go unarmed into the strongholds of many gangs without encountering any difficulties.

Once a bandit gang near Ban Bay (P'ing-hsiang) asked Ly Mung Sang, one of our reliable sympathizers, to extend us an invitation to visit their stronghold.

We knew that this band was large and also engaged in opium smuggling. They were well armed. They wanted to find a route through Cao Loc (Lang Son province) into Vietnam to carry out a big raid. We were planning to discover this route ourselves so we wanted to meet the bandit chief. I discussed with Ha Khai Lac about collecting money from the villagers to buy weapons from this gang. Our goal was to buy weapons and to find a route to Cao Loc--so that if anything happened we could withdraw through this route to avoid enemy repression temporarily. But this was not the main thing.

Ha Khai Lac and I left, following a guide. At the sentry station the guide handed us over to another fellow and went back. Each guard knew only the area in which he lived and was forbidden to penetrate deeper, beyond his own perimeter, in order to keep the locale of the bandits' headquarters secret. We went through four guard stations similar to this one. Suddenly in the mountain a shot rang out to alert the bandits inside.

The bandit chief, a big, fat, muscular and handsome man came out to greet us. He said, "I've invited you here mainly to get to know you, so that in the future if we run into each other, we won't shoot one another by mistake. The Chiang soldiers can never set foot here. Even if they can get here, they won't be able to come out alive."

In our conversation, we explained to him what it meant to make revolution. He showed that he understood a little. Especially when we explained why and because of whom the people suffered and did not have enough to eat, he approved of our making revolution to overthrow the French. However, he did not mind the Japanese entering Indochina, and since he belonged to the faction of Wang Ching Wei,[8] he just grunted in a noncommittal manner when we talked about "the need to carry out a revolution to overthrow the ruling clique."

He said, "If you want me to do anything else, I'll do it. It's difficult to make revolution. Whenever you need weapons, I'll donate them to you," he said, laughing, "because if the Vietnamese revolution succeeds you won't forget me, will you?"

The underlings brought meat and wine. The bandit chief poured a cup full of wine and invited us warmly to drink, "Let's recognize each other as brothers!"

Gradually, when he saw that we had a good grasp of military and political matters, and could argue logically, he asked us to join his staff as advisors. He said eagerly, "Please join us."

I said, "We need weapons now. Can you buy some for us?"

He accepted cheerfully. "That's easy. Just have the money ready. Or I can loan the weapons to you if you need them. I can't spare many, but I can always loan you a couple."

Through our talk, he got to understand us better. During the whole time we spent in his stronghold he never showed any signs that he had changed his attitude toward us. The feast lasted two or three hours. He introduced us to many bandits, and those who had the same clan names as Ha Khai Lac and I accepted us as their brothers.

When the feast came to an end, the bandit chief saw us off, whispering as though he still had many things to talk with us about but could not mention them in front of so many people. He accompanied us all the way to the last guard station and then turned back--something that he had never done before for anyone.

So we had won over the bandits in the two districts of Lungchou and P'ing-hsiang. We even propagandized a number of Chiang soldiers who had deserted and hidden in the mountains; gradually they became enlightened and did a few things to help the AFNS. The bandits' raids decreased. The villagers' sufferings were alleviated somewhat, and their confidence in us was strengthened as a result. From them on the AFNS could move around freely to operate. The bandits' domination over the people in this area weakened gradually.

---

8. Wang Chi Wei was a collaborator of the Japanese and headed the Japanese-sponsored government which was established in Nanking in 1940. (Trans.)

* * *

A series of letters sent by Ha Cham, Voong Tai and Thai Long from Vietnam made us very happy and confident. The AFNS's policy of withdrawing the main body to the border while leaving a section dispersed among the population to carry out armed propaganda and to set up grassroot bases among the masses had been correct. It was then around September 1942. After the communication route linking us with Doong Hinh, Hoi Hoan, Binh Gia, Bac Son and Vo Nhai was established, all the comrades operating in this area sent out reports. They were unanimous in their assessment that "the Vo Nhai movement was recovering rapidly, and requested the AFNS to urgently send cadres back."

"The situation had become relatively stabilized, and the liaison route had been opened"; this made us feel even more encouraged. In moments like these, we felt that we could go without food and work for hours without getting tired. At this time, the AFNS Command Staff (composed of comrades Chu quoc Hung, Nong Thai Long, Le Duc Ton and myself) was still staying in Bo Cuc. The situation demanded an accurate and timely decision--which meant we must establish a communication route to link us with Binh Gia. For this reason, brothers Hong Thai and Nhu Hoa who came from Binh Gia were sent back there.

Our plan was to send the AFNS back a section at a time. When they reached their destination, each section would send us a report through a special communication channel. The liaison agents would have to go all the way from the Vo Nhai-Trang Xa area to reach us here in Bo Cuc. In order to facilitate this work, we would have to string our forces all the way from the border to Binh Gia to form a corridor which would start in Na Hinh, go to Hoi Hoan and then Binh Gia. At the same time we should build up grassroot bases in Binh Gia. We would send the brothers who came from Bac Son back to their home area. Another number would go back to Vo Nhai. Those who came from Phu Thuong would go back to link up with Lau Thuong and La Hien. Another number would return to Trang Xa with the mission of consolidating and expanding the local infrastructure, and establishing contact with the movement in Lang Muoi village. Another number would return to Cay Thi and then proceed to Phu Binh and Yen The (Bac Giang province). Another group of cadres would go outside the Bac Son region to establish contact; wherever they went they would set up infrastructure, make propaganda, consolidate the local organization, maintain secrecy, start training classes for self-defense and combat self-defense units, and propagate the Viet Minh Program.

I returned to Bo Cuc to inform the AFNS brothers in the cells operating in Ban Trang, Kheo Meo, Tham Th'lang, Ban Khiec, Na Slieng, Ba Nac, and Doong Hinh, of the news.

The cells were located about a kilometer or less--as the crow flies--from each other. In some cases, they were separated only by a hill. All of them were overjoyed when they heard the news. The cells vied with each other to be the first to go back, telling each other "we'll go back first, and then you follow us." They had been away from their country for almost a year, and were all homesick. They were worried about their families, and also concerned about the fact that the movement did not have enough cadres. They missed the crop and vegetable patches, the ricefields, the gardens, the forests and mountains, and the streams that flowed behind their houses. Some comrades were so excited they could not sleep the whole night.

The brothers streamed in to see the Command Staff and demanded to be included in the first group that went back. It was not that they were unaware of the difficulties and dangers waiting for them back home. They just knew that their love for their homeland would transmit to them a new vigor for combat which would be immensely more powerful than anything they had experienced before. Only those who had been forced to live in a foreign country could understand the power of this feeling.

We held a general meeting to discuss how many groups would go back and where each one should go. The question of who would go back first depended on the nature of the mission involved and the qualifications of each cadre. This was the logical thing to do, but in order to make the brothers accept our argument in their hearts as well as in their minds, the Command Staff had to expend a lot of energy to explain and reason with them and motivate them, so that they would accept to stay behind and work with peace of mind. Those brothers who were allowed to go back were happy like "horses returning to their stables." The Command Staff advised those returning of the need to investigate carefully the areas where they were going to operate. They all listened and acted accordingly (this was why all the brothers went back safely and none was lost to the enemy).

In November 1942, comrades Voong Tai, Duong Cong Binh, Ha Ky, Hong Hai, Quoc Vinh, Hong Thai, Khoa and Doanh went to Hoi Hoan to meet comrades Nong Thai Long, Ha Cham and Phu Phong to discuss the task of consolidating this area further, and then moved straight back deep into Vietnam.

Comrades Doanh and Hong Thai stopped in Binh Gia to consolidate the infrastructure there.

Comrades Quoc Vinh, Binh and Khoa were assigned to consolidate the base in Bac Son.

Le Duc Ton and the other comrades returned to Vo Nhai. I moved back and forth between Na Hinh and Lungchou, and stayed in Bo Cuc and P'ing-hsiang wherever my presence was necessary. In short, I went wherever I was needed.

After many waves of terrorism, our homelands were in ruins and looked desolate. On the old platforms blackened by smoke and fire, only flimsy huts had been built as temporary shelters against the sun and rain. However, one fortunate thing was that the rice had ripened, and the ears were heavy with plump grains. Next to piles of straw, the villagers were threshing rice in the fields, over the old wooden *loong*[9] scorched by fire or new ones which had been hastily built and which still showed the knife marks. At night, the villagers streamed in to see the AFNS brothers. Old comrades met again. Mothers and sons, wives and husbands, brothers, saw each other again. The news raced through the girls whose boyfriends were in the AFNS faster than an electric current. They came to ask who had returned and who had not. The women whose husbands or sons were in jail and had been exiled to faraway places also came, so that the joy of meeting the comrades would displace the sadness over their separation from their husbands or sons.

---

9. A tool in the form of a boat, covered with bamboo woven mats on both sides, which the Nung people used to thresh rice in the fields. (Footnote in text.)

Many children and old people had become crippled by the beatings and tortures inflicted on them, and it tore the brothers' hearts to see them in this condition.

The brothers talked with the people. Previously, some villagers had feared that if we fled deeper into the forest we would not have anything to eat or would have to eat leaves to survive. Now they saw us coming back after we had not only stirred up the movement along the border, but also expanded the movement at home deeper and wider. So, they became more enthusiastic.

Each night, the conversation lasted far into the night.

The brothers immediately set to work. Brother Du, Mrs. Sang, Sisters Quan, Thu and Pinh, who had been assigned to stay behind and operate in extremely difficult conditions, had managed to maintain and preserve the movement and the infrastructure intact, and consolidate it, gave a report on the local situation. They all met to discuss a new plan of action. A liaison agent was sent to the border to ask the remaining AFNS brothers to return to the country right away. Other liaison agents were sent to establish contact with the Central Committee and the AFNS groups in Dai Tu and Son Duong. The cadres parted and set out in many directions. An atmosphere of excitement prodded everyone to act boldly.

Also in November 1942, in Kheo Meo, we met again comrades Duong Nhat Quy and Phuong Cuong. They had been sent by the unit in Tuyen Quang and Thai Nguyen to contact us. They had openly bought tickets and took the bus to That Khe and then secretly crossed the border and made their way to Bo Cuc. They told us that the revolutionary grass-root bases in Dai Tu, Dinh Hoa, Yen Son, Son Duong and Cho Don had been expanded and consolidated. But there were not enough cadres to keep up with the rapidly expanding movement. The masses were anxiously waiting for more AFNS members to come back. The brothers and sisters in those areas were in good health, and had not suffered any losses. So, we had a full and clear understanding of the situation in the three provinces of Lang Son, Tuyen Quang, and Thai Nguyen, and part of Bac Can province (Cho Don).

In January 1943 the second AFNS group composed of comrades Hoa, Trieu Khanh Phuong, Voong Nhi, Hoang Xuan, Hoang Thuong, Coong, Mung and To set out to return to the country.

We would never forget the days we spent among the local Chinese people. Even at the start of these days full of hardships, the affectionate relationship between the "water and the fish" had been beautiful. The formation of the revolutionary forces under the leadership of our Party marked the beginning of a new relationship between the people and the troops, full of so many moving stories which later on became frequent occurrences during the Resistance.

Whenever I went to Lungchou on mission, I stayed and ate with the family of Nung Nhi Sao, a very good sympathizer who did his utmost to help the Vietnamese revolution. During one of my trips to Lungchou, I stopped in Nung Nhi Sao's house and then went to Mrs. Au's[10] house to

---

10. Mrs. Au was a Vietnamese who had married a Chinese. Brother Lam Phu Thinh adopted her as his mother and had introduced me to her. Each time I passed

fetch Hoang Thuong who was staying there to cure his night-blindness, so the two of us could go on mission together. We spent the whole day climbing hills and crossing streams, our feet were lacerated by the sharp and pointed rocks. At dusk, Thuong could not see and groped along, so I had to lead him by the hand. The comrade who was acting as our guide was from this area, and he took us to Lam Cooc village, nestled in a small valley.

Lines of grey rocky mountains loomed all round. The terraced fields of rice, corn and beans lined up like steps on a ladder. That year there was a bumper harvest of kanari fruit. After the fruit were picked, the huge and tall kanari trees looked shabby and ragged, shorn of leaves. We stepped into a house surrounded by walls, with a tiled roof, as solidly built as an old shrine. A candle made of kanari sap burned in a red glow on the table, emitting a smell of acrid smoke.

The old lady who owned the house was over 50 years of age. She was small but still strong, and wore Nung clothes dyed in Chinese blue, but her hair was wrapped in a piece of cloth and coiled on top of her head in the Vietnamese style. When the guide introduced us as Vietnamese revolutionaries, she suddenly clasped our hands tightly, and tears welled up in her eyes. It turned out she was Vietnamese and had come from as far away as Bac Ninh province. When she was still young she was kidnapped by a child-stealer who took her here and sold her. After many adventures, she got married and settled down here. Her oldest son was at home, and he warmly talked with us. The old lady insisted that we stay for a couple of days, so she could assuage her thirst for the company of her compatriots.

She spoke a mixture of Nung and Vietnamese: "It's because you're making revolution that you had the chance to come here."

Her oldest son and a few other people in the house went out. In just an hour they came back with two huge pike, each weighing up to five or six catties. We asked and found out that the fish came from their own pond. The three of us joined them to lend a hand in cooking. The oldest son went out again in a hurry, saying over his shoulder, "I'm going to get some wine!"

The old lady went to the garden to gather fresh herbs, and came back smiling happily. "Later on, the brothers in the village will come here to talk with you."

After a few days of travelling, our limbs were rubbery with fatigue. The delicious food was almost ready when suddenly there were thudding footsteps at the gate, and then a voice called out to the old lady urgently, "The hamlet chief said soldiers from Lungchou have arrived to check the village."

We started and wondered what the soldiers had come here for. To arrest us? This could not be, since we had legal papers. There was nothing for us to worry about. The old lady looked at us, full of apprehension. The oldest son came back with the wine, followed by a few neighbors, and said that "soldiers from Lungchou had come here to arrest deserters."

---

through, I came to visit her. While working in the fields Hoang Thuong came down with night-blindness. Mrs. Au bought chickens and pig's livers to feed him for months, and put medicine in his eyes to cure them. (Footnote in text.)

We still felt worried. Although we had legal papers, the soldiers would become suspicious if they came to the house and found out that we were strangers here; they might cause trouble and interrogate everyone. Besides the soldiers who were wont to extort money might threaten to arrest us in order to annoy our host family. I told Thuong, "We don't know what's going to happen. The soldiers can misinterpret our presence here, and if they tell us to go back to Lungchou with them for the time being we'll be in deep trouble. It's alright for us, but we might implicate the villagers. Let's avoid them. Since they're looking for deserters, they won't remain here long. If we stay here and they arrest us, it will be really silly. Let's go away to avoid them, and then see what we can do."

I told the oldest son to lead us into the mountains. I led Thuong who had night-blindness, and groped my way behind.

It was very dark. We waited for a long time, and then dozed off. Suddenly there was a noise at the top of the slope. We answered in the manner we had agreed to in advance. The oldest son emerged, carrying a rather heavy basket. He opened it, and there were a container full of rice and a tureen of soup, still hot. There was also a large dish of fish salad, with all the necessary accompanying spices and condiments, and a flask full of wine.

He then turned around and went back to the settlement. A while later, he returned and told us that the soldiers had gone back to Lungchou. We went back to the house and talked with a number of villagers until very late in the night. Many of them promised that when we came here to operate they would take us to the houses of their acquaintances in this area so we could build up grassroot bases. They expressed their longing for the Chinese Red Army and their sincere support for the Vietnamese revolution.

After spending almost a year among the people in Bo Cuc canton, strong bonds of affection attached the AFNS to the villagers and weighed heavily in their hearts when they left [to return to Vietnam]. We remembered that whenever we came back from a mission--whether at twilight or in the middle of the night--after having braved the wind and rain, and slipped past the rifle muzzles of the enemy posts, the moment we stepped into the house, our hearts were filled with warmth. Everyone in the family crowded around us, asking questions. The children were full of joy, pulled at our clothes and told us everything that had happened. The first question that was asked was always: "Have you eaten?" If we had not eaten, the mother immediately brought out some rice and fried an egg she had just picked out of the hen's nest and which was still warm to the touch. We did not mind eating whatever the people could scrape up for us. Whenever there was anything to do around the house or in the fields, we would do it. Whenever we had a free moment, we helped the people by doing odd jobs, such as weaving baskets, or repairing ditches. We stayed for such a long time with them that they thought of us as members of their own families. They missed us whenever we were away.

If everyone in the family was out working in the fields when we came back from a mission, we automatically set about sweeping and putting the house in order, drawing water and cooking rice. If there was no milled rice left, we pounded paddy in the mortar pit. The villagers told us to feel free to pick the vegetables in their gardens and to catch the fish in their ponds to cook. On feast days, or on the anniversaries of their ancestors' deaths, the villagers always insisted on waiting for us to come back and join them before they would pick up their chopsticks and bowls and start eating. If we could not make it back, they saved the best morsels for us. If we were busy and had to be away on these occasions, the people felt very sorry that we had missed the feasts, and regretted this for a long time.

Many Chinese families wept when the AFNS left to return to their country. In these past months, the AFNS had become close to the people here and had been a part of the life of the families who had housed and fed them, and of the whole village which had sheltered and protected them. These families and the villagers had become emotionally attached to them. Right at the start, when the AFNS set foot here, the people sincerely considered us as friends caught in the same plight, and as comrades who shared the goals of their struggle. Gradually, the longer we stayed, the more accustomed the people became to our presence, and the better they got to know us, and we became like members of their own families--like their own children and brothers.

Now that the AFNS brothers were gone, the villagers suddenly felt lost and nostalgic. The houses and settlements seemed empty. The old men and women no longer had the brothers around to ask questions about what was going on in the settlement and in the village. The children missed the easy-going "uncles" who loved to play with them. The youths in particular missed the brothers and friends who had helped them see what the purpose of their life should be, and the ideal of the revolutionary struggle. A few girls who had secretly fallen in love with the AFNS fighters, moved around looking distracted.

About ten families had hinted to some AFNS brothers that they would like to have them as sons-in-law. These "fortunate men" had to refuse tactfully, saying that they were so burdened with revolutionary work and had to move around so much that they could not afford to think about their personal life. But some of the old people said, "But no one is asking you to stay here and live with us. We are parents, and it is our duty to find a husband for our grown daughter. Just marry her so that your life is at least settled in that respect. Then you can go wherever you want and stay away as long as you want. Our daughter is enlightened, and she won't try to keep you here."

The brothers were stuck for an answer; in the end they had to plead for a delay: "We must ask the Command Staff about this."

The people really had sincere intensions, and all we could do was to thank them profusely and explain tactfully to them that the brothers still had a long-term mission to carry out on the road toward the liberation of our nation and class, and this was why they could not think of marrying and starting a family.

We would never forget the affection and love the villagers had for us, and the favors they did for us. To repay these favors, the AFNS comrades swore to remain for the rest of their life the faithful servants of the proletariat and the laboring masses.

CHAPTER VIII

We still had not succeeded in establishing contact with the Central Committee. For over a year now, although we were far away from the Central Committee, we had based our actions on the spirit of its 8th Resolution, on the instructions of the Old Man in Pac Bo, and on the instructions and guidance that the Central Committee comrades gave us when they were in Bac Son. We continued to operate on our own and generally speaking the results had been favorable, but we could not assess these results accurately since we did not know what the situation was in the whole country. Over half of the AFNS unit had returned to Vietnam. A new period of activities began for us. If we did not find out about the situation in the country and in the world, and if we could not exchange experiences with other areas, then it would be difficult for us to set forth clearsighted policies and concrete plans of action to perform our task.

I recalled that once in Pac Bo, after asking me about the Bac Son-Vo Nhai movement and about the enemy repression there, the Old Man said that in order to consolidate and expand the movement, our activities should not be restricted to one locality. We must maintain smooth liaison between all echelons, from top to bottom. If this was accomplished, instead of being uncoordinated and haphazard, the revolutionary leadership would be unified and the deployment of cadres would accurately meet the requirements of each area since it would be based on the strength or weakness of the movement there. The revolution could only succeed if communication and liaison was good.

Even if we returned to Vo Nhai, it would still not be easy for us to contact the Central Committee in the delta. At the time, a section of the Central Committee and of the Viet Minh General Headquarters was stationed in Cao Bang province, and the Old Man was there also. The AFNS Command Staff decided to send Ha Khai Lac and me to Cao Bang in all urgency to report on the tasks we had completed, study the experience of the Cao Bang movement, obtain documents and request new operating instructions.

I handed over the job of leading the AFNS and the Permanent Liaison Office to comrade Chu Quoc Hung. I had managed to wrangle passes allowing us to go from Chinghsi to Cao Bang. This trip was full of dangers. Recently, the Chiang Kai Shek security police had tightened their surveillance of the AFNS, because they sensed that Communist influence had penetrated deeply among a portion of the population living along the border. From now until all the AFNS members could return to Vietnam, the KMT might resort to some sort of sabotage. At this time, the end of the year was approaching and the Tet (New Year) Festival was drawing close. It was the 12th lunar month, the month when crimes reached their peak,[1] and so the roads were very dangerous--murders and

---

1. Usually, robberies and thefts reach their peak at this time of the year as the criminals try to obtain enough money to celebrate the New Year Festival. (Trans.)

robberies occurred frequently, even in broad daylight. Also, in Chinghsi we would have to guard against the Vietnamese KMT and the Vietnam Revolutionary League who were relying on the support of the Chiang Kai Shek regime to kidnap and murder Viet Minh cadres. Once we crossed the border into Vietnam, we would have to watch out for the lackeys and security police of the French and the Japanese, especially since we were unfamiliar with the terrain and the population in Cao Bang. We told the comrades staying behind that if we failed to make it back after Tet, they should all return to Vietnam to operate and propel the movement forward.

Around the middle of the 12th lunar month (January 1943) the two of us set out from Lungchou. The road stretched on endlessly, climbed toward mountain passes and crossed clearings, surrounded on all sides by an unbroken mass of mountains and forests. A drizzle seemed to hang its fine strands of water in the air and the wind howled in the mountain hollows. We passed Pao Hi, Sang Cam, and then arrived in Sec Lung. We stopped at a three-way intersection. Two roads spread in front of us. One was a shortcut through a portion of Vietnamese territory which jutted into China--it would take us less time to reach Chinghsi through this road, but we might easily be captured by the canton and village militia chiefs. The other went through Chinese territory and was a meandering road which would take us out of our way and which was not completely safe either. We thought it over, and in the end--in order to avoid a lot of anxiety about our safety--we decided to follow the roundabout road which would take us through nineteen passes and thirty ravines--a detour of twenty kilometers which would require us to climb passes and negotiate steep slopes.

After three long days on the road, we reached Chinghsi town at dusk. We were tired and hungry. Our clothes were filthy and covered with dust. We did not know our way and felt very lost, like all strangers coming to a town from afar. If we kept wandering in the streets like this, something might happen to us. If by chance we ran into the group of Tran Bao--a crony of Nguyen Hai Than[2]--we would certainly fall victims to their cruel actions. In this strange place, our acquaintances were few and not entirely reliable. I thought, "I must enquire and find out where Vi Duc Minh lives. We must find this out quickly, so we will not have to wander in the streets . . . this is not a good thing to do. And when we find his house we must come in secretly." This comrade was a Nung and knew brother Hoang Van Thu. He had also done a few minor things to help Chu Quoc Hung recently. However, he was working for the Chinese Kuomintang.

Seeing me, Minh was both happy and worried. He asked, "Where did you come from?"

I answered, "From down there."

Seeing the expression on his face and the glances he cast around, I asked right away, "It's not convenient for us to stay here. Do you know what else we can do?"

Right at that moment, his wife came out of the kitchen. Seeing us strangers, she became agitated, and her eyes clearly showed her worry. Vi Duc Minh suggested, "Go to the boarding house in Chinghsi."

---

2. Leader of the Vietnamese Revolutionary League. (Trans.)

Hearing this, his wife knew who we were and asked him, "What happens if they check papers?"

I nodded and said, "I've got papers."

Minh said to his wife, "Do we have any rice left?"

"Yes, but we don't have any food to go with it," she replied uneasily.

Minh went and fried an egg for us to eat with the cold rice. He said, "At present the Tran Bao and Nguyen Hai Than group is aggressively looking for our brothers and kidnapping them. They've adopted the cry, 'If the Viet Minh remain, we'll have to go; and if we remain, the Viet Minh will have to go.' They've come to my house frequently to check on me."

We understood his situation. He singlehandedly worked to support his wife. Chinese money was worthless then, and it was really quite good of him to give us cold rice and fried egg to eat. Anyway, we had come to see him mainly to obtain information.

He took us to a boarding house located at the entrance into town. The rent came to two-thirds of the money we had in our pockets. We stayed awake the whole night, unable to go to sleep, consumed by worry that something unexpected might happen.

The next day, we hurriedly got up and left at daybreak. It was freezing cold, we each had only some thin and flimsy clothing on, and had to quicken our steps to keep warm. We emptied our pockets, but found that we only had enough money to buy each three cakes to eat. This was all the food we had to last us for over a day, the time it would take us to reach Pac Bo. But the hope of meeting the Old Man and the Viet Minh General Headquarters dissolved all worries and difficulties. Last year, after spending just a couple of months with the Old Man and being taught and nurtured by him, I found that my level of understanding was raised tremendously. His high forehead, his quick steps, his old but clean Nung clothes, and his bamboo stick--this image of the "big Boss"[3] seemed to appear before my eyes and beckon me.

I wondered whether his health had improved this year. Although he was old and weak, he worked a lot harder than we. "He's old, but he works so hard. I'm young, so shouldn't I exert myself a lot more?" I kept asking myself this question. As I walked, I arranged in my mind all the things I should report and the problems I must consult the Old Man about so that he could show me how to solve them. I did not feel tired at all, and I felt that my steps were firm and that I was full of vigor.

We passed Liutung. We were near the border and Pac Bo. I was thrilled and excited, like a son who had gone away for a long time and was returning home to his native village. I had passed through this way once before. Just as we entered a crossroad in the trail, someone

---

3. "Ông Ké Thượng Cấp": "Ông Ké" is a term used by the Nung to designate a respected old man with good reputation in high position. "Thượng Cấp" literally means "upper echelon." (Trans.)

rushed out. It turned out to be comrade Phung Hec.[4] What luck! He was with comrade Le Quang Ba's[5] Section, and in 1941 he had accompanied us from Pac Bo to Cao Bang, to That Khe, and then Bo Cuc. He took us to the house of an acquaintance in a small Chinese settlement to sleep. That night the owner of the house ground some corn and made corn gruel, and even produced a few cups of wine to treat us. Everyone stayed up and talked till very late.

The next morning, Phung Hec took us to Pac Bo. We crossed a mountain peak, and were coming down the slope on the Vietnam side of the border when we saw a short and fat man approaching from a distance. I turned and asked Phung Hec, "That looks like comrade Ba, does it not?"

"That's him all right!"

Phung Hec cupped his hands and called out to Ba in a loud voice. Comrade Ba rushed toward us, clasped my hand and smiled: "From afar I saw a bony man with a straight and stiff neck, and I knew right away it must be you! Where are you going?"

I answered immediately, "I've come back here to look for the Big Leader, and ask his instructions."

"He's gone far away on mission,"[6] Ba replied.

"When will he come back?" I asked.

"He's gone very far away. No one knows when he'll come back."

Ha Khai Lac and I were both dumbfounded and bewildered. I looked at comrade Ba and saw that he was looking fixedly at us, with a great deal of sympathy. I asked, "Well, is there anyone of the highest rank in charge here now?"

"I'm the only man here."

I asked, "Are there any comrades from the Central Committee and the Viet Minh General Headquarters in this area?"

"Yes, but they are about two days' walk from here," Ba replied and then asked me, "Will you go if it takes another two days?"

"Definitely," I said positively. "We'll have to go even if it's further than that."

Then Ba said warmly, "Come down to the village with me! Eat something first. Rest a while. We'll have to get a liaison agent for you, and you won't be able to leave till this evening."

---

4. Phùng Héc means someone who makes his living by repairing pots and pans. People got used to calling him by this name and stopped using his real name. (Footnote in text.)

5. Le Quang Ba was then Secretary of the Soc Giang District Party Committee in Cao Bang province. (Footnote in text.)

6. Ho at that time was in jail in Liuchow (Kwangsi province) having been arrested by the Chinese KMT in 1942. (Trans.)

The five of us--Le Quang Ba, Phung Hec, Ha Khai Lac, a comrade acting as Ba's bodyguard and I--edged our way along the stream down to the house of comrade La Thanh, the leader of the communication cell in Pac Bo settlement. Ba told me softly that our side had just eliminated Quyen, a canton militia chief notorious for his cruelty in Ha Quang who had murdered many cadres. He said that this was only the first warning to the security police and other lackeys.

The two of us only had time to ask each other with excitement about a few of the tasks we had completed, and did not have time to talk about our families and other personal matters. We would have liked to spend a couple of nights confiding in each other.

When Ha Khai Lac and I finished eating, the liaison comrade arrived. Darkness began to fall when we reached the ricefields. We exchanged the passwords for the trip. Ba shook my hand: "Go now while it's still early, so you can make it to your destination in time. When the Big Leader comes back, I'll report to him what you've told me."

For that whole night, we walked up and down hills, through the settlements of Hoang, Na Ma, Dao Ngan, and Bo Lech. After crossing a few knolls, we arrived at a liaison station. We stayed in a few isolated houses, protected by sentries inside as well as outside. The local comrades took special care of us, so we ate and slept well. We spent the whole day resting there.

The sun came out and it became warm. The landscape was beautiful here, with deep green and lush forests, with grass hills on which buffaloes were grazing, with apricot, plum and cherry blossoms. The air here was light and pure, and everyone felt invigorated. The boys and girls went to the Nuoc Hai market, exchanging courting songs.

At night, we resumed our journey, and arrived in Lam Son, Hoa An District, the next morning. Around us were hills covered with elephant grass and ferns, and a chain of reddish rocky mountains. The liaison agent took us to the house of comrade Quoc Vuong in the settlement. The sugar canes were luxuriant and dense, two fat and heavy buffaloes were slowly pulling the shaft of the sugar cane mill next to a huge pan bubbling with cane syrup. The next morning we followed the liaison agent up to a stone cave.

That night, comrade Vu Anh came to see us. He had not changed since I last saw him in Pac Bo, he still had the same stocky and short build, the two thick and long eyebrows, and the same resounding voice. He recognized me at once. He happily shook hands with all of us, and asked us what we wanted. I reported to him about the situation since the eight months of guerrilla warfare in Trang Xa and told him about our purpose in coming here.

He listened and said when I finished, "Rest assured and stay here a while. In a couple of days someone will come out and work with you."

Two days later, four brothers came from the Lung Hoang cave to meet us. Two of them--Pham Van Dong and Hoang Van Hoan--I had already met, and the other two I had never seen before.

Pham Van Dong had on a few occasions explained Marxism-Leninism to me in Pac Bo.

Hoang Van Hoan squeezed my hand and said, "It's been a long time! How have you all been?"

It was rather dark in the cave. The two brothers invited us to sit down and introduced the others one by one to us. It was then that I realized the two brothers I had never met before were Vo Nguyen Giap and Hoang Duc Thac (alias La).

The meeting was very instructive and interesting.

I reported first. I talked about the evolution of the AFNS from the time it was formed, the repression of the French and the Japanese, the eight months of struggle in Trang Xa-Vo Nhai, the temporary withdrawal of the AFNS to the Vietnam-China border. I presented clearly the political and military line of the AFNS in general as well as the concrete measures and actions we had taken. Finally I mentioned the difficulties that were confronting the AFNS, especially now that it was returning to the country; in this new phase of operations, it was absolutely necessary for us to understand the situation inside as well as outside the country, reestablish contact with the movement in other areas in the country in order to adopt appropriate policies and measures and to devise closely coordinated plans.

While they were listening to my report, the brothers kept looking at me and then at each other. When they heard how the enemy had wrecked and burned down villages, how we had lived during the eight months of guerrilla warfare, about the problems concerning our everyday life, the constant moving of our camps, and the development of grassroot bases, some of the comrades wept.

They asked me in minute detail about our experience in resisting repression, in carrying out guerrilla warfare, in proselytizing enemy soldiers, maintaining and consolidating grassroot bases, and also about our diplomatic experience in dealing with the Chiang regime and the Chinese bandits.

After that brother Hoang Duc Thac gave a report. He talked about the situation of the movement in Cao Bang province. From a few test areas, the movement had expanded rapidly over a wide region. The self-defense units were very active. The tasks of maintaining communication, protecting the camps and eliminating traitors were being carried out satisfactorily. The National Salvation organizations composed of all elements in society--old people, young people, women and children--had expanded to the entire province, including even the high plateaus inhabited by the Meo and Yao ethnic minorities. There were villages and districts that were "completely Viet Minh" where all the people had joined the Viet Minh movement. A "two gills"[7] administration had taken shape; the village and canton chiefs continued to attend meetings in the district and province capitals but governed in accordance with the line and policy of the revolution. In some areas, the Village Viet Minh Committees had to directly come out and solve problems because the population only had faith in them. Preparations for the insurrection were proceeding with urgency.

Hoang Van Hoan, Pham Van Dong and Vo Nguyen Giap filled us in on many important questions. As I listened to them, I felt my mind becom-

---

7. Like a fish with two gills, these areas now had two separate and parallel administrations (French and Viet Minh). (Trans.)

ing clearer and clearer, and I told myself, "There are still a lot of things that the AFNS must learn from these comrades."

The meeting also discussed the situation inside and outside the country. The general situation was favorable to us in many respects. Our enthusiasm and confidence was reinforced because the exchange of ideas had helped us to see the situation more clearly. The achievements of the AFNS and of the movement in Cao Bang province mutually reinforced and encouraged each other. I came to the profound realization that if the primitively armed revolutionary units knew how to rely solidly on the people and apply guerrilla warfare tactics with ingenuity, they could certainly set up bases in the countryside and in the jungle and mountain areas, maintain firmly and expand their forces in order to gradually weaken by attrition and destroy the imperialist forces armed with modern weapons. The self-defense units in Cao Bang province and the AFNS had proved this. In order to firmly maintain and expand the revolutionary bases, it was necessary to strongly motivate the people, and on this basis to tightly coordinate the political and military struggle. These experiences would be very useful to the forthcoming phase of operations, and at the same time they encouraged us boldly to expand the movement and clear a route to move southward to the delta.

After this exchange, in accordance with the spirit of the 8th Resolution, the meeting decided to perform four major tasks:

(1) Maintain firmly the infrastructure in the border region, and clear a route from there to Binh Gia, Bac Son, and Vo Nhai.

(2) Set up new infrastructure in Cao-Bac-Lang, Tuyen Quang, Thai Nguyen and Bac Giang provinces, consolidate the existing infrastructure and link up the liaison routes.

(3) Proceed with the formation of the Southward March Shock Units, under the direct command of comrade Vo Nguyen Giap. The AFNS would dispatch a squad to Cao Bang to join hands with the comrades in Cao Bang to clear and open a route to the delta. From the Bac Son-Vo Nhai war zone, the AFNS would open four routes to move northward and link up with the Southward March prongs jabbing their way toward the South. These four routes would be:

    (a) From That Khe and Dong Khe up toward Cao Bang.

    (b) From Hoi Hoan, Binh Gia up toward Van Mich and Na Ri.

    (c) From Vo Nhai up to Na Ri.

    (d) From Cho Chu up to Cho Don and Cho Ra.

(4) Try to reestablish contact with the Central Committee in the delta.

With this concrete direction of operation, we felt greatly reassured and encouraged. We must take action immediately. The 23rd day of the 12th lunar month--the day on which the Kitchen God returned to heavens to report to the Emperor of Jade--had passed.[8] It would not

---

8. The Kitchen God keeps track of all the affairs in each family, and at the end of the year returns to heavens to report to the Emperor of Jade. (Trans.)

be possible for us to reach Lungchou before Tet. But be that as it may, we had to leave because the brothers in the unit were anxiously awaiting our return. At this juncture, we could not afford to lose even one day.

Before we left, Hoang Van Hoan (alias Ly Quy Hoa) gave us many political and military documents, as well as souvenirs such as pictures, books and newspapers, and flags that Chang Fa-k'uei and other Chinese KMT organizations had presented to the Viet Minh Diplomatic Delegation in China.[9] These objects later on proved to be very useful for the AFNS who used them in their mobile exhibition during armed propaganda missions. The brothers also gave us 100 Indochinese Piastres to cover our operation expenses and 40 Piastres to the AFNS as a token of solace. However, we did not spend this sum on ourselves and added it to our operating funds.

Brother Vo Nguyen Giap asked, "Do you need our assistance in anything else?"

I said, "In our propaganda work, and in our training, we badly need a map to talk about the situation in the world. This map must be easy to look at and easy to understand, and it must be easy to carry around and must include all the continents of the world. We haven't succeeded in finding one like this anywhere. If you have one, please give it to us."

Brother Pham Van Dong said, "We don't have one like that here either. But if you need it, we'll draw one."

He pulled out color pencils and started to draw on a white sheet of paper. I had only finished the fourth years of Elementary School, so I was very impressed with his drawing skill. I watched every movement of his hands which glided the crayons in clear lines, and looked at him with great pleasure. He colored the Soviet Union red. I thought, "When we talk in front of the people, this will have a great impact. With this, the people will see where our country is located, and what its position is," but I did not say this out loud. As for Khai Lac, he kept gushing to me, "I wonder how advanced this man's education is to give him such a fantastic memory! He can just pick up a pencil and draw, and he doesn't even have to erase anything and draw over again!"

When Pham Van Dong finished drawing, he picked it up, looked at it, and then gave it to me: "Use this for the time being."

I smiled as though to say, "This will do very nicely indeed! I can't ask for anything better!" (This map was later on reproduced in many copies and distributed to propaganda cells to use, and proved very useful.) We rested and relaxed. Once in a while, if a new idea occurred to us, we would bring it up and discuss it. Our camaraderie became even more intimate and warm.

After our work was completed, we got ready to leave. At nightfall, the brothers gave a dinner for us right in the camp office. More accurately, it was really a banquet, because we had chicken, pig's feet

---

9. The Chiang Kai Shek regime had presented these gifts when the Viet Minh maintained a Diplomatic Delegation in Chinghsi. (Footnote in text.)

braised with bamboo shoot, fried fish, sticky rice flat cakes, glutinous rice, and steamed rice pancakes with pork, shrimp and mushroom filling.

The moment of parting came. Each brother clasped our hands tightly. Each of their gestures, actions and words expressed their attachment and affection.

We went from station to station. We came to a liaison station every five or ten kilometers. Along the way, at each settlement and during each leg of our journey, villagers asked us to rest in their houses and offered us food to eat or wine to drink--some gave us steamed glutinous rice mixed with beans, and sweet soup, some gave us rice flour balls in syrup to eat. It turned out the local people had been told in advance that "two comrades from Bac Son would be passing through." So, every two or three kilometers we inevitably ran into a "special liaison station," and we were invited inside to partake in a meal, prepared in advance and waiting for us. Faced with this precious feeling on the part of the local people and comrades, we could not refuse. If we could not eat much, we made an effort to eat a little. Just a bite here and a bite there was enough to give us indigestion. In some places, we could not possibly eat everything, and our guide had to take the food along. When we reached the settlement of comrade Nong Cong Dung, we met a cadre who asked us to heal the leg wound of a local comrade. We asked and found out that this cadre had been shot in the leg when the self-defense comrades tried out their rifles. It was impossible to take him to the hospital because he would be uncovered right away. I asked about the wound, and then told the comrades to go and look for *Co Slam Ca*--a medicinal herb that grew in the forest. This herb would draw out and absorb all the gunpowder and the leg would heal.

When we were on the last leg of our trip, we could not take along all the gifts the people had donated to us and had to leave them behind. Besides, our mass bases did not extend to this area, and our guide must be unencumbered so he could go and reconnoiter the route.

The way the people in our mass bases had treated us during each stretch of our journey showed us that the level of enlightenment of the people was quite high. In these "completely Viet Minh" villages and districts, the Viet Minh movement in the form of National Salvation organizations, joined by all social elements, had sunk deep roots and expanded over a wide area. The comrades in Cao Bang province had performed skillfully the task of leading and organizing the mass bases. We felt that we must learn a lot more, so that on our return--together with the other brothers--we would be able to propel the revolutionary movement in Vo Nhai-Bac Son decisively forward.

In Pac Bo, we stopped to rest and eat with Le Quang Ba. I told him about all the things I had not had time to talk about when I passed through the last time, and especially about stories concerning the Old Leader. I said goodbye to Le Quang Ba, and climbed the mountain into China. We went to Liutung to spend the night.

The next day, we crossed Chinghsi and stopped to rest about ten kilometers from there. Learning from the experience we gained on our way down, we took precautions in order to avoid falling into the hands of Tran Bao's gang--we would be in grave danger if they caught us.

On the third day, we walked till late in the afternoon. Near Pao Hi (on the road from Chinghsi to Pao Hi) we ran into a group of KMT soldiers going in the same direction. We merged with them, walking behind, hoping this way to avoid the robbers and bandits active in these last days of the Lunar year. To our astonishment, when we entered a town, every family hurriedly slammed their doors and windows shut. To the people, the Chiang soldiers were just day robbers--even more brazen then the bandits. The soldiers got angry, cursed the people loudly, and started to smash things. We hurriedly detached ourselves from the soldiers, otherwise the people might take us for Chiang security policemen and we might lose our lives unjustly.

On New Year's eve, we arrived in an area in Thuong Kim district. Each settlement, each village, each town and city that we passed was bustling and noisy. Children wore beautiful clothes, and laughed and played with joy. Married couples, carrying chickens in baskets and leading their children by the hand, headed for their in-laws' houses to celebrate Tet. Seeing these families gathering together for Tet, we thought of the AFNS brothers in Bo Cuc canton who must be waiting for us to come back. As we walked along, I told Khai Lac, "These guys back there must be thinking that something has happened to us."

Khai Lac nodded his head and said, "The villagers in Na Slieng, Kheo Meo and Ban Trang settlements must be anxiously waiting for us also."

We talked about Mr. Nong Nhi Co in Lungchou who had a Nung wife. This was a good family, every brother--starting with Hoang Van Thu--who passed through Lungchou always went to stay in his house. When we left he had told us, "You can go wherever you want, but you must come back at Tet!"

We walked in the midst of red streamers sprinkled with gold dust-- with the black and shiny ink still fresh on the Chinese characters-- which were pasted to the door of every household, and in the midst of lanterns of every shape and style, burning brightly in a festive atmosphere. But the two of us were shivering with cold and hunger. It would take us more than half a day to reach Lungchou. We must find a place to sleep. We asked five or six families, but none of them allowed us to spend the night in their houses. We knew the people believed that "the person who spent the night in the house on New Year's eve and left on the day of Tet would take the good fortune of the family for the new year with him." The people observed this taboo and did not want us to sleep in their houses.

We passed the gate of a house with two compartments. It was not completely dark yet. We looked inside, and saw an old lady, a young woman, a young man and a small child. After a moment's hesitation, I mounted the porch and said, "We are from Lungchou. We're going back there for Tet, but can't make it in time. We don't have a place to sleep. Please let us spend the night here, old lady. We can sit here on the porch, and lean on the house. We'll leave for Lungchou tomorrow."

The old lady did not turn around, and addressed us from inside the house, "It's New Year's eve, who's going to let you sleep in their house?"

She talked in the Nung dialect.

I said boldly, "I know that. But it's not good for us to stand here in the street for a long time. People might think we're bandits, and that's not good."

I pointed to the spot where I was standing and continued, "You can let us rest right here."

The old lady then turned around and said, "If you're in such a difficult situation, you can come in."

Her words were like music to our ears, and Khai Lac and I went in. Outside the bedrooms, the only furniture in the house consisted of a bamboo cot and an altar. Incense smoke shrouded the altar on which were placed a chicken, glutinous rice cakes, and sticky rice flour cakes.

The atmosphere in the house remained cold and silent after we had come in and sat down for a while. Everyone ignored us completely, including the young woman and the young man. We understood the custom here, and did not resent their attitude. The young woman stood up and lit joss sticks. I looked up at the altar, and saw that the ancestors of both the wife and husband were represented. I understood why the young man did not say anything. I told myself, "He must be a son-in-law who has come here to look after the family in the place of the old lady's son."

I broke the oppressive silence: "If you have any cakes, please sell us a couple. We had a few balls of rice, but we ate them all."

The old lady said slowly, "I don't have many cakes, but if you're hungry I'll give you a couple to eat."

I put out my hands to receive the cake which exuded the fragrance of the glutinous rice. There was only one light in the house, the one on the altar. We peeled off the banana leaves and ate the cake while the old lady's family ate in the compartment in the back of the house.

The rice grains warmed our bellies. We waited till it was very late and then went to bed, sleeping on the bamboo cot.

The wind was blowing strongly outside. We lay on our sides, close to each other to keep warm. The cot was very narrow, but we still had room to spare! When one of us wanted to turn, the other had to turn also.

We were tired, but could not go to sleep. The transition hour between the old year and the new year was drawing close. I missed my family and my home village. I thought of the previous Tet in Phu Thuong and Bo Tat, and then of Tet last year spent in Trang Xa--although our life was full of privations and our struggle was full of difficulties then, we had the company of the brothers in the unit in happy as well as in sad moments. This year, when Tet came, we were lying here. It would take us another half day to reach Lungchou. I wondered whether anything would happen to us on the way there.

The first day of Tet arrived. We got up very early. To partly repay the old lady for her kindness in allowing us to sleep in her house and feeding us, we gave her two piastres. This sum was quite large for us at that time. She refused, but we left the money and said goodbye.

The streets were deserted. The wind blew chilly and desolate.

Our clothes covered with dust, we walked briskly, our hearts filled with excitement at the thought of the task we would soon carry out.

We arrived in Lungchou past noontime. We went to Mr. Nong's house to rest. The moment he saw us, he said reproachfully, "Where have you been all this time? You've been moving around all your life, but you must know that you should come back early for Tet at the end of the year."

Ha Khai Lac smiled and said, "Well, this is still quite early for us. It was lucky we didn't bite the dirt when we went through Chinghsi. We didn't even have the luxury to think about celebrating Tet."

On the altar were two fat and golden boiled capons, each with a rose stuck in its beak. A fragrant cooking aroma wafted from the kitchen. Mr. Nong brought out two plates filled with cakes and said, "Eat a couple of these for the time being, but save your appetite for the meal."

I said softly to Khai Lac, "Let's eat as much as we can hold, and then leave. Let's not wait for the meal."

Khai Lac nodded.

After we finished eating, I told Mr. Nong, "On the occasion of the new year, we wish your whole family good health, good luck and good fortune in your business. We have to go!"

Mr. Nong was so angry he almost shouted, "You're not going anywhere. You've just come back, and before your seats get warmed up you want to leave, what do you think you're doing? Revolution is a long-term business, and it doesn't matter if you lose a day or two. You must stay here and celebrate Tet, at least until the second day of Tet, and then you can go wherever you want to go."

Mrs. Nong was opening a trunk in her room, her key ring tinkling. She hastily ran out, and locked the front door, absolutely refusing to let us leave.

In the end, we had to confess that we had just returned from a conference far away, that we had promised the brothers to be back before Tet, and that if we came back late the brothers would all have left to go on mission and we would not be able to communicate the new tasks to them--and this would foul up everything.

I added to comfort them, "Well, you've seen that we've made it back in good health, with our bodies in good condition, and you know now that the movement has expanded over wide areas. I'm sure you share our happiness."

Mrs. Nong handed us a few cakes to take along and eat on the road. We did not dare to offend her, and accepted one. This couple reluctantly let us go, but they followed us with their eyes full of attachment.

* * *

Like horses returning to their stables, the closer we got to our destination the faster we walked. We arrived in Ban Khiec[10] at eight o'clock in the evening, and entered Pinh Chi's house. The whole family was eating and drinking with the AFNS brothers. They all shouted with joy when we entered. Sister Pinh Chi immediately took the bowls and tray of food away. According to the local custom, when precious guests appeared in the course of the meal, the family had to take the tray of food and the bowls away--even if they had barely started eating--and bring out new bowls and a new tray of food to invite the guests to join them. We drank and played charades, and the gay banquet lasted far into the night.

On the second day of the year Quy Mui (February 1943) all the AFNS brothers still remaining in Bo Cuc attended a meeting during which the resolution adopted by the conference held in Lung Hoang cave was communicated to them. A plan of action was drawn up and each man was assigned a task in order to implement the resolution.

On the third day of Tet, we parted and set out to carry out our mission.

---

10. Ban Khiec, the stopping point of the AFNS on our friends' soil has now become a vast reservoir, part of a large-scale hydraulic project. The vestiges of backwardness, poverty and hunger had sunk deep under the water. The people of Ban Khiec have moved elsewhere to set up a new village where they lead a life of welfare and happiness under the leadership of the Chinese Communist Party headed by the respected and beloved Chairman Mao. After the August Revolution succeeded, and prior to 1964, I had the opportunity to return to Bo Cuc. The villagers from that area who used to know us had come to visit us a couple of times. Our meetings were full of joy and happiness. As the saying goes, "misfortune does not last forever, and is inevitably replaced by a period of bliss." The beautiful spirit of internationalist proletariat solidarity between our two Parties and countries is further strengthened by this friendship. (Footnote in text.)

CHAPTER IX

The Lung Hoang Conference resolution gave the AFNS the responsibility of establishing contact with the Central Committee in the delta, setting up a base area, and clearing two routes: from Thai Nguyen to Cao Bang, and from Thai Nguyen to the delta.

To carry out this resolution, the AFNS Command Staff set forth as the task for the forthcoming phase of activities the establishment of a new base area in Dinh Hoa. We felt that with the favorable development of the movement at this time and the good terrain in this area which leaned against a vast mountain chain--the Hong Mountains--we could set up a large base camp.

Since my return from the Lung Hoang Conference, I had been thinking a great deal about brother Hai Cao--a comrade who had operated with me in Thai Nguyen before, and who had been arrested and jailed by the enemy in the Ba Van prison camp. He had operated in Ninh Binh province in the years 1937, 1938 and 1939. His wife was from Lang Moi village where my wife was living, disguised as the "concubine" of a man named Trieu in order not to arouse the suspicion of the security police and to carry out revolutionary activities. I wanted to go to Lang Moi for two purposes: to take a look at the situation and the grassroot organization in this area, and to find Mrs. Hai Cao in order to establish contact with the Central Committee. In addition, I would take this occasion to visit my wife and find out how she was getting along. I told the AFNS Command Staff about my intention, and they approved it.

I was as familiar with the roads from Bo Cuc to Dai Tu as I was with the lines on the palm of my hand. I left Bo Cuc to return to Vietnam after the Quy Mui New Year festival (February 1943). Whenever I passed through an area where the AFNS Command Staff had--in accordance with the Lam Son [i.e., Lung Hoang] resolution--planted cadres as "stakes" to consolidate the grassroot bases and to expand the movement--I would hold meetings with the local cadres to learn about the current situation and discuss with them about the direction of their activities and the methods they were applying to carry these out. Then I would continue on my way. In Binh Gia, I discussed further with comrade Hong Thai the task of clearing the corridor connecting Bac Son-Vo Nhai with Na Ri (Bac Can province), and checked to see how the linkage of Trang Xa and Yen The was progressing.

The problem of conducting military and political training classes for each region was becoming urgent. Every area was complaining about the shortage of cadres.

I set foot in Vo Nhai at the end of February 1943. The two slopes of the mountain, deep green with vegetation, embraced the fertile ricefields. I had been gone for only one year, but it seemed as though I had been away for a very long time. Now, returning to this land which had given birth to the AFNS Second Platoon and which had heroically fought against an enemy many times stronger, I wanted to look--until my longing was assuaged--at the green color of the forest and trees, the ricefields and crop patches, and the people who had sacrificed themselves and their houses to protect the revolution. As a native of Vo Nhai, I wanted to express all my feelings and my affection for the ethnic minorities who lived here. But whatever I wanted to tell them came down, in the end, to urging them to seize power for only with the revolution in power could the ethnic minorities achieve material well-being and escape repression and exploitation. In order to reach this goal, they would have to bear hardships and difficulties temporarily and to carry out a revolution because the enemy had not yet been wiped out.

In Vo Nhai, I met with the local brothers in the Tham Phie Khao cave in Na Khao. Then I organized a meeting to see the villagers. After that I went to La Hien and passed through Dong Hy to establish contact. Then I went to Phu Luong to start a training class, and then on to Dai Tu to assign various tasks and at the same time to grasp the situation in Dinh Hoa in order to set a date for our moving there.

After a couple of exhausting days and nights climbing mountains, crossing forests, slipping through enemy checkpoints, lacking sleep and food, I reached Dai Tu at the end of the 3rd lunar month in the year Quy Mui (April 1943).

Dai Tu was one of our grassroot bases. Brothers Duong Nhat Quy, Thuong, Hoa, Tai and I walked all night, and when we arrived in Lang Moi village, the moon was beginning to set. A large road cut through this village. In the morning, this road would be crowded with people. If they saw our group dressed entirely in black, carrying cloth bags, and well equipped with weapons, it would not be very good for us. So, we told each other to quicken our steps.

For a long time now--ever since my wife and I had to part because the enemy intensified their repression--I had been looking forward to this day. Now finally, on one of my missions I was permitted to pass through this area to see her. My heart was filled with a feeling of anxiety and agitation, difficult to describe. If I counted the duration of our separation by the moon, then it had been seventeen moons since we were last together.

Before we knew it, we were there. Brother Nhat Quy signalled to us to stop. I looked up at the night sky. The cold and bright quarter moon was still there. We stood in front of a tightly shut wooden gate. One or two dogs were growling somewhere close by, but had not started to bark. Nhat Quy knocked on the gate panel according to the secret signal. The growling was replaced by furious barking, coming from all directions. Someone inside the house was coming out. Judging from the footsteps, I knew two people were advancing toward the gate. The wretched dogs continued to bark. A woman's voice ordered the dogs to remain quiet. I started; "It sounds like An!" At that precise moment, the gate opened a crack and then swung wide open: a man appeared in front of Nhat Quy, and obliquely behind him was a woman. In the pale moonlight I looked at the man who was wearing an old set of brown clothes, and I knew right away that he was a Vietnamese from the delta. I asked myself, "It this Trieu, the man who agreed to let my wife pretend to be his second wife?" Nhat Quy had told me a little about Trieu's family. His family was a grassroot base in Lang Moi village. He and his wife were childless and so had adopted two children, a boy and a girl.

The man recognized Nhat Quy, but when he saw bobbling behind Nhat Quy many mem all dressed in black, carrying neatly packed bags and weapons, he looked surprised. The dog continued to growl somewhere in a dark corner. Again I heard a voice hushing the dog. I wanted to cry out, "An! An! Do you recognize me" but I restrained myself in time, "This is not the right moment." The man spoke quickly but softly in the accent of the rice-growing delta, "Brother Nhat Quy! Please come in! Comrades, please come in!"

Then he turned around, and Nhat Quy and we followed behind.

The room was pitch black. A dot of light, the size of a pea, flashed into a higher flame.

I could see clearly the woman who had just lit the lamp, and my eyes followed each of her movements avidly.

We huddled close together in the shadows. I forgot my exhaustion when I saw my wife in her brown Vietnamese blouse. I heard my wife whisper to Nhat Quy, "Where did you come from?" Nhat Quy answered softly, his voice rasped as he whispered, "From Dai Tu!" My wife again whispered, "Do you want to eat?" Nhat Quy nodded and whispered to her the number of people who were accompanying him.

After introducing us to brother Trieu--it was then that I was certain about the identity of the host--Nhat Quy told him about our mission. Trieu seemed to be used to these nocturnal visits. He did everything softly, and only spoke when it was necessary to do so. And when he spoke, he talked very softly, as though he feared that any noise, no matter how small, might carry outside.

In a short time, food was brought out. There was only one dish: chicken braised with sour bamboo shoot. A soft voice speaking in Vietnamese dialect but still retaining a trace of the highland accent said, "Please come and eat while it's still hot."

My wife and I looked at each other quickly, but did not utter a word. We kept silent, but we understood each other's feelings. She still remembered that I liked sour bamboo shoot, a dish which embodied the warm feelings of our homeland.

Day was beginning to break by the time we finished eating. Trieu told us briefly about the local situation. He jerked his chin toward the outside and continued, "We're close to the main road here, so they keep close watch on the village. But nothing has happened so far. The neighbors are all enlightened people. There's nothing for you to worry about, comrades. Tomorrow I'll go to see you and we'll discuss things further."

I asked, "Where would be a convenient place for us to stay for the moment? How can we contact you?"

He answered, "It's better to take precautions. Take cover in the crop patch behind my house. We'll send people to check on the situation around there and ensure your safety."

Then he led us into the patch in the rocky mountain covered with trees behind his house. We looked for a flat spot to lie down to sleep, but sleep eluded us. Nhat Quy and a few other brothers walked around to check the surroundings. I took out my map to study the terrain.

That night we met comrades Mua, Duong, Trieu, Vu and Dien--the Party members in Lang Moi village--to exchange information on the situation. We were very happy to find out that the local infrastructure was working with efficiency and urgency. Then we went to the house of brother Nhi and sister Len, which was located in a more isolated area, and was therefore a more convenient place for us to meet our comrades and the masses, but to reach it we had to cross a ricefield. We found that it was relatively safer for us to stay in the caves and in the forest, but it was not convenient for us when we needed to see the masses. We found that Mr. Chan's house, on the other side of the Ta Ma bridge, was the most convenient place because we would not have to cross the road or the ricefields to reach it, thus avoiding large crowds of people one of whom would be bound to detect us. We would only have to go across the mountain, go down a slope and we would be there. This way we could keep our presence secret and we would be in a favorable position to take action if there was a sudden alert.

We organized many meetings and drew up many plans, consolidated existing grassroot bases, investigated and studied new ones, expanded the movement to Na Khao, toward Coc Lung and Bai Hoi, and moved it gradually into the Hong mountain chain. With regard to the plan to reestablish contact with the Central Committee, we talked about Mrs. Hai Cao.

The brothers had not paid much attention to her. She was from the delta, and had followed her husband to Lang Moi village to settle. She was an enlightened person. It was brother Hai Cao himself who had recruited the present Party members in Lang Moi village into the Party. After her husband was arrested, she worked very hard to raise her two children.

I asked, "What type of person is she? Is she a Party member?"

"Not yet, but she's a good person, and does not pay attention to anything outside her work through which she earns a living," comrade Duong answered.

"Does she often go to visit her husband?" I asked again.

"We haven't seen her go at all."

I thought, "This means we've now found the first link in our chain," and then proceeded to draw up a plan through which the brothers could motivate her to go and visit her husband, and give her the money she would need to make the trip.

The brothers talked and talked with her until they ran out of things to say, but she still did not dare to go. We were in a predicament. But we must persuade her at all costs. First, we must overcome her reluctance and then find someone to go with her.

While discussing who could do this job, someone mentioned Mrs. Me. This woman was a widow and an experienced petty merchant. She was articulate and very alert. A comrade who had been deep in thought nodded his head and said, "With this stone we can kill two birds!" What he meant was that if we used Mrs. Me, we could accomplish two things. First, Mrs. Me would accompany Mrs. Hai Cao, and second Mrs. Me had been a frequent visitor to the house of Mr. Tu in Bai Hoi--this way, [through Mrs. Me] Mr. Tu could become a very reliable grassroot base for us. (Later on, Mr. Tu was the man who guided a number of brothers who had escaped from the Cho Chu prison camp and led them to our base in safety.)

We assigned to Duong and his wife, and to Trieu, the task of enlightening Mrs. Me.

After propagandizing and educating her, motivating and encouraging her with relatively satisfactory results, Duong came to report to us.

One evening, I went to see her at Duong's house. Before she could express her surprise, I asked her immediately about her business, her profits and losses, and how she was living. I did not forget to tell her that I was a good friend of Duong and his wife, and of Trieu. She stared at me fixedly. Then she slightly bent her tall and slender body and said sadly, "Whenever I go to the market, I have to pay bribes coming and going, so I earn practically nothing."

I mentioned the state our country and our families were in--how our country had been lost to the foreigners and how our families had been dispersed. I also pointed out to her that the only way for us to survive was to take part in the salvation of the country.

She sighed, "Even if we women want to save the country, what can we do?"

"That's not correct! The whole population--men and women--can help save the country. Everyone can do something. Even if you only do small things, such as helping the cadres in their activities, you're helping save the country. To help us relay a bit of information, or deliver a letter--that's also saving the country."

She became bolder: "What do you propose I should do then?"

I looked at her intently, nodded my head and said, "You can do anything. It all depends on whether you're determined or not. If you're determined, you'll think up ruses to accomplish what you want to do. If you lack determination, you'll act very clumsily."

She sat still, listening to me, the expression on her face showed that she was moved. I went on, "To make revolution, we must bear hardships. After hardships will come happiness. Only then will our happiness be long lasting."

At that instant, her eyes shone brightly. She said excitedly, "What job do you want to give me?"

"Can you go to Thai Nguyen?" I asked.

She answered without hesitating, "Yes."

I told her, "That's excellent! Let's wait for the right occasion."

After that meeting, I told Duong and his wife to continue watching Mrs. Mr. She appeared extremely agitated and restless, a complete change from her usual behavior. She boasted to Duong and his wife, "Brother Tan Hong[1] has pointed everything out clearly to me." The

---

1. Chu Van Tan's alias. (Trans.)

brothers who kept an eye on her reported that "she was dying to be given a mission."

As for Mrs. Hai Cao, the brothers expended a lot of energy trying to persuade her to go, but she was still hesitant. She was afraid that if she too was arrested her two children would be left by themselves, with no one to take care of them. In the end, she understood the need for her to make the trip, but she was afraid to go by herself. I proposed that Mrs. Me go with her. The brothers approved of my idea, and so did Mrs. Hai Cao.

One day I went to see Mrs. Me at Mr. Chan's house. I told her about Mrs. Hai Cao. Tears welled up in her eyes, and she said, "Her situation is even more pitiful than mine. I feel very sorry for her."

So, the problem of finding liaison agents to take a message to the Ba Van prison camp had been resolved. Now, we must quickly carry out a new task which was to investigate and find out whether Hai Cao--since his arrest--had retained the indomitable spirit of a Party member. At the least, we must know what his attitude inside the Ba Van prison camp was. This task also required time and delicate handling. We could not do it by ourselves, and had to appeal for help from the local Party members. If we did not perform this task well, the two women liaison agents could be arrested and tortured, and not only would our work come to naught but we might be put in danger as well.

I drew up a new plan of action for myself and asked the local Party cell to lend me a hand.

A few days later, the local comrades completed their investigation of Hai Cao's attitude at my request. He had not changed.

I wrote a letter to him:

> Brother Hai Cao,
>
> You and I have not seen each other for a long time. I have just come back from a mission far away. The movement is now strong and widespread, and is progressing well. We must contact brother Hoang Van Thu. Please forward this letter to him through the communication channel.
>
> Signed: Ba[2]

Then I wrote another letter to the Central Committee. Both letters were written on thin paper, in very small letters, then rolled up tightly like a caterpillar's nest, and tightly sealed.

That evening, Mrs. Me came to the rendezvous spot to meet me. My aim this time was to reinforce her spirit, educate her further, and assign her this task. At first, I only talked about her business and her health. After a long while, noticing that I did not mention what we had discussed in the previous meetings, she asked me, "What was it you wanted me to do?"

I looked at her and said sternly, "The organization today has given you a mission. Go with sister Hai Cao to the Ba Van prison camp to

---

2. Another of Chu Van Tan's aliases. (Trans.)

visit her husband and hand him this letter--I thrust the letter in front of her eyes and repeated each word clearly because I was afraid that she was too moved to have heard everything--you'll accompany sister Hai Cao to the Ba Van prison camp to visit her husband and hand him this letter. Pretend to be sister Hai Cao's cousin on her mother's side. When you see him, just talk normally, you don't have to mention anything. If you can pass him this letter, then you will have accomplished your mission."

Very intelligent and alert, she inserted the letter addressed to Hai Cao inside the border of her scarf, and hid the second letter in the hem of her brown blouse. I described the man to whom the letter was addressed so she would not be surprised when she met him, and so she would not hand it by mistake to another person.

Before she left, I gave her additional instructions on how to maintain secrecy, and said, "If you can keep the whole thing secret, you'll succeed."

We provided the two women with everything they needed to make the trip without any hitches. We considered that the task was accomplished and only waited for the "good results."

A week passed.

One night, the local infrastructure reported to us that Mrs. Me and Mrs. Hai Cao had come back. I hurriedly went over. Mrs. Me handed back to me a rolled up message. I took it; it had not been opened! No one had touched it. What did this mean? "Why did Hai Cao refuse to accept it?" Many questions crowded in my mind. The results were far from what we had expected.

Mrs. Me said, "Brother Hai Cao only accepted the one addressed to him. After he finished reading it, he asked me, 'Who told you to give me this letter? What was he like? How old was he? How come he knew me?' I told him exactly what I knew. He looked at me for a long time and did not say anything. Then he told us to wait for a couple of days. He refused to accept this letter" (Mrs. Me pointed at the rolled up message I was holding). "I waited for two days. That brother Hai Cao--he was exactly as you had described to me--very hot-tempered! I had just asked him why he refused to take the letter when he brushed me aside as though I was a pest and his face flushed with anger: 'Just take it back! I haven't decided what to do.' He looked very intimidating. I didn't dare to ask any more questions."

I had asked Mrs. Hai Cao to go so Mrs. Me could use her as an excuse to see Hai Cao and hand him the letter. I was sure the two women were not lying. I reviewed each of Hai Cao's gestures and words, as Mrs. Me had just described to me. Though I had not been present at the encounter, I could guess how Hai Cao felt when he received the letter I wrote him. The name "Ba" and the sentence "returned from mission" were not good enough guarantees to reassure him that the letter had not been faked. Suppose I had been in his position, the letter and the messenger would certainly make me wonder also, if not find the whole thing suspect. As I thought about this, I heartily approved of Hai Cao's high revolutionary spirit of vigilance. In jail, one could not let oneself be easily persuaded. If you did, you would violate the principle of operation and harm the Party. I must do something to make the brothers in the prison camp believe the message so "they would accept to help me."

173

Seeing me standing still and silent, Mrs. Hai Cao was close to tears. "I saw my husband, but I failed to accomplish the mission that the organization had given me. I felt very bad about this, but did not dare to ask my husband to explain."

I said, "I thank both of you. That's alright. Go home and rest now. There's no need for you to tell anyone about this, alright?"

(I had guessed right. Later on, after he got out of jail, brother Hai Cao told me this story from beginning to end. It turned out he was half doubtful and half believing when he got my letter, especially when he saw that Mrs. Me was the messenger. When he was still operating in Lang Moi village--before his arrest--though he was in charge of propaganda and had recruited Duong and his wife, and Trieu into the Party, he never liked Mrs. Me because she was a merchant, and as such he considered her unreliable, unlike the peasants. Hai Cao took my letter to report to comrade Tran Huy Lieu[3] who was then in the Leadership Committee in the prison camp. Comrade Lieu read the letter and then told him, "We'd be finished if this came from a security agent!" After many bloody experiences, our brothers who were held in the prisons of the French and Japanese fascists had learned to be cautious.)

A few days later, after preparing them ideologically in a more thorough fashion, and after instructing Duong and his wife to do all they could to help these two newly recruited liaison agents, I asked Mrs. Me, "Would you dare to make a second trip?"

She thought it over for a while, and then answered, "I can go. Show me what to do, and I'll do it."

I asked Mrs. Hai Cao once more, "How about you?"

"It's alright with me. This time I'll ask my husband for a detailed explanation."

I shook my head. "All you'll have to do is to go there. You don't have to ask any further questions. Just act normally, like you did the last time. If anything comes up, sister Me will take care of it. Besides, there won't be any hitches this time."

I said this to put their minds at ease for the trip. Their willingness to go was good enough--I thought--it was better for the two of them to go than for us to select two new people; we would have to start all over from scratch, and this would take a lot more time and effort. I went back and talked with the brothers in the local Party Chapter to see whether they could think up a good plan. I tried to recall everything I knew about Hai Cao--even minor details which would be insignificant in normal circumstances--and then wrote him a personal letter, besides the one addressed to the Central Committee:

Brother Hai Cao,

In August 1939, the guava fruit were at their ripest. You came to see me. You passed through Mit's house in Dinh Ca, and then came

---

3. Tran Huy Lieu became the Minister of Propaganda in 1945. He was appointed as the head of the Historical, Literary and Geographical Research Commission of Vietnam in 1956. He became the Director of the Historical Institute of Vietnam in 1959 and a member of the Standing Committee of the National Assembly. (Trans.)

to my house. But there were too many people in my house then, so I had to take you to Duc Ton's house. You and I walked from his house and climbed the mountain in the back of the house, following a trail. When we reached a bamboo grove surrounded by many guava trees, we stopped to discuss our mission. As we talked, I pulled down the branches and plucked the guavas which I handed to you to eat. Do you still remember?

The situation has now improved. I've just come back from a mission outside, and must contact the Central Committee. Please forward this letter immediately. This will decide the fate of the movement here, and I hope you'll do your best to help.

Signed: Ba

I handed the well-sealed letters to Mrs. Me to deliver to brother Hai Cao. The two of them left, and the days following their departure were days of tense waiting. I was confident that Hai Cao was still loyal to the Party and that he would certainly act in accordance with my request. Time seemed to go by too slowly. Right after the women left Lang Moi village, though I knew it would take them some time to reach destination and to get to see Hai Cao--even if nothing happened, it would still be a long time before they got back--I could not help but expect some news each evening, each night.

They returned a few days later. I immediately went to Mrs. Me's house. She felt in her scarf and then handed me a rolled up letter, saying excitedly, "Brother Hai Cao accepted the letter! Here's his reply."

I was so happy I wanted to shout. Although I tried to calm myself, my hands shook with emotion when I held his letter. I opened it gingerly. It was a tiny piece of paper, but it must have taken him a long time to find it. Even the pencil he had used to write these words must have been difficult for him to get hold of in a prison like the Ba Van camp.

Brother Ba,
I've received your letter. I've forwarded it, as you asked. Wishing you good health.

Signed: Hai Cao

The letter was very brief, but my heart was invaded by an extraordinary warm feeling. This meant brother Hai Cao had recognized me.

So, my letter was on its way, but no reply was forthcoming. Day and night we waited anxiously for a liaison agent from the delta, like the parched earth longing for rain.

The Party infrastructure and the mass movement was expanding wider every day and was being consolidated. At this time, the region from Bai Hoi--the center of our base area--to Coc Lung, Na Khao, etc., had become solid grassroot bases. Wherever we went, we made propaganda and organized the masses.

At that time, the rice grains were still green in Coc Lung. We were absorbed with our work. One rainy afternoon, brother Duong--his pants rolled up to his knees, leaning on a bamboo stick, his face aglow with excitement, came to see me. I asked, "What's up?"

"There's a letter," he answered, breathing heavily, "and there's someone looking for you."

"A man or a woman?" I asked immediately.

"A woman."

"A highland woman or a delta woman?"

"A delta woman," brother Duong said as he shook out a rolled-up letter, and gave it to me.

I opened it. It was a letter written from Lang Moi village, the writing was delicate and wiggly.

"There's an urgent business. Please come back right away."

Duong looked outside, and cried with happiness, "It's stopped raining, let's go!"

We arrived in Lang Moi village in a flash. With three long strides, I was in Duong's house.

It was then seven or eight o'clock at night. The house was lit only by a small lamp. In this orange light, a young woman, her head covered with a scarf, wearing a light brown blouse with a round collar, was sitting next to a bamboo cot. I took the initiative and greeted her first. "You've just come up here?"

She looked at me and said, "I just got here late this afternoon." Then she asked right away, "Are you brother Ba?"

"Yes."

She looked at me, her head cocked to one side, as though listening intently to the timbre of my voice. As for me, though I was happy about her arrival, I remained on my guard. I asked, "Are the brothers in good health?"

"They're alright."

She studied me carefully--from my hair to the clothes I was wearing--bit her lips and then asked suddenly, "Do you know brother Hoang Van Thu?"

"I know him a little," I answered modestly.

Her eyes seemed to rivet on me even more, and she again asked, "What kind of a man is brother Hoang Van Thu?"

This time I answered clearly and positively, "Brother Hoang Van Thu used to stay at my house often. While he was operating overseas, some explosives he was testing exploded and hit one of his eyelids, leaving a small scar. He's of average height, with slightly protruding cheekbones, with black and stiff hair, and thick eyebrows."

Brother Hoang Van Thu must have described how I looked and what my voice sounded like to her before she went off on mission. Her face now became radiant, she batted her eyelashes as she looked at me, and seemed to trust me more. She looked at Duong's family sitting in a corner of the house, and then put two packages of "Basto" cigarettes--one intact, one opened--on the table and said, "The brothers sent these cigarettes to you."

I understood the hint, shook the cigarettes from the opened package and pulled out one. I squeezed it. There was nothing inside. I took out a second one; it felt slightly stiff. I broke it in two. A rolled up message, the size of a toothpick, jutted out. My heart was filled with an overwhelming happiness. The letter was written on paper used to roll cigarettes. It was in Hoang Van Thu's handwriting, and he had signed his name. I looked up and saw the liaison agent smile with joy. She was as happy as I was. I read and reread the letter many times:

> Brother Ba,
>
> I've received your letter. This in itself is a good thing. The movement down here is progressing well, and is expanding. The task of proselytizing enemy soldiers is proceeding satisfactorily. Your and the brothers' return is timely and advantageous for us. We can't come up at the moment. When we can arrange it, we'll come to see you. For the time being, you must expand the movement, and do it discreetly and secretly. At the same time, concentrate your forces to open the Northward march routes. The infrastructure in the Cho Chu prison camp has a link with the outside. We won't assign you this task now, but will give it to you later. You must keep this extremely secret. Only you should know about this.
>
> I hope the movement will expand. I'll introduce you to this "link" in my next letter.
>
> Signed: Vân[4]

Were my eyes blurred by emotion, or had the tiny lamp lowered its flame? These were instructions from the Central Committee, relayed by Hoang Van Thu on its behalf. I remained silent for a long time, and then asked the liaison agent a question which I felt was superfluous after I said it: "How's the movement down there coming along, comrade?"

She miled and said, "The letter must have mentioned it."

I also broke out into a happy smile. From then on, we expressed our true comradely feelings to each other. I asked her again, "Is Van alright? Have you spent much time with him?"

"He's in good health, comrade. I'm a liaison agent, so sometimes I stayed close to him, and other times I had to be away."

"How about Truong Chinh, Hoang Quoc Viet and Tran Dang Ninh? Are they in good health?"

"Yes, they're all in good health."

My thought turned to the brothers living in the delta. The enemy was even more numerous and more thickly deployed there than here, but these brothers neither had enough weapons to defend themselves nor did they have the protection of the forests and mountains as we did up here. In the delta, the only thing they could do was to try and avoid running into the enemy, while up here we could--when necessary--attack the

---

4. Hoang Van Thu's alias. (Trans.)

security police searching around, or ambush the soldiers on their way to sow terrorism. Not only were we armed, but the hearts and minds of the people were turned toward the revolution.

I asked the liaison agent, full of worry, "Are they tracking the brothers down there fiercely?"

"It's quite bad, comrade. Fortunately, the people are very good, and always alert them so they can hide whenever there is something afoot," she answered with great pride.

I looked at her with fondness and admiration--this intelligent and heroic girl who had dared to make her way through the wolves armed to their teeth to reach the area where I lived. Her presence and the mission she was performing reminded me of Old Mr. Thu Son's instructions when I left Pac Bo: "Maintain tight liaison, make quick decisions, and communicate decisions in time." The night was far advanced, but we wanted to go on talking. However, she would have to leave early tomorrow morning. I told her to go to bed. I went to another house, lay down to rest for a while and then got up to write my second letter to Hoang Van Thu.

My heart was in each word, each sentence I wrote him:

Brother Van,

There's a relatively large infrastructure network around Cho Chu town. There are many reliable grassroot bases in this Yao minority area. Dai Tu has been restored. The movement in Vo Nhai is stronger and more widespread now, and has expanded into Yen The and Dong Hy. Please send a liaison agent there to establish direct contact and get to know the situation first hand. The route to Cao Bang we've cleared all the way to Cho Don, and we are now pushing it toward Cho Ra. The movement is now so vast. There's an acute shortage of cadres. Please help us.

I propose that you brothers move to the base area. We have adequate forces to ensure your safety.

Ba

I reread the letter one more time. If Hoang Van Thu were here, I could report to him more minutely, with more details. On this small piece of cigarette paper--to make it easier for the liaison agent to slip the message through enemy lines--there was just not enough space for me to express how much I longed to see these brothers again. I rolled up the letter, stuffed it into a cigarette, and then put the cigarette in the still unopened package, and sealed it with a stamp-- the way it had looked originally.

I had just lay down on the bed when the roosters began to crow noisily.

* * *

Lang Moi village, on an autumn morning in 1943.

The liaison agent left for the delta, carrying our letter. I followed with my eyes the silhouette of this alert and heroic girl until she disappeared from view. I recalled the evolution of the mission and struggle of the AFNS and of the local people against the French colonialists and Japanese fascists, and their lackeys. I felt very proud and realized how accurate old Mr. Thu Son's words had been: "It's dangerous to make revolution. The enemy's tricks are extremely cruel and cunning. We must remain alert, we must persevere, we must be brave, and we must not give up in the face of force and violence. With our heads holding up the vault of the skies and our feet planted on the earth--only with a position as firm as this could we win over the people. Also, we must maintain secrecy, know how to protect ourselves, and heighten the people's vigilance." Lang Moi village used to be deserted, but now it had become a link in our communication chain, nestled right in the middle of a thick network of grassroot bases. The mass movement and the Party infrastructure had become rather strong. The Dinh Hoa region became the center of our base area. The National Salvation Army had matured in the course of their struggle and had become the key armed forces of the mass movement. From the base area, the infrastructure had expanded everywhere.

The more I thought about this, the more enthusiastic I became.

A long time later, another woman liaison agent came to Lang Moi village to see me and give me a second letter from Hoang Van Thu. He wrote:

Brother Ba,

The Cho Chu prison camp now has a liaison agent. They have also set up an infrastructure to proselytize enemy soldiers. You comrades should contact them in order to join forces to propel the movement forward. The cadres [you need] are right there in the Cho Chu prison camp.

With determination, clear the route from Bac Son to Cao Bang as soon as possible.

I'll come to the base area very shortly.

Vân

It seemed I could see Hoang Van Thu looking at me with his bright eyes shaded with thick eyebrows. I felt immensely encouraged because from now on we would have direct guidance from the Central Committee, and also because the movement was expanding rapidly.

CHAPTER X

At the end of 1943 I received a letter from Vo Nguyen Giap, sent through a special communication corridor.

The letter was very brief:

> Brother Tan Hong,
>
> I'll come down to see you around the last week of the 11th Lunar month. Will discuss the situation and the mission then.
>
> Signed: Văn[1]

To make it easier for Vo Nguyen Giap to make the trip and return to his area, I told him I would meet him in Khuoi Ta. He would come down from Ban Pinh and Ban Pai. I would come up from Khuoi Phat through Coc post. Previously, whenever we wanted to go from here to Cao Bang, or from Cao Bang down here, we had to cross into China and then circle back around; this made us waste a lot of time and effort. After the Lung Hoang conference, the Northward March and Southward March prongs had made it possible for us to make the trip through routes lying within the country. A political corridor had been cleared, which linked the two base areas of Cao Bang and Bac Son-Vo Nhai, thus creating the conditions for the establishment of the Liberated Zone later.

Our group included comrades Hoa, Thanh, Hong Thai and a few comrades who had just returned from combat operations to clear the routes from the North down here. They were brothers Nhat Quy, Hoang Thuong and Ha Cham. All of us were armed--some carried muskets, others carried Dop 3 rifles, and I carried the Pac-hooc submachine gun I had been using for a long time. We spent hours walking in the night, wading up the stream against the current. The stream was small, but the bed was covered with jutting rocks which made it difficult for us to progress. Once in a while we ran into a cataract and had to make a detour. We moved like this for 8 or 9 kilometers, and then climbed onto a gently graded mountain covered with walnut and *hong sac* trees. There was a Meo settlement on the mountain top. This was Khuoi Ta, the spot chosen as the meeting place for Vo Nguyen Giap's group and ours.

In this period, every area was bustling with preparations for the insurrection.

That afternoon--I no longer can remember what day it was, all I can recall was that the fields had recently been harvested, and that the stumps of rice stalks were still fresh--I looked outside and saw the healthy *hong sac* trees bathed in sunlight. I was sitting and working when an AFNS fighter came in to announce that "Brother Vo Nguyen Giap has arrived!" I was overjoyed, and hurriedly went out with the rest of the brothers to greet him.

---

1. Vo Nguyen Giap's alias. (Trans.)

There he was! He looked the same as when I last saw him at the Lung Hoang conference. The local people, hearing that guests were arriving, looked out from their windows or came out to their fences to take a look, or stood in their courtyards and looked out.

We shook hands warmly. We both asked the same question simultaneously: "Are you alright, comrade?" We looked at each other for a long time and then smiled with happiness.

After that moment, I suddenly heard a shout of joy, "Uncle!"

Someone grabbed me. I turned around and cried out, "Nephew Hien! Why have you been so discreet?"

"I was waiting for the two Command Staffs to shake hands [before I made my presence known]," Hien said laughing. "I saw you from afar and recognized you at once. I wanted to hug you right then and there!"

Hien was among the AFNS comrades we assigned--after the Lung Hoang conference--to help Vo Nguyen Giap in his Southward March. Now he was accompanying Vo Nguyen Giap here. He looked much more mature and tougher after a year on mission. I was happy that he had made progress thanks to Vo Nguyen Giap's guidance.

The comrades in Vo Nguyen Giap's group told us about their trip from Ban Pinh and Ban Pai to here, climbing hills and crossing streams. They took the Bach Thong route, and walked two or three nights through areas inhabited by the Man Tien[2] minority. The last night they covered the final stage of their journey, and crossed Coc village.

I took them inside the house. The host was sitting on a bed. Brother Vo Nguyen Giap greeted him in Yao dialect, "You're staying home?"

The host, seeing that the newly arrived guest who was dressed differently from the local people could speak the local dialect, stared at Vo Nguyen Giap and then said, "Yes, I'm staying home. You just got here?"

"Are the children out playing?"

"Yes, they've gone out to play."

I introduced him to the host, "This is a comrade who's just arrived from Cao Bang."

"Good. Sit down. Have some water. If you're hungry, have some food."

Vo Nguyen Giap smiled kindly. "We've just eaten. When we're hungry we'll eat again."

"Alright!" the host replied.

Then the two of them discussed farming and hunting, and seemed to hit it off famously.

---

2. A Yao sub-group. (Trans.)

* * *

The next morning, after our meal, we went to the crop patch to hold a meeting at around eight or nine o'clock. Even though our host was a trustworthy sympathizer, we could not discuss important matters in this villager's house.

There was a hut in the field where the villagers kept a small amount of paddy and where they put their small children to shield them from the sun while they worked in the fields. But the hut was too small and we could not all come in to sit down. We went down, near the clearing, and held our meeting in the shade of huge trees with thick foliage. We cut down leaves and spread them on the bank of the stream. Our group included comrades Nhat Quy, Cham, Thuong and Hoa.

Vo Nguyen Giap's goal in coming was to find out about our situation down here, from all points of view. Then he would go to the delta to report to the Central Committee about the situation in the two base areas of Cao Bang and Bac Son-Vo Nhai.

To start the meeting, I reported on the situation down here, especially about the continuing effort to clear a route to Cao Bang, the Northward March problem, and the question of cadres.

Brother Vo Nguyen Giap listened attentively and asked for details about our communication with the delta and our liaison with the Central Committee.

In accordance with the spirit of the 8th Central Committee Resolution on the question of "maintaining and developing the guerrilla base in Bac Son-Vo Nhai, and at the same time making resolute efforts to consolidate and expand the Cao Bang base, and consolidating these two bases to transform them into the epicenter of the task of making military preparations for an insurrection in the Viet Bac Zone," we discussed many important questions dealing with the activities of these two bases.

Brother Vo Nguyen Giap said, "The general situation is very good. The movement in Bac Son-Vo Nhai and in Cao Bang has spread to large areas. We should continue to consolidate the region of Cho Don-Yen Son-Dai Tu-Phu Luong into a corridor leading to Vo Nhai, we should direct our operations toward the delta and at the same time focus our attention on consolidating the liaison route to Cao Bang; further south we should also organize prongs to attack toward the lowlands. In this way the two bases would be linked and the War Zone would expand all the way to Tam Dao. In particular, we should make sure that the liaison route to the Standing Committee of the Central Committee was completely cleared so that agents could move back and forth whenever necessary, in order for us to have close coordination with the movement in the whole country."

He stopped, thought for a while, looked at me, and then said excitedly, "I'll go back to Cao Bang to discuss and hand over my responsibilities to the brothers, and then I'll come back here right away. Then both of us can go and report to the Standing Committee."

He also proposed that on his return we would review a few important problems, such as the preparations for the insurrection, the clearing of communication routes--especially the liaison route to the delta--and the training and formation of cadres.

The meeting adjourned when our shadows stretched out on the field. We walked side by side from the field back to the house. Giap was very happy, and his face shone with joy. My heart too was filled with a special joy and confidence. Not only had the movement expanded tremendously, but also we had succeeded in contacting the Central Committee--we could now picture the creation of a "three-legged" position formed by the three centers of Cao Bang, Dinh Hoa-Son Duong, and Bac Son-Vo Nhai, operating in coordination, and all three able to reach the Central Committee in the delta.

We parted and promised to meet each other again shortly. Right after that, however, the enemy launched a large-scale campaign of repression thrusting into Cao Bang-Bac Can. The Southward March routes from Cao Bang were cut in many places. And Vo Nguyen Giap and I could not meet again in Khuoi Ta as we had promised each other.

* * *

The task of mobilizing the people in the Bac Son-Dinh Ca region was pushed ahead and produced good results. National Salvation associations and Viet Minh Committees were organized in every village, and gradually replaced the enemy government. The people supplied the guerrillas quite adequately from all points of view, and helped the revolutionary armed forces to expand continuously.

Side by side with the expansion of the AFNS, self-defense and combat self-defense units were set up along the length and breadth of the base area, and were given intensive military training.

In February 1944, Hoang Quoc Viet arrived in Khuoi Phat (Yen Son district, Tuyen Quang province). Comrade Cam accompanied him.

Hoang Quoc Viet still looked the same as he did two years ago. The only change was that he now wore a cap with a visor, brown clothes and slippers. He was more cheerful than in the old days, because the atmosphere nowadays was full of joy and enthusiasm; the revolutionary movement was expanding strongly and at the same rate everywhere. Many cadres inside the prisons had established contact with the infrastructure outside. The AFNS had expanded strongly and linked up with the areas of Tuyen Quang-Thai Nguyen and Cao Bang, creating a liberated zone. Spring was returning and the traditional New Year festival was drawing close.

The last time we managed to contact the Central Committee after being cut off for two years, we could do it only by letter, but now the Central Committee had sent someone here. We would receive guidance from the Central Committee again. It seemed to us that the mountains and forests were covered with a beautiful green cloak, that the skies and earth appeared more joyful, and the *hong sac*, walnut, *lat* and ironwood trees stretched themselves with vigor to greet the visitors.

In Khuoi Phat, the AFNS Command Staff reported to Hoang Quoc Viet about the general situation, and about the major events which took place after his departure for the delta, about our shortcomings and good points, and about the lessons drawn from the things that the AFNS had done. It was difficult to grasp the situation of the grassroot bases on both sides of the Hong mountain chain. In addition, the Bac Son-Vo Nhai, Dai Tu-Dinh Hoa-Son Duong-Yen Son also needed close guidance, but we did not have enough cadres--and furthermore our capacity and capability was limited. The route to Cao Bang had been blocked, and the AFNS was doing their best to reestablished this link.

Hoang Quoc Viet listened, nodded and then interrupted, "The Central Committee also needs the organ up there in Cao Bang very badly."

I added, "The Tuyen-Quang area now has a widespread infrastructure network. The number of AFNS members has also increased tremendously. Their operation area would be widely expanded. According to our calculation, besides the brothers in the AFNS Second Platoon, there is over a squad of men newly arrived from Cao Bang; on the Tuyen Quang side, we have comrades Ha Cham, Thanh, Phuong Cuong, Chu Phong, An, La, Le, Tai, Bao Tien and a number of other men--about three squads. The Tuyen Quang area has expanded, and so will the Trang Xa-Vo Nhai area. We think that in this new situation, we should set up an AFNS Third Platoon. We would like to have the opinion of the Central Committee."

Hoang Quoc Viet said, "We feel greatly encouraged in the course of this visit with you comrades. I agree with your assessment as well as with your plan to expand the movement. Our operation area is now very vast and our responsibilities are very heavy. I approve of the formation of another AFNS platoon. What will its mission be? I think it should be as follows. One, to continue consolidating and expanding our forces, to transform this region into a third base, expand the movement, open a route Northward, and at the same time thrust down and open a route into Dai Tu to be closer to the Central Committee, to clear a route to Lap Thach (south of Tuyen Quang), protect the base area, and organize special liaison agents to protect the leading comrades moving back and forth. Second--and this is a rather important task--to counter the enemy repression and terror. As you have reported, the enemy in Dinh Hoa and Coc post have arrested some of our people. We have had the experience of Bac Son. The third mission the Central Committee assigns to you comrades is to establish contact with our brothers in jails and prison camps and to bring them out."

He stopped for a while and then went on, "There's one thing I'd like to inform you. The North Vietnam Region Party Committee is planning to bring comrade Vinh out of the Tuyen Quang jail. She is a liaison agent of our Party, and I'm sure you have never met her. The Central Committee has already contacted the infrastructure in charge of proselytizing the enemy soldiers in Tuyen Quang. The North Vietnam Region Party Committee has given this task to Cam alone: how to bring her out into our War Zone."

We studied together the measures to implement faithfully the three tasks that the Central Committee had assigned to the new AFNS platoon. We informed the AFNS fighters and asked them to go to Khuoi Kich to attend the ceremony setting up the AFNS Third Platoon. While waiting for the group operating in Tuyen Quang to return, the AFNS fighters who gathered here from various areas would go through a military training course before they were presented to the Central Committee.

When they learned the significance of this training and especially when they heard that a representative of the Central Committee would be here to attend the ceremony, the new as well as the old AFNS fighters were filled with an extraordinary enthusiasm.

* * *

Hoang Quoc Viet and the AFNS Command Staff discussed the new task. We spread out to operate all the way from Khuoi Phat to Khuoi Kich to make preparations for the ceremony setting up the AFNS Third Platoon.

Everyone felt very proud, and was restless in anticipation of this historic day. In only a few days, representatives of the people in the Son Duong area would arrive in the hundreds to attend the ceremony. We were not afraid of enemy sabotage in this area; our only concern was to let the people see clearly in this ceremony the strength of the AFNS and reinforce their confidence in the revolution.

Khuoi Kich was a small settlement deep in the forest, inhabited entirely by the Yao minority. To go from Son Duong to Khuoi Kich, one had to go for 20 kilometers before reaching Kim Long (i.e., Tan Trao) and then walk for another two or three kilometers through the forest to arrive at destination. The movement here was expanding but there was a shortage of cadres.

A stream flowed through this settlement. The brothers cleared a large area on the bank of the stream, and posted sentries to provide protection. When they heard the news, the people in the surrounding areas were very happy and donated a whole patch of manioc, baskets and baskets of pumpkins and squashes, and dozens of pigs and chickens, and other food supplies.

The preparation which was most time-consuming was the teaching of military movements. Among the new members of the AFNS were those who had gone through the difficult period of combat and had borne hardships and overcome difficulties; others were remnants from the Bac Son uprising, while the rest were veterans of the eight-month guerrilla warfare in Trang Xa. Most of them had studied basic military movements, but not all of them could execute these movements skillfully.

I told the brothers, "The people will be watching us. We are the revolutionary army. It wouldn't look too tood if we march out of step or carry rifles improperly during the parade. I have never studied in any military institutes either. But whatever I learned from brothers Phung Chi Kien and Luong Huu Chi years before I'll pass on to you."

Ha Cham nodded and said, "That's fine! Everything will be alright if you can teach us."

The others agreed. They all made an effort. They practiced individually and in groups--the commanders as well as the unit members practiced. They practiced during rest periods and reviewed what they had learned while standing guard, so that they could quickly reach the level at which they could march in step and parade nicely. One comrade volunteered for guard duty every day. The brothers were surprised and wondered what he was up to, so they hid and watched. It turned out he volunteered for guard duty in order to get a good rifle, and he only felt good when he could practice the movements he had learned with a good rifle.

Everything was ready, in time for the appointed day.

The deep Khuoi Kich forest, normally very mysterious and rarely frequented, now resounded with many different ethnic dialects, with the calls of "comrade!" and with happy and relaxed laughter. Dozens of bright red flags glowed in the light which filtered through the foliage. Every face shone with joy and happiness.

It was then around three or four o'clock in the afternoon.

"Attention everyone! Line up in three horizontal rows! Assemble!" The solemn shout silenced all noises.

The AFNS obeyed the command and lined up in three rows, while the people--their ranks also in good order--stood in the back. They all looked toward the largest red flag with the yellow star. The flag reflected in every eye, and every heart was moved and filled with a great pride. The national anthem rose, and shook the mountains and forests:

> Onward march the Viet Minh troops
> Sharing a common desire to save their country
> Their footsteps
> Resounding on the long and rugged road.

High and low voices, female and male voices, rasping and clear voices--today they seemed to blend with each other in an extraordinary manner and became one voice singing about saving the fatherland, and sharing an unshakable faith.

This army with the people standing close by its side to provide heartfelt support looked very heroic and full of strength. How lovable and admirable these men looked! Present today were members of the AFNS First and Second Platoons, the brothers who had just returned from Cao Bang, and even the brothers who had just come from the infrastructure in many settlements and villages to join our ranks. A large number of them were here today to appear before the Party and the people's representatives.

At the end of the saluting the flag ceremony, Hoang Quoc Viet--on behalf of the Central Committee--recalled in a clear and resounding voice the contributions of the two AFNS platoons and of the local people who had protected and supported the armed forces to which their children belonged, and expressed sorrow over the loss of the brothers who had sacrificed their lives since the Bac Son uprising to the present.

Hoang Quoc Viet's voice suddenly became choked. "Comrade Hoang Van Thu is a leading cadre of our Party. The imperialists have captured him. They tortured him savagely. But he refused to talk. They tried to exploit the love he had for his family and for his father to shake his indomitable spirit of struggle, but his spirit remains as hard as steel, and his loyalty to the Party and the people remained as spotless and as crystal clear as a mirror. They could not break him with either torture or violence, so the cowardly imperialists condemned him to death. We swear not to live under the same sky with the imperialists! Emulate the heroic and indomitable example of comrade Hoang Van Thu! We are determined to avenge him!"

Hoang Quoc Viet's voice became hard and cold. A solemn, somber and majestic atmosphere enveloped all of us. Though Hoang Quoc Viet had told me this in advance and had added, "They've passed this sentence, but perhaps things wouldn't come to that. We'll try every means possible to save him," an acute pain shot to my heart. Tears streamed out of my eyes. I did not want to believe that the imperialists would spare the life of an outstanding leader of the Indochinese Communist Party like "brother Van." But I continued to hope, and to believe that the utmost efforts of the comrades in the delta could commute this death sentence. (Later, I was told by the brothers that Laneque--the head of the French Sûreté notorious for his cruelty--had said, "Unless we kill Hoang Van Thu the Indochinese revolution will succeed.")

I remembered that Hoang Van Thu had written me not long ago, "I'll come to the base area very shortly." That letter--I did not suspect then--was Hoang Van Thu's last words to us. He had lived with us in those days and months when we were surrounded by the enemy on all sides, when our armed forces were still weak and inexperienced in combat, and when our War Zone was still small. Under the guidance of the Central Committee and thanks to the resoluteness of the ethnic minorities around our base area, the Party's armed forces came into being and gradually expanded, but now that we had a strong and solid base area to ensure the safety of the Central Committee brothers, Hoang Van Thu could no longer come to be with us.

Hoang Quoc Viet brushed away his tears. As he had said, our pain on this day would certainly be transformed into strength and hatred to crush our enemies--the colonialists and imperialists. There was no doubt about this. The AFNS was ready.

On behalf of the Central Committee, Hoang Quoc Viet recognized the AFNS Third Platoon. Its mission was clear. He said, "The AFNS Third Platoon Command Staff will include comrades Trieu Khanh Phuong, Chu Phong and Phuong Cuong. Show that you're worthy of the task that the Party has assigned to you. Be brave in the face of the enemy! You must be resolute and cautious, and try at all costs to avoid arbitrary and reckless actions. You must be close to the brothers in the unit and take good care of them. You must be united with the ethnic minorities here."

He stopped, and looked at all of us, one by one. He motivated the old fighters and encouraged the new ones. "Everywhere in the world our enemies are losing. In our country the revolutionary movement is spreading. In the highlands as well as in the lowlands, unrelenting struggles have broken out everywhere. We are strong everywhere, and the enemy will surely be annihilated."

These words of our Party penetrated deep into the heart of each man. Everyone felt honored, understood his heavy responsibility, and was confident that the Party's predictions would come true.

"The Army for National Salvation fighters will unite with each other and with the people to become a bloc of steel, and will heroically complete the task that the Party has assigned to them." This was what I promised to the Party and to the people.

Comrade Vinh, the Central Committee's communication and liaison agent recently rescued from the Tuyen Quang jail who had been living in the War Zone for the last couple of days and who had thus seen the hardships, the difficulties and the privations of life in the mountain areas--the terrain was rough, and going anywhere always meant climbing hills, wading in streams and crossing forests, not to mention running into wild beasts--was very moved and expressed her opinion. "It's only by living here that I've come to realize how large our armed forces in the War Zone are. When I return to the delta, I will do my best to motivate the women's movement there to increase their support to the War Zone."

After Vinh had spoken, the villagers expressed their opinion. They promised to march side by side with the AFNS, behind the flag of the revolution, to win independence.

The words of the Party, of our people and of the army were engraved in everyone's mind. The ceremony ended with the parade of the AFNS. Solemn shouts arose.

The whole platoon quickly executed the order of their commander, and lined up in rows at proper intervals.

In a flash, the AFNS changed their formation, and--well armed--began to move, their thudding steps stamping the ground in cadence, though they were all barefoot. Their movements were vigorous and well practiced.

"Line up in three rows! Open fire in sitting, kneeling and standing position!"

I was shouting these commands, but deep down I was still worried that the brothers and sisters would execute the orders improperly and in disorder. But they all did their best to reproduce what they had learned. Their ranks in order, they correctly deployed in three rows and fired in the sitting, kneeling and standing position. Their eyes seemed to burn with anger as they aimed at points which to them must represent the enemy.

As the military commander at that moment, I felt very proud of my unit and of my comrades. I was certain the brothers and sisters shared my feelings. I turned toward the comrade representing the Central Committee and toward the people attending the ceremony, raised my hand to the level of my eyebrows and saluted in the military style.

The people watched the exhibit of military movements, following each gesture closely, pointing, praising and approving, and smiling with enthusiasm. (We were then in the phase of secret activities, so there was no applause and no noisy acclaim.) Now, remembering the unit as it was on that day, I find it simple, immature, and primitively armed. At that time, however, the ethnic minorities and we felt very proud because our revolutionary army looked very impressive and imposing.

At the end of the ceremony, the AFNS and the people sang a few songs together and then ate a "meal of unity." There were about a hundred people attending. The tables were very simple and were made of wood and bamboo sections, and were lined up one next to the other in a long and orderly row. Everyone had to stand, but it was all very gay. The people put food in the AFNS fighters' bowls, scooped up heaping bowls of rice for each other, wished each other good health, and expressed the hope of killling many of the enemies. Talk and laughter resounded.

After the meal, we again gathered on the parade ground, and celebrated with songs. Songs such as "Let's All Join the Red Army," "The Brothers in the Guerrilla Unit," "The Revolution Is Rising Everywhere on All Five Continents," and "Unsheathing Our Yard-long Swords, We'll March Forward Together," were sung and resung in many different dialects.

The festivities lasted till late at night, and no one left early. However, the hour of parting drew near. The people and the fighters were reluctant to say goodbye. Some carried torches, others said goodbye, crowding around in groups and talking noisily; the Tay and Nung dialects were fast and resounding like echoes bouncing off a rocky mountain, the Yao dialect was warm and slow, and the Kinh dialect was like a bird song. The guerrillas and the people of all ethnic backgrounds who had come to attend the meeting promised that the next time they met they would prolong the festivities longer and eat a bigger meal of "people-army solidarity."

The line of torches lit up the twisting trails along the stream bank, and led the groups of people back to their far away settlements where they would assume their task of expanding the movement. The Khuoi Kich forest seemed to echo still the resolute promises of the Army for National Salvation.

* * *

The AFNS Third Platoon immediately set about to study and discuss their tasks. Brother Hoang Quoc Viet taught the AFNS about the revolutionary ideology and spirit of the Party, and contributed ideas crucial to the implementation of our tasks. We would split up and go to Tuyen Quang, Bac Can and Thai Nguyen to carry out our new mission. I myself would take charge of two squads and move gradually to the Northwest of Thai Nguyen province, that is to say the region of Dai Tu and Phu Luong, and to Tuyen Quang to carry out the following tasks: one, to develop and consolidate a new movement to solidify the base area; second, to consolidate the military as well as the political forces side by side; three, to march Northward and continue to clear a corridor to Cao Bang to link up with the Southward March unit.

Two days after the ceremony establishing the AFNS Third Platoon, comrades Hoang Quoc Viet, Hoa, Cham, Vinh, An, Thanh and I returned to Lang Cam village from Khuoi Kich to be in time for the opening of the conference to discuss the tasks of Subregions A and B. Subregion A was the area on this side of the Song Cau river and consisted of Binh Gia and Bac Son (Lang Son province), Vo Nhai and Dong Hy (Thai Nguyen province), and Huu Lung and Yen The (Bac Giang province). Subregion B was on the other side of the Song Cau River and consisted of Phu Luong, Dai Tu and Cho Chu (Thai Nguyen province), Cho Moi, Cho Don and Cho Ra (Bac Can province), and Son Duong and Yen Son (Tuyen Quang province).

Lang Cam village, on top of Chua mountain, was a small settlement consisting of only five families, but it covered a larger area than many other settlements. It was because of this factor that we had a safe place to stay. Frequently, groups of ten and sometimes twenty cadres came here to meet and eat. This was the place that had welcomed us many times in the past after we had overcome difficulties and hardships. The AFNS had used Lang Cam as a springboard from which to expand the movement over the entire area.

This conference was also organized in Lang Cam. It was well attended and included even the comrades from Vo Nhai district led by brother Quoc Hung. The movement demanded that we discuss more difficult and more complicated problems. The tasks of the two Subregions A and B, the consolidation of the liaison corridor between these two subregions, the liaison route linking us with the Central Committee in the delta, the continued clearing of the route to Cao Bang, the consolidation and expansion of the grassroot bases, the formation and nurturing of cadres, and the underground activities--these were all major and urgent problems paving the way for the military and political struggle to seize power.

After this conference, a number of AFNS brothers and sisters were assigned to remain in Lang Cam village to operate. To implement the resolution of the conference--with the exception of the brothers who took Hoang Quoc Viet and sister Vinh to the delta--we all set out to carry out our tasks.

We took Hoang Quoc Viet and Vinh all the way to Vo Nhai where we met a number of villagers, discussed the bright and encouraging situation of the movement everywhere, motivated and encouraged the people to keep up their struggle against the enemy. After that, we reluctantly parted. Hoang Quoc Viet and Vinh returned to the delta; the people of Vo Nhai remained in the War Zone, and I along with a few other brothers left to go on mission.

Full of enthusiasm for their new tasks, the brothers wanted to get back to their areas of operation quickly, but they also felt very attached to their blood comrades, and to the affection and love of the grandmothers, mothers, sisters and brothers in Lang Cam, this out of the way but very cozy and warm village. Also--and who could have guessed--it was in Lang Cam that the love between Hoang Quoc Viet and Vinh blossomed and has remained undiminished to this day.

The bamboo forest on the Chua mountain stretched out their arms as though to wave goodbye to us as we climbed down the mountain. We spread out in different directions, but we all carried with us an unshakable confidence that the revolution would succeed.

*   *   *

The AFNS Third Platoon was split up into squads, and each squad was put in charge of a separate area. Each comrade in the Platoon Command Staff took direct charge of a squad.

Comrade Le Duc Ton, one of the three comrades commanding the AFNS Second Platoon, was put in direct charge of Dinh Hoa. At this time, Dinh Hoa had become a center of enemy soldier proselytizing efforts, and was a liaison chain linking up with the Command Committee within the prison camp. Also the mass movement there had expanded greatly. After spending some time in Dinh Hoa, I went down to Ban Pinh and Ban Pai, and then went up to Cho Chu. In this period, Hoang Thuong and Nhat Quy were still in charge of the Northward March route.

In May 1944 I left to attend the conference of the North Vietnam Region Party Committee. This was an extraordinary meeting, to be held in Hiep Hoa district (Bac Giang province), to listen to the reports on the situation in every area. However, since a number of comrades in the North Vietnam Region Party Committee could not make it in time, the official conference of the North Vietnam Region was set for August. Before I left to attend this conference, I told Le Duc Ton, "Go ahead and get them out [of jail], [even if we can spring loose] only ten or fifteen it would be good enough." Le Duc Ton understood clearly what I meant, nodded and said, "You can go to the conference with peace of mind. I'm facing a shortage of cadres also. What more could I ask than to have them out to help me?" Since Hoang Van Thu wrote that "the cadres [you need] are now in the Cho Chu prison," and had the letter delivered to us by a special liaison agent, we had been paying close attention to the Cho Chu area. Also, the woman who brought the letter from the Central Committee to us turned out to be the comrade in charge of enemy soldier proselytizing at the central level. We hoped to obtain this number of cadres whom the Central Committee had planned to assign to our area to reinforce it. So, on my way to attend the North Vietnam Region Party Conference this time, the joy of seeing the ever expanding and strengthened movement made me walk on and on without feeling the cramp in my legs.

The North Vietnam Region Party Conference was again organized in Hiep Hoa. I even saw Truong Chinh and Van Tien Dung,[3] etc., at the conference. The conference officially adopted the divisions into Subregions A and B, and assigned responsibilities for the implementation of the policy to help the cadres escape from the two prison camps of Ba Van and Dinh Hoa.

I rejoiced inwardly, and anxiously waited for the end of the conference so that I could go back and organize for the implementation of this important resolution of the North Vietnam Region. The conference was almost over when a comrade said, "Tomorrow night, there'll be a jail break from the Ba Van prison camp." I looked at him, stunned, and thought, "Ba Van and Dinh Hoa should escape at the same time. If Ba Van is coming out tomorrow night, even if I had supernatural power I wouldn't be able to organize an escape from Dinh Hoa in time." As though to stress this point so that the brothers in charge of Ba Van would keep it in mind, the comrade repeated, "Tomorrow night there'll be an escape from the Ba Van prison camp." At that moment I understood very well that to get our brothers out of the imperialists' jails was an enormous task of investigation, reconnaissance, and devising the best and most effective way to take them out in order not only to liberate those who escaped but also to keep the identities of the brothers helping in the escape who remained in jail and of our contacts secret.

---

3. Van Tien Dung was born in 1917 in Co Nhue (a suburb of Hanoi). A weaver by trade, he participated in the revolutionary movement as early as 1936. He joined the Indochinese Communist Party in 1937, and became a member of the Hanoi Party Committee in 1938 as well as Secretary of the Hanoi Workers' Union. Arrested twice by the French in 1939, he was condemned to two years at hard labor. In September of the same year, while being transferred from Son La prison to the Hanoi Central prison, he managed to escape. In July 1943 he helped set up Party organizations in the provinces of Ha Dong and Bac Ninh. In 1944, he became Secretary of the North Vietnam Party Committee. Arrested again by the French in August 1944, he was sentenced to death but escaped from prison and resumed his revolutionary activities. In March 1943, he was a member of the Standing Bureau of the Revolutionary Military Committee of the North and was given the task of organizing the Quang Trung military zone. He led the armed insurrection of 1945 in this area. In November 1946, he was Head of the General Political Department of the Vietnam People's Army and Assistant Secretary of the Standing Bureau of the Party Committee in the Vietnam People's Army. In 1947, he was promoted to the rank of brigadier general. In late 1949, he was Political Commissar for the third military zone. In December 1950, he was the commander of the 320th Division. At the Second Party Congress in 1951, he was elected a member of the Central Committee. Van Tien Dung is now a Colonel General, a National Assembly deputy, a member of the Central Committee, an alternate member of the Politburo, a member of the National Defense Supreme Council, and the Chief of the General Staff of the Vietnam People's Army. (Information obtained from *Vietnam Advances*, No. 7 [Hanoi, 1963], p. 23. Trans.)

But I don't know why I was complaining that day. "If the Ba Van group escapes first, they might run into obstacles when they come out. . . . How come they're not going to wait for the others [in Dinh Hoa]? We don't have enough cadres. . . ." However, the North Vietnam Region Party Committee had made up its mind and all areas involved would have to do exactly as planned.

[On my way back] after the conference, when I reached Cay Thi I sensed a change in the atmosphere. In La Hien, I saw soldiers standing guard everywhere; I asked a sympathizer named Ba who was a militiaman to go and check the main road leading to Phu Luong. I stayed about 100 meters from the district seat to wait for news. Ba came back and told me that all kinds of soldiers and militiamen were standing guard and maintaining security. When he asked, some refused to explain, but others said that "prisoners had escaped from Ba Van." I knew very well then that our brothers in the Ba Van camp had successfully escaped from jail, and that the enemy had been panicking and trying to deal with the situation since that night. I was happy for these comrades, but I was concerned about my area and about Duc Ton who had stayed behind. I wondered whether he had been alert and fast enough to take advantage of the situation to carry out our plan. "When a beast is snared, the rest of the flock is alerted and bolt away"; the jail-break in Ba Van would make the wolves tighten their security around the Cho Chu prison camp. "But there's nothing to worry about," I thought, "the AFNS is neither afraid of difficulties nor deterred by hardships, and it is determined to make sacrifices and heroically complete the task assigned to it by the Party." My thoughts coincided with the lyrics of a song which any AFNS fighter--man or woman--loved to sing; it was the song, "Let's Join the Red Army." Also, these lyrics reflected the same sentiments as the oath of the AFNS.

A few days later, all the soldiers were withdrawn and I returned to Le Duc Ton's place. The moment I saw him, I asked about the question we discussed before I left to attend the North Vietnam Region Party Committee conference. Duc Ton, the expression on his face unchanged--I couldn't tell whether he was happy or sad--told me, "I've been waiting for you to come back to do it." He was still his curt self, but he always stood by whatever he said. Anyone who came into contact with him and heard him talk for the first time must think that he was an arrogant man. That was his personal trait, but whatever he did he insisted on doing well. I understood Le Duc Ton had a good reason to wait for me to come back before carrying out our plan, because the situation had changed, and he should not act recklessly. I nodded and told him, "Alright, let's talk it over and then do it." He did not say a word to that. That was just the way he was!

* * *

We did not manage to get our brothers out of the Cho Chu prison camp until October 2, 1944. There were twelve in all: comrades Song Hao,[4] Hien Mai,[5] Ta Xuan Thu,[6] Trung Dinh, Chi, Black Phong, Nhi Quy,

---

4. Song Hao is now a Lieutenant General in the DRV People's Army. He was promoted to this rank in 1959. He is now a member of the Workers' Party Central Committee, head of the Political Department of the High Command of the People's Army, and National Defense Deputy Minister. (Trans.)

5. Le Hien Mai is now a Major General in the DRV People's Army, a permanent member

Khang, Mon, Son, Chu Nu and Tung--all outstanding cadres of our Party. I thought, "If our War Zone gets them it would be like a gift from heavens." At that time, to tell the truth, even a gift from heavens could not match these brothers. We made careful preparations and carried out our plan neatly and swiftly. The comrades who escaped included members of the Party Branch Committee and its Secretary, comrade Song Hao. We arranged to have old Mr. Tu wait for them in Bai Hoi, near a stream which flowed beneath the road, a few kilometers from Khuon Linh. Old Mr. Tu took them further inside where Le Duc Ton[7] was waiting for them near a huge tree. He handed to each of them a grenade and told them about the planned march. They left at once because it was not a safe spot. Duc Ton and Mr. Tu bypassed the trails and led the brothers into the dense forest, in the direction of the chosen target area.

Near midnight, they reached the bank of the Song Day river. It was a starless, moonless, and pitch-dark night. Suddenly they saw the glare of a torch in the river. Duc Ton signalled to the brothers to halt while Mr. Tu, his rifle at the ready, moved ahead to reconnoiter. A while later he came back and said, "It's Hong Hai[8] catching fish!"

It turned out that Hong Hai, who was to act as guide, had waited for so long that he finally decided to cut bamboo branches--there were thick bamboo forests on both banks of the river--to make a torch and catch some fish in order to put the waiting period to profitable use. He was a member of the AFNS Second Platoon and a Yao, and was very tall and big. The youth who had been so absorbed in thought while standing guard on that day not long ago[9] had now become a cadre of high prestige in the area. He took over as guide from Mr. Tu from there on. They arrived in Ban Pai the third night.

The enemy meanwhile discovered that "Communist prisoners had escaped." Province troops had been moved to Ban Pai along with hundreds of militiamen who had been assembled here. All trails were watched. The enemy had strung out strings to detect traces of the escapees. The infrastructure reported that "soldiers from Cho Chu were in pursuit and had almost caught up with the escapees here. The villagers in Ban Pai were being intensely questioned."

The whole group had to stop to find ways to cope with the situation. At the same time, a Southward March squad moving down also found its way blocked. In the face of this difficult and complicated situation, they unanimously decided to "take cover in a slash-and-burn field far away, and patiently wait for the enemy to withdraw to resume their march." Hoang Hai led the brothers to a very distant mountain peak

---

of the Central Military Party Committee, Vice Director of the General Political Department, and a member of the Central Committee of the Workers' Party. (Trans.)

6. Ta Xuan Thu is now a Major General in the DRV People's Army. (Trans.)

7. Le Duc Ton is now in charge of the Standing Committee of the Viet Bac Autonomous Region Party Committee. (Footnote in text.)

8. Hong Hai is now a member of the Fatherland Front in the Viet Bac Autonomous Zone. (Footnote in text.)

9. See Chapter V. (Trans.)

densely covered with vegetation. As a Yao, Hong Hai was used to climbing mountains, but the Kinh comrades were only used to walking on level surfaces, and so this trip was particularly trying for them.

They had to withstand countless hardships and privations--they had to go hungry and thirsty, but thanks to the resolute efforts of the Ban Pai villagers to protect and assist them, the comrades made it safely to the War Zone. (For seven days the enemy failed utterly to find any traces of the group and to obtain information from the people, and so--frustrated--they had no choice but to go back to Dai Tu, Cho Chu and Son Duong.)

At that time, I was staying in Van Minh village, near Van Lang. For almost ten days--since I sent Duc Ton, Hong Hai and Mr. Tu to pick up the brothers--I had not been able to get an untroubled sleep at night, especially when I heard that enemy soldiers in Bac Can, Thai Nguyen and Tuyen Quang had been ordered by Hanoi to "recapture this group of Communist prisoners and bring them to Cho Chu." After I heard that the enemy had withdrawn, I spent every night sitting by the fire, waiting. I longed to hear Le Duc Ton's curt style of speech: "Hey buddy, I've brought the comrades here!"

That night, like the other nights, I was waiting, sitting next to the fire. Suddenly I heard a voice at the foot of the stairs. "We're here, comrades."

It was Duc Ton! Our brothers had arrived. I jumped up and walked toward them. The small house on stilts shook slightly. The light from the fire lit up each beloved face. I saw all twelve comrades were there. I was extremely moved, and I said, my voice shaking with an uncontrollable emotion, "So, you've made it out here! The movement needs you badly, comrades."

The local infrastructure had cooked chicken rice soup to treat the guests. We sat in a circle around the fire, eating the hot soup, talking, confiding in each other.

The next day, the North Vietnam Region Party Committee assigned a number of the comrades to operate in the Quang Trung subregion (still referred to as Subregion A at that time), and the rest to operate in the Nguyen Hue subregion (i.e., Subregion B). Comrades Song Hao, Hien Mai, Ta Xuan Thu, Trung Dinh, Chi, Tung, Mon and Phong were assigned to the Nguyen Hue subregion. Comrade Song Hao was the Party Secretary, in charge of all aspects in the subregion. Duc Ton went with them. He was then in charge of building up the grassroot bases in that area along with comrade Trieu Khanh Phuong.

* * *

We continued to operate around the Hong mountain chain.

After our brothers escaped from jail, the French colonialists sent their soldiers and reactionary henchmen out to arrest and torture people living in the Cho Chu area. They accused the people of "being the accomplices of the Communist prisoners, helping them to escape, and failing to report to the authorities." Lang Coc was caught in the enemy's terrorism, and some people were arrested and killed. The mad and frenzied struggle of the enemy was the same as in any place where the revolutionary movement was developing strongly. The wave of terror spread rapidly to all areas: Cao Bang, Bac Can, and Lang Son.

We split up and merged with the grassroot infrastructure to operate. At the time, the cadres in the War Zone cinstituted a significant force. In addition, the AFNS Third Platoon consisted mostly of comrades who had fought in difficult and complicated situations and had earned a great deal of experience, so what could the enemy do to cope with them? While assigning comrade Trung Dinh[10] to remain in Dai Tu, the North Vietnam Region Party Committee transferred a few brothers to the Kim Long (Tan Trao) area to join comrade Le Duc Ton in expanding the grassroot bases and set up a revolutionary administration. Ta Xuan Thu, a number of brothers and I were transferred to the concentrated armed propaganda unit to propagandize and educate the people and at the same time to organize exhibits to show the people the expansion and strength of the revolutionary movement in the whole country, as well as the ever growing prestige of the Viet Minh.

As early as May 1944, on the basis of the Party Central Committee's policy, the Viet Minh General Headquarters had already issued orders to prepare for the insurrection, and pushed more strongly ahead the expansion of our forces in order to launch an insurrection to seize power.

At the end of May 1944, in the exhilarating atmosphere of implementing the new directive from the Viet Minh General Headquarters, the news that comrade Hoang Van Thu had been executed by the French imperialists in Bach Mai sowed sorrow in the entire War Zone and sharpened the hatred of everyone toward the French and their lackeys. Comrade Hoang Van Thu had sacrificed his life, but the example of his indomitability in the face of the enemy would shine forever for us to emulate and to disregard our own lives to fight for the Party and for the people.

On August 10, 1944, the Party Central Committee issued an appeal calling on everyone to prepare arms and drive the common enemy out of the country. To carry out the Party Central Committee's policy, the AFNS intensified their efforts to push strongly ahead their preparations for the armed insurrection. In the revolutionary base areas, the masses were ready to rise up. However, we were then still in the period of preserving and building up our forces, and getting ready for the launching of the insurrection.

In October 1944, under Japanese fascist pressure, the French fascists launched a large-scale mop-up operation into Vo Nhai. This was the third large-scale terror campaign launched against this region. Full of hatred for the enemy, the AFNS and the revolutionary masses were prepared to fight in that situation. However, instead of tightly coordinating the political struggle with the armed struggle, and using the political struggle as the key action to counter enemy repression and to protect the people, the subregion leadership committee led the people into the forest, launched an armed struggle, proceeded to eliminate a slew of traitors, carried out continuous ambushes, attacked posts, cut off the communications lines of the enemy, etc. This struggle against enemy repression took on the character of an insurrection. The Standing Committee of the Central Committee, on the one hand, upheld the revolutionary spirit of the masses, but on the other criticized the errors and shortcomings of the struggle. The Central Commit-

---

10. Le Trung Dinh was the Deputy Secretary of the Thai-Meo Autonomous Region Party Committee in 1959, and became the Tay Bac Autonomous Region Party Committee Secretary in 1962. (Trans.)

tee quickly dispatched cadres to Vo Nhai to help and overcome the limited and narrow view and the impatience and recklessness [of the sub-region leadership] and in general succeeded in preserving the revolutionary grassroot bases and maintaining the revolutionary forces to await a more favorable opportunity.

(Later, I heard that in the Cao Bang base area, the Cao-Bac-Lang Inter-province Party Committee, since July 1944, had assessed that conditions for the launching of an armed insurrection were ripe. Preparations for the insurrection were feverishly pushed ahead. The Inter-province Party Committee intended to call a final meeting to decide on the date and time of the insurrection. Exactly at that moment, comrade Ho Chi Minh returned from China and ordered them to postpone it in time. He felt that the Cao-Bac-Lang Inter-province Party Committee's policy to launch an insurrection was only based on the local situation, and had failed to take into account the concrete situation in the whole country, and that the Committee had only seen a part, and not the whole, of the situation. He said, "At the present time, the phase of peaceful development of the revolution has passed, but the period for a general insurrection has not yet arrived. If we continue now to operate by political means alone, we won't be able to propel the movement forward. If we launch an armed struggle now, each time the enemy comes the people will have to flee into the forest, and we will run into a lot of difficulties. We must do it in such a way that we can continue to carry out military actions while enabling the people to stay where they are to produce, and while reinforcing our sentinel system and vigilance to prevent the enemy from arresting and harming the people who are active in the movement." Then he proposed a solution: "Our armed forces are at present both small and dispersed. We should assemble the bravest cadres and fighters, and gather the best weapons to create a concentrated unit to operate. We will use military actions to spread the influence of the revolution deep and wide among the masses. Attacks should be carried out with the aim of creating a good political impact, and in this way we will expand our grassroot bases and develop our armed forces. We will set up a Liberation Army." This enlightened assessment of Ho Chi Minh helped Cao-Bac-Lang to avoid huge losses.)

* * *

Winter 1944.

The rifle shots annihilating the Phai Khat and Na Ngan posts reverberated. The province and regular troops coming back from combat spread the rumor among their ranks that "the Communist gentlemen have revolted in Cao Bang and killed the French in the posts, but they let Annamese soldiers go unharmed." The villagers heard this rumor when they went to the market and reported this to the cadres on their return. I immediately thought of the comrades in Cao Bang: Hoang Duc Thac, Pham Van Dong, Hoang Van Hoan, Vu Anh, and many other brothers. I thought most of all about Vo Nguyen Giap. Since our historic meeting in Khuoi Ta, I had not had any news from him during the time when the French imperialists zeroed in on Cao Bang as the center of their terror campaign to attack and destroy the revolution, and at the same time to set up a sort of rear base for them in case they had to retreat [under Japanese attacks].[11] Now, hearing the rifle shots in Cao Bang which

---

11. The Vichy government in France collapsed in July 1944. In Indochina, relations between the Japanese and French administration became very tense, and a Japanese attack on the French forces appeared possible. (Trans.)

were felling the enemy, I guessed that Vo Nguyen Giap "was doing something big." The brothers up there had raised their voices! When I heard their rifle shots, my heart was filled with happiness and jubilance. A few comrades coming down from up north also said that the "Vietnam Propaganda and Liberation Army" had been set up under the instruction of comrade Ho Chi Minh. The ceremony marking the formation of the unit had been held in a forest lying between the two cantons of Tran Hung Dao and Hoang Hoa Tham on December 22, 1944. The unit included both men and women, and even had a Party Chapter. It was rumored that Vo Nguyen Giap, Son Hung and An were in this unit. I suddenly recalled how these beloved comrades had looked. Son Hung and An the previous years had been chosen to go abroad to study; they must have completed their training and now had joined the Vietnam Propaganda and Liberation Army. And Vo Nguyen Giap, he must still remember the places and the settlements he had passed through, such as Ban Pinh, Ban Pai, Bang Bang, and the name Thang Loi (Victory) he had given to Nghia Ta village.[12]

Comrade Ho Chi Minh! Old Mr. Thu Son! The Cominterm Representative! So, this Old Man "who had gone on mission far away until no one knew when" must have returned to Cao Bang. How encouraging! When I was in Pac Bo, I wanted to see him every moment of the day; I wanted to visit him all the time, and if I did not see him, I felt that something was missing, and I thought of him and missed him all the time. If I was absorbed in work, then I did not think of him, but the moment I sat thinking idly, I began to miss him. The situation in the world was changing rapidly, and becoming favorable to the revolution. In addition, the movement in the country was expanding. The Old Man was back in Cao Bang now. With him taking care of the masses, the cadres and the national movement, the Revolution would certainly triumph.

At that moment, I just wished I could grow arms hundreds of miles long so I could stretch them across the deep forests and the high mountains to hug my brothers and comrades in a tight embrace to express this extraordinary happiness and enthusiasm of mine. "When I see Vo Nguyen Giap again, I must remember to ask him to tell me about old Mr. Thu Son's return to the country," I told myself.

* * *

Just as our Party had anticipated, the sharp contradictions between the Japanese and French in Indochina, and the deteriorating situation of the Japanese in the Pacific forced the Japanese fascists to overthrow the French in a coup d'etat to monopolize Indochina for themselves.

In the night of March 9, 1945, the Japanese opened fire on the French and simultaneously attacked them all over Indochina. The French resisted feebly in Hanoi, Lang Son, Hue, and Ha Giang. French civilians were arrested by the Japanese. French troops quickly surrendered, or fell apart, or fled to Southern China. Wherever the residue of French forces fled, they robbed the people and compelled the people to wait on them. Before fleeing, the French in Cao Bang threw grenades into the prison and killed over 100 Vietnamese political prisoners.

---

12. This is the village where Vo Nguyen Giap and Chu Van Tan met in December 1943 to inaugurate the corridor linking the two bases in Cao Bang and Bac Son-Vo Nhai. (Trans.)

At the precise moment when the Japanese attacked and overthrew the French in Hanoi, the plenary conference of the Standing Committee of the Central Committee began in Dinh Bang village (Tu Son district, Bac Ninh province), presided over by comrade Truong Chinh, the Party Secretary General. The conference lasted from March 9 to March 12. The conference analyzed the key factors which had forced the Japanese to overthrow the French and take over Indochina for themselves. The conference assessed that the coup d'etat had created a profound and serious political crisis, and that conditions were rapidly becoming ripe for the launching of the insurrection. It was a "pre-insurrection period" and the task of our Party was to launch a high tide of struggle against the Japanese to save the country, and to lead the entire population to make urgent preparations and proceed toward a general insurrection to seize power nationwide. The conference decided to change all forms of propaganda and motivation, to organize and struggle in a manner appropriate to the pre-insurrection phase, especially to strongly motivate the masses to boldly pour into the streets to demonstrate, break open the imperialists' rice storehouses to solve the problem of famine, in order to "launch a high tide of struggle against the Japanese to save the country; and this will serve as the overture to the general insurrection. This high tide could take the form of illegal activities such as noncooperation, strikes of workers and market vendors, and disturbances, and move on to higher forms, such as demonstration, armed show of force, and guerrilla actions." The conference assessed that launching guerrilla attacks to liberate each region and expand the base areas, keeping up and expanding guerrilla warfare, must be our nation's method of struggle to "take the initiative in driving the Japanese aggressors out of the country."

The Standing Committee of the Central Committee issued the directive that "while the French and Japanese were shooting each other, the action was ours to take."

The coup d'etat of March 9, 1945, quickly brought about the pitiful collapse of the French colonialists' government, but the Japanese fascist militarists did not succeed right away in setting up a smoothly functioning machinery of domination. This situation created objective conditions favorable to the preparations for our people's general insurrection.

In Subregion B, on hearing the news of the Japanese facists' attack on the French, the leadership committee decided to motivate the people to rise up and seize power in the villages and hamlets, and to attack Son Duong district for the first time (13 March). Immediately thereafter, the AFNS attacked Cho Chu and coordinated with the popular uprising to achieve success in Cho Chu (25 March), Dai Tu (29 March), Yen Son (1 April), and Yen Binh (18 May). In Cho Chu, the AFNS liberated about 30 revolutionary cadres jailed there. At the same time, the AFNS disarmed the remnants of the French army fleeing through Thai Nguyen and Tuyen Quang to cross into China. The most notable achievements were the ambushes that the AFNS carried out against Japanese troops in Deo Khe, in the course of which a large amount of weapons and other military equipment and materiel were seized.

The revolutionary fervor of the masses in Subregion B rose very high. National Salvation associations and self-defense units developed rapidly and were consolidated. Subregion B had a favorable terrain and could communicate easily with the Central Committee's Standing Committee stationed near Hanoi.

In Subregion A, the AFNS went on the attack and established revolutionary government in many areas in Thai Nguyen and Lang Son provinces, such as: La Hien, i.e., the Vo Nhai district seat (19 March), Trang Xa (23 March), Dinh Ca (10 April), Mo Ga (15 April), Vu Le (16 April), Nam Nhi (17 April), Bac Son (18 April), Binh Gia (29 April), and Bang Mac (2 May). The AFNS coordinated with the Vietnam Liberation and Propaganda Army unit advancing down from Cao Bang to liberate Trang Dinh, Diem He and Thoat Lang. The AFNS also sent a section to coordinate with the combat self-defense units of Bac Giang to attack Yen The for the first time (1 April), Huu Lung (15 April), Bo Ha (18 April), Mo Sat (19 April), Luc Ngan (30 May), and Pho Yen (3 June). The District Chiefs of Huu Lung and Luc Ngan surrendered to the Viet Minh. In many areas, the AFNS broke into paddy depots and distributed the paddy to the people.

Our momentum was unstoppable. Viet Minh committees were set up in many districts, from the banks of the Lo River to Route 3, and southward almost to the Vinh Yen province capital. In the Le Loi War Zone, the Cao-Bac-Lang Inter-province Standing Committee met on March 10, 1945, and decided to:

(1) Immediately overthrow the regime of French domination in the countryside, and set up--depending on the situation in each area--popular government at the village, district, prefect or province level.

(2) Assign cadres from the Propaganda Unit to local armed units to organize Liberation Army units and prepare for direct attacks on the Japanese.

(3) With regard to French troops, the policy was not to attack them in their retreat; on the contrary, resolute efforts would be made to appeal to them to collaborate with us to organize a resistance against the Japanese.

To carry out this policy, the Vietnam Propaganda and Liberation Army split up into many sections, and spread out to various areas to lead the popular uprising. One section went to fight in Bao Lac (Cao Bang province) and then advanced toward That Khe and Binh Gia (Lang Son province), and coordinated their action with the AFNS. Another section moved toward the Vietnam-China border to attack the Soc Giang post and liberate Ha Quang district. After that, they continued their advance toward Bac Quang (Ha Giang province). The main body of this army, led by Vo Nguyen Giap, advanced toward Ngan Son district, surrounded the Ngan Son post and called on the enemy to come out and surrender. The French post commander came out with this entire contingent to surrender to the Viet Minh. Afterward, they moved to liberate Cho Ra, Phu Thong district, Cho Don-Na Ri (Bac Can province) and Chiem Hoa (Tuyen Quang province). Wherever they went the Vietnam Propaganda and Liberation Army was widely acclaimed by the masses carrying red flags with the yellow star and primitive weapons, and they cooperated with the people to disarm the militia, seize the seals and certificates of the local officials, punish the traitors, and set up a revolutionary government. In each and every area, the Vietnam Propaganda and Liberation Army paid special attention to the development and consolidation of the various National Salvation associations, and took special care to expand the combat self-defense and the guerrilla units to protect the newly established popular government.

* * *

I will never forget that memorable last day of March 1945.

A section of the Vietnam Propaganda and Liberation Army led by brother Vo Nguyen Giap arrived in Cho Chu.

More than a year before, Vo Nguyen Giap and I had met on a high mountain peak, in a small Meo settlement, and in a situation in which we had to keep our presence secret.

This time, in this new situation of surging power and strength, we again met, on the soil of newly liberated Cho Chu, and this time around we were accompanied not just by a handful of cadres, but our meeting was also the meeting of two armies. What happiness it was for me to meet Vo Nguyen Giap again in broad daylight, right in the middle of a bustling and crowded market. There were so many things we wanted to tell each other!

Who could have guessed that what I had wished for at the end of last winter would come to pass within three months. So, the Vietnam Propaganda and Liberation Army and the AFNS had met. And the two comrades who had met in the Lung Hoang conference and became attached to each other since then, and who had been concerned about each other during the enemy wave of terrorism, found themselves face to face again, each man now stronger and more enthusiastic than before. We clasped hands tightly, laughed happily, and looked at each other with eyes bright with joy.

At the end of the year before, I had vaguely heard that the Vietnam Propaganda and Liberation Army had been set up. Now, meeting Vo Nguyen Giap in Cho Chu, I finally found out about the concrete instructions of comrade Ho Chi Minh on December 22, 1944, and about the expansion of this army and its combat activities during the past few months.

I was extremely happy. Happy because I met Vo Nguyen Giap again. Happy because the movement in Bac Son, in Cao Bang, and in the whole country was developing rapidly. Happy about the expansion and strength of the Vietnam Propaganda and Liberation Army and of the Army for National Salvation. I was confident that the Vietnam Propaganda and Liberation Army would be able to achieve what Uncle Ho had said: "... this army is the beginning of our Liberation Army; it will be able to move from North to South and go everywhere in our country."

Comrade Ho Chi Minh's instructions concerning the formation of the Vietnam Propaganda and Liberation Army made me think about the situation and the mission of the Army for National Salvation in the past and from now onward. The principle that armed propaganda and political activities were more important than military activities, that propaganda was more important than combat, that military operations would be used to protect, consolidate and expand our political base, and at the same time to consolidate and expand armed units and paramilitary units, not only applied to the Vietnam Propaganda and Liberation Army but also lit the way for the Army for National Salvation in all its activities.

Remembering that comrade Le Quang Ba had said, "The Big Leader had gone on mission far away, and no one knew when he would come back," I asked Vo Nguyen about this. He nodded his head and laughed happily, but we were then standing in a crowded market and it would not be convenient for him to talk. So, he promised to tell me many stories about Uncle Ho since his return to Cao Bang on another occasion.

On a grassy field in Tong Quang, we held a meeting between the two armies to hear the news about the situation in the world and in the country, and also to assess the situation and discuss the opportunity to launch an uprising. We sat in a circle. Attending the meeting were Vo Nguyen Giap, Pham Van Dong, Song Hao, Khang (an alias adopted by Hoang Van Thai at that time), Trung Dinh and myself. The women attending the meeting included Thanh, Can, Loan and Ngoc. Vo Nguyen Giap presided over this meeting, and proposed that I speak first. The other brothers also spoke, focusing on the situation in the world and the opportunity to launch an uprising. Afterward, the two armies linked forces and together carried out an attack on the Japanese at Kilometer 31 on the road to Bac Can, and after that they split to carry out civilian proselytizing activities.

While on mission, I received a letter convoking a meeting of the Standing Committee of the Party Central Committee. The Standing Committee called a North Vietnam Region Revolutionary Military Conference in Hiep Hoa (Bac Giang province), presided over by comrade Truong Chinh, the Party Secretary General. The conference lasted six days, from April 15th to 20th, 1945. This was the first important military conference of our Party.

Brother Truong Chinh directed this conference.

Vo Nguyen Giap reported on the situation of the movement in Cao Bang-Bac Can, and on the activities of the Vietnam Propaganda and Liberation Army there. I reported on the situation of the movement and the activities of the Army for National Salvation in Thai Nguyen-Tuyen Quang. This conference gave me an overall view of the situation everywhere in the country. It was only then that I understood that a high tide of anti-Japanese resistance was rising forcefully from North to South. Many armed demonstrations, each 2,000-3,000 strong, had moved to attack and seize rice depots in the plantations of French reactionaries and depots belonging to the Japanese to distribute rice to the poor people in Bac Ninh, Bac Giang, Ninh Binh, Thai Nguyen provinces, etc. Many areas in the midlands had set up National Minorities' Liberation Committees. Political prisoners in Nghia Lo (Yen Bai) rose up and smashed the jail. In addition to the armed forces of the Party in Viet Bac, there were many self-defense and combat self-defense units in the midlands, in the delta, and even in the big cities. In Quang Ngai province, guerrillas also emerged; this was the guerrilla unit of Ba To. In the South, the Viet Minh were active in My Tho and in the Lower Mekong Delta region (Hau Giang).

The conference pointed out the weaknesses and strengths of the anti-Japanese resistance for the national salvation of the Indochinese people. The conference affirmed: "the situation had placed the military task above all other important and urgent tasks at this juncture. Resolute efforts must be made to expand guerrilla warfare, build up the base areas to resist the Japanese, in order to make preparations for the General Uprising and seize this opportunity in time." With regard to this military task, we all felt that it was necessary to define clearly and assign specific tasks to each War Zone; to clear communication and liaison corridors linking up the War Zones of North, Central and South Vietnam; to build up base areas to resist the Japanese; unify, consolidate and expand the various armed forces; unify military command; organize special armed units, etc. In accordance with the Resolution of April 1945, the Vietnam Propaganda and Liberation Army and the Army for National Salvation were merged. The conference designated a North Vietnam Revolutionary Military Committee (Ủy Ban Quân Sự Cách Mạng Bắc Kỳ) to command the War Zones of North Indochina (the Le Loi, Hoang Hoa Tham, Quang Trung and Tran Hung Dao War Zones), and at the same time this committee also had the task of providing military assistance to the entire country. The Central Committee appointed comrades Vo Nguyen Giap, Van Tien Dung, Le Thanh Nghi,[13] Trang Dang Ninh, and Chu Van Tan to this committee. With regard to the question of cadres, a number of outstanding members of the various armed forces would be selected and trained to become unit commanders and political officers; anti-Japanese military and political training schools would be set up; people of talent would be recruited; students would be recruited to go to the War Zones for military training; and the cadres would be militarized.

A new atmosphere full of enthusiasm and confidence pervaded everywhere. There were so many things to do. We had the impression that time was fleeing too rapidly.

* * *

After attending the North Vietnam Region Revolutionary Military Conference, Vo Nguyen Giap returned to Cho Chu (Dinh Hoa) exactly on the International Labor Day of May 1st. Carrying out the Resolution of April 1945, he convened a conference in Dinh Bien Thuong to officially announce the merger of all armed forces, and clarify the brothers' ideological understanding concerning their immediate and long-term tasks. Besides Vo Nguyen Giap, the other key cadres included comrades Hien Mai, Mon and Khanh Phuong.

After that, we heard the news that Uncle Ho was coming down from Cao Bang to the lowlands, and Vo Nguyen Giap galloped off on a horse toward Deo Re Pass to welcome him.

We continued to operate in the Cho Chu area. A few days later, a letter arrived from Vo Nguyen Giap saying, "Make preparations to welcome the Old Man." Brother Quang Trung and we moved our troops to Deo So and deployed them to protect the route Uncle Ho would take and to welcome him. Later on, however, another letter of Giap arrived reporting that "Uncle Ho had taken the route further inland. He would go to Son Duong." We turned around and went back, passing Deo Re Pass, going down to Dinh Hoa, into Thanh Dieu and Luc Ra, and then on to Hong Thai to welcome Uncle Ho.

He stayed for a few days with a grassroot base family in Kim Long settlement (Tan Trao) and then moved to a small hut built on a hill

---

13. Le Thanh Nghi was born in 1911. He worked as an electrician in Hong Quang district from 1927 to 1930, and carried out revolutionary activities among the miners. In 1929, he joined the Thanh Nien Party, and in 1930 the Indochinese Communist Party. He was in prison from 1930 to 1936. During the Popular Front period, he worked to set up trade unions, working people's associations and Party cells. He was in prison again from 1940 to 1945. He escaped from jail in early 1945. From 1946 to 1951 he was Secretary of the Party Bureau, Chairman of the Administrative and Resistance Committee and Political Commissar of the Vietnam People's Army for the Third Zone. He has been a member of the Politburo since 1956. In 1955, he became the Minister of Industry. He is now a Vice-Premier of the DRV. (Trans.)

slope. At this time, comrade Nguyen Luong Bang[14] coming from the delta, and comrade Hoang Quoc Viet recently returned from abroad also came to Tan Trao.

Uncle Ho chose Tan Trao as his living and working headquarters to guide the movement in the entire country and to make preparations for the National Congress.

After listening to the reports on the general situation in the country and on the North Vietnam Region Revolutionary Military Conference, he issued the following instructions. Since the liberated area in the North Vietnam Region included almost all the provinces of Cao Bang, Bac Can, Lang Son, Ha Giang, Tuyen Quang and Thai Nguyen, and a number of adjacent areas in the provinces of Bac Giang, Phu Tho, Yen Bai and Vinh Yen, and since these areas were all linked together, a large revolutionary base should be set up and designated as the Liberated Zone (Tan Trao was chosen as the capital of the Liberated Zone). It had been correct to unify all the armed forces and place them under the direct command of the Central Committee. This army should be called the "Liberation Army" because the term "liberation" was both simple and easy to understand, precise and penetrating--it denoted clearly the goal of fighting the French, driving out the Japanese, liberating the country, and aspiring for national independence.

To carry out these instructions, on June 4, 1945, the Viet Minh General Headquarters convoked a conference to officially announce the formation of the Liberated Zone, which was put under the leadership of the Provisional Command Committee, and which should be firmly consolidated from the political, military, economic and cultural points of view to become the springboard for the March Southward and the liberation of the whole country.

At that time, the concrete situation in the War Zones and the areas within the Liberated Zone was very urgent. Comrade Vo Nguyen Giap was designated as the Permanent Officer of this Committee to maintain liaison with the Central Committee in the delta and also with comrades Le Thanh Nghi and Tran Dang Ninh in Bac Giang on the one hand, and to maintain liaison with the provinces of Cao Bang and Bac Son on the other hand.

In the Liberated Zone, the People's Revolutionary Committees elected by the masses were carrying out the ten big programs. These were:

(1) Liquidating the Japanese forces, eliminating traitors and punishing criminals.

---

14. Nguyen Luong Bang was born in 1905 in Thanh Mien district, Hai Duong province. He joined the revolution in the 1920's, and was active in Canton, Shanghai, Haiphong, Hanoi and Saigon. He was arrested by the French in Shanghai at the end of 1930 and deported to Haiphong. He was sentenced to life banishment and jailed in Hanoi. He escaped, but was arrested again and was imprisoned in Son La. He escaped in 1943, and remained on the outskirts of Hanoi to carry out revolutionary activities along with Truong Chinh. He became the Party Treasurer in 1944. After liberation he became the DRV Ambassador to Moscow in 1952, Director General of the Central Inspectorate in 1957. He is now the Vice President of the DRV. (For a more detailed account of Nguyen Luong Bang's early biography, see his article in *A Heroic People, Memoirs from the Revolution* [Hanoi: Foreign Languages Publishing House, 1965].) (Trans.)

(2) Seizing the properties of the traitors and of the lackeys of the foreigners, and--depending in each situation--using them as the common property of the people or distributing them to the poor.

(3) Instituting universal suffrage and other free and democratic rights.

(4) Arming the masses, motivating the people to support the guerrillas and join the Liberation Army to resist the Japanese.

(5) Organizing the clearing of land, encouraging production, and creating a self-sufficient economy for the Liberated Zone.

(6) Restricting the number of work days, and carrying out social security laws and the relief of people afflicted by calamities.

(7) Redistributing communal ricefields, reducing land rents and interest rates, and postponing the repayment of debts.

(8) Abolishing taxes and labor conscription, and making plans for a light and unique progressive taxation.

(9) Fighting against illiteracy, and organizing popular military and political training classes for the masses.

(10) Equality among all ethnic groups, and equal rights for men and women.

A new Vietnam was born. A section of North Vietnam was placed under the revolutionary government. Over one million people began to enjoy a new life brought by the Revolution.

With the merging of all armed forces, the Liberation Army became fairly large, and was split up into detachments. Almost all the former members of the Vietnam Propaganda and Liberation Army and of the Army for National Salvation became command cadres.

The problem of forming and training cadres became very urgent. At the beginning of July 1945, in accordance with the Resolution of the North Vietnam Region Military Conference, a Resist-Japan Military Academy was set up under the direction of Hoang Van Thai, in order to train platoon leaders and platoon political officers. The school was set up in Khuoi Kich, on the bank of a stream, where the Yao woman had witnessed the ceremony establishing the AFNS Third Platoon. The students were selected from the ranks of the Liberation Army and the youths from the delta who had been introduced by the National Salvation Associations.

The popular government in the Liberated Zone was reorganized by elections, with universal suffrage. Each village had a National Salvation Council Hall where the people frequently came to attend meetings, to listen to reports on the situation, and to discuss affairs of public interest.

* * *

Right after learning of the complete disintegration of the Japanese aggressors and of their surrender to the Soviet Union and to the Allies, on August 12, 1945, the Provisional Command Committee of the

Liberated Zone issued the order for a general uprising to the Liberation Army, to the self-defense units, to the People's Revolutionary Committees and to the entire population in the region.

On August 13, 1945, the National Party Congress opened in Tan Trao. Attending the Congress were representatives of Party Headquarters in all three regions of Vietnam--North, Central, and South--and also a number of representatives operating abroad.

In this extremely urgent situation, the Congress worked for three days. In order to provide correct leadership to ensure the success of the general insurrection, the Congress set forth three principles:

(1) *Concentration*: concentration of our forces on major tasks.

(2) *Unification*: unification of all military and political means, and unification of leadership and command.

(3) *Timely action*: acting in a timely manner, and not losing any opportunity.

The Congress emphasized that "we must concentrate our forces in critical areas to attack" and "we must attack and immediately seize the areas where we were sure of success, whether urban areas or the countryside."

Right in the night of August 13, 1945, the Insurrection Committee, set up by the Viet Minh General Headquarters, issued its Military Order No. 1, ordering the launching of the General Insurrection.

Right after the National Congress broke up, a People's National Congress also convened in Tan Trao on August 16th. This Congress chose the national flag and national anthem, and designated the Vietnam National Liberation Committee, that is to say the Provisional Government, with comrade Ho Chi Minh as President.

Implementing the order of the Liberated Zone's Provisional Command Committee issued on August 12th, and of the Insurrection Committee, units of the Liberation Army captured one after another the Japanese posts still remaining in the provinces of Cao Bang, Bac Can, Thai Nguyen, Yen Bai, etc., and then advanced to liberate the towns and cities.

On August 16th, a unit of the Liberation Army under the command of comrade Vo Nguyen Giap coming from Tan Trao, advanced and attacked the Thai Nguyen province capital to open the route to Hanoi.

On August 17th, the Liberation Army attacked the Tuyen Quang province town. The Japanese fascists returned the fire, but in the face of the overwhelming force of the revolution, they had to offer to negotiate, and on August 21st, the Viet Minh seized power in the province.

The Liberation Army was advancing in the surging revolutionary storm. Every Communist Party member, every Viet Minh fighter, and the population in the whole country showed their determination and their firm spirits in heroically fighting for the cause of national liberation, in accordance with President Ho's instructions:

> At this moment, the favorable opportunity has arrived. No matter
> what the sacrifices, even if the entire Annamite Chain has to go up
> in flames, we must maintain our determination in order to win back
> our national independence.

* * *

Already 24 years have passed since those days. Viet Bac--the cradle of the Party's first popular forces--has gone through many changes. I still feel very moved whenever I recall the months and years I spent living in the Khuoi Noi clearing, in the Khuon Manh forest, on the bank of the Khuoi Kich stream--the places which witnessed the formation ceremonies of the Army for National Salvation First, Second and Third Platoons. The images of the beloved dead comrades are still engraved in my heart: brothers Hoang Van Thu, Tran Dang Ninh, Phung Chi Kien and Luong Van Chi. They were the first leaders and commanders of the Army for National Salvation; they were the men who were deeply loved and protected by the Viet Bac ethnic minorities, and who were feared by the enemy.

General Chu Van Tan in a discussion with Mr. Chuyen, a Professor from Hanoi, and George Kahin, outside of a cave in the Vu Nhai area of Thai Nguyen province, September 27, 1972.

As the offshoot of the Bac Son uprising, the evolution of the Army for National Salvation was closely linked to the movement in Bac Son. The AFNS cadres and fighters were the men and woman of the ethnic minorities who shared the fate of an oppressed Vietnam, but who--reached by the light of the Party, educated and trained, organized and nurtured--took up arms and marched forward toward the revolutionary goals of the Party.

Brought to life and nurtured by the Party, through their activities to implement the revolutionary task in the Liberated Zone, the AFNS worked with devotion and accepted sacrifices, showed their utmost loyalty to the Party, and penetrated deep into the masses of the ethnic minorities.

The AFNS accomplished their historic mission. In each of their phases of operation, they scored specific achievements. The reason for this was that the AFNS received extremely lucid leadership from the Party Central Committee and relied on the people of the ethnic minorities for support.

Right after its formation, the AFNS received the special attention and care of the Party Central Committee in all fields. The Party leadership was the factor determining the successful evolution of the AFNS. With the resolutions and instructions of the Party lighting the way, the AFNS overcame innumerable difficulties, and advanced step by step. It was thanks to the Party leadership that the AFNS, right from the start and forever afterward, acquired, firmly maintained and developed the good political quality of a revolutionary army--an armed force belonging to the people and serving the people.

Protected by the ethnic nationalities, firmly planted on the soil and the political grassroot base that had brought it to life, the AFNS effectively became a force that any cunning and savage enemy would have feared and respected.

Each success of the AFNS, from small ones to big ones, sprang from the people and was achieved with the help of the people. To carry out the instructions of the Party, the AFNS combined more and more tightly the task of motivating the masses and building up the political grassroot bases with the task of consolidating the armed forces and fighting.

The maturing of the AFNS was also closely linked to the development of various revolutionary armed forces in the whole country, with the revolutionary movement and with the armed force in the War Zone of Cao Bang, and in particular with the Vietnam Propaganda and Liberation Army.

The resolution of the Lung Hoang conference opened up a new era in the development of the AFNS. After June 1945 the AFNS merged with the Vietnam Propaganda and Liberation Army to become the Vietnam Liberation Army. The activities of the Vietnam Liberation Army spread beyond the confines of the Viet Bac War Zone, to implement correctly the instruction of President Ho Chi Minh: ". . . to move from North to South, all over our country."

Under the leadership of the Party and President Ho Chi Minh, our people and our people's armed forces advanced from one victory to another bigger victory, and helped the August Revolution to succeed. Looking at the red flags with the five-cornered yellow star now fluttering proudly everywhere, from the mountains to the delta, I cannot help but remember with emotion the AFNS comrades and the people who had sacrificed their lives for the country. Even though they cannot see now with their own eyes the imposing and awe-inspiring position of Vietnam today on the China Seas, the bulwark against imperialism headed by the American imperialist aggressors who are being defeated, they did perceive in those days when they had in their hands only primitive weapons, muskets and spears, the bright future of their country and fight without a thought to their own survival.

Whenever I recount these past events, I always remember these comrades, and I hope I have described [adequately] on their behalf a few of the phases of struggle in order to help the youths of today understand more about the early beginnings of our army.

I do not have the ambition to mention here the lessons taught by the Army for National Salvation or to draw experiences [from their activities] because this could constitute the substance of another book. I am only presenting here some of my own deep and unforgettable memories.

There are many things that the long passage of time has made me forget, and so there might be many omissions. Besides, these are only the main events of which I was personally aware. As to the many things that the AFNS comrades did while they were dispersed, I did not know them all. If there are any errors or omissions, I hope other comrades will supplement this book with their knowledge.

                                                      Fall 1969
                                                      Recorded by Ngoc Tu

CORNELL UNIVERSITY SOUTHEAST ASIA PROGRAM

I. SOUTHEAST ASIA PROGRAM DATA PAPERS,
Including Cornell Thailand Project Interim
Reports Series and Linguistics Series

II. STUDY AND TEACHING MATERIALS,
Thai Cultural Readers, Indonesian Lessons,
Thailand Map Series and 16 mm Rental Film

III. CORNELL MODERN INDONESIA PROJECT PAPERS,
Bibliography Series, Interim Reports,
Translations and Monographs

CORNELL UNIVERSITY SOUTHEAST ASIA PROGRAM

IN PRINT

I. SOUTHEAST ASIA PROGRAM DATA PAPERS -- 120 Uris Hall, Cornell University, Ithaca, New York 14850

Number 18 CONCEPTIONS OF STATE AND KINGSHIP IN SOUTHEAST ASIA, by Robert Heine-Geldern, 1956. (Fourth Printing 1972) 14 pages. $2.00.

Number 30 A SIMPLE ONE, The Story of a Siamese Girlhood, by Prajuab Tirabutana. 1958. (Second Printing 1967) 40 pages. $2.00.

Number 46 AN EXPERIMENT IN WARTIME INTERCULTURAL RELATIONS: PHILIPPINE STUDENTS IN JAPAN, 1943-1945, by Grant K. Goodman. 1962. 34 pages. $2.00.

Number 47 A BIBLIOGRAPHY OF NORTH VIETNAMESE PUBLICATIONS IN THE CORNELL UNIVERSITY LIBRARY, by Jane Godfrey Keyes. 1962. 116 pages. $3.00.

Number 49 THE TEXTILE INDUSTRY -- A CASE STUDY OF INDUSTRIAL DEVELOPMENT IN THE PHILIPPINES, by Laurence David Stifel. 1963. 199 pages. $3.00.

Number 51 MATERNITY AND ITS RITUALS IN BANG CHAN, THAILAND, by Jane Richardson Hanks. Cornell Thailand Project, Interim Reports Series: Number Six. 1963. (Second Printing 1968) 116 pages. $2.50.

Number 54 CATALOGUE OF THAI LANGUAGE HOLDINGS IN THE CORNELL UNIVERSITY LIBRARIES THROUGH 1964, compiled by Frances A. Bernath, Thai Cataloguer. 1964. 236 pages. $3.00.

Number 55 STRATEGIC HAMLETS IN SOUTH VIET-NAM, A SURVEY AND A COMPARISON, by Milton E. Osborne. 1965. (Second Printing 1968) 66 pages. $2.50.

Number 57 THE SHAN STATES AND THE BRITISH ANNEXATION, by Sao Saimong Mangrai. 1965. (Second Printing 1969) 204 pages. $4.00.

Number 60 VIETNAM'S UNHELD ELECTIONS: The Failure to Carry Out the 1956 Reunification Elections and the Effect on Hanoi's Present Outlook, by Franklin B. Weinstein. 1966. 65 pages. $2.00.

Number 61 RAJAH'S SERVANT, by A. B. Ward. 1966. 204 pages. (Second Printing 1969) $2.50.

Number 62 CHECKLIST OF HOLDINGS ON BORNEO IN THE CORNELL UNIVERSITY LIBRARY, compiled by Michael B. Leigh. 1966. 62 pages. $2.00.

Number 64 MILITARY OPERATIONS IN BURMA, 1890-1892: Letters from Lt. J. K. Watson, K.R.R.C., edited by B. R. Pearn. February 1967. 72 pages. $2.00.

Number 65 ISAN: REGIONALISM IN NORTHEASTERN THAILAND, by Charles F. Keyes, Cornell Thailand Project, Interim Reports Series: Number Ten. March 1967 (Second Printing 1969) 97 pages. $2.00.

Number 67 ACCOUNT OF A TRIP TO THE COUNTRIES OF SOUTHEAST ASIA FOR THE LIBRARY OF CONGRESS, AUGUST-DECEMBER 1965, by Cecil Hobbs. June 1967. 92 pages. $2.00.

Number 68 THE BARITO ISOLECTS OF BORNEO: A CLASSIFICATION BASED ON COMPARATIVE RECONSTRUCTION AND LEXICOSTATISTICS, by Alfred Hudson. Linguistics Series I. 1967. 112 pages. $2.00.

Number 69 YAO-ENGLISH DICTIONARY, compiled by Sylvia J. Lombard and edited by Herbert C. Purnell, Jr., Linguistic Series II. March 1968. 363 pages. $3.50.

Number 70 AKHA-ENGLISH DICTIONARY, compiled by Paul Lewis. Linguistic Series III. June 1968. 363 pages. $3.50.

Number 71 AMERICAN DOCTORAL DISSERTATIONS ON ASIA, 1933 -- June 1966, INCLUDING APPENDIX OF MASTER'S THESES AT CORNELL UNIVERSITY 1933 -- June 1968, by Curtis W. Stucki. October 1968. 304 pages. (Second Printing 1970) $4.00.

CORNELL UNIVERSITY SOUTHEAST ASIA PROGRAM

IN PRINT (cont'd)

Number 72 EXCAVATIONS OF THE PREHISTORIC IRON INDUSTRY IN WEST BORNEO, Vol. I, RAW MATERIALS AND INDUSTRIAL WASTE, Vol. II, ASSOCIATED ANTIFACTS AND IDEAS, by Tom Harrisson and Stanley J. O'Connor. April 1969. 417 pages. $5.00 each set.

Number 73 THE SEPARATION OF SINGAPORE FROM MALAYSIA, by Nancy McHenry Fletcher. July 1969. (Second Printing 1971) 98 pages. $2.50.

Number 74 THE ORGANIZATION OF THAI SOCIETY IN THE EARLY BANGKOK PERIOD, 1782-1873, by Akin Rabibhadana. Cornell Thailand Project, Interim Reports Series: Number Twelve. July 1969. (Second Printing 1970) 245 pages. $3.00.

Number 75 WHITE MEO-ENGLISH DICTIONARY, compiled by Ernest E. Heimbach, Linguistics Series IV, August 1969. 497 pages. $5.00 each.

Number 77 GOLD AND MEGALITHIC ACTIVITY IN PREHISTORIC AND RECENT WEST BORNEO, by Tom Harrisson and Stanley J. O'Connor. 331 pages. $4.00. 1970.

Number 78 THE NEW YEAR CEREMONY AT BASAK (SOUTH LAOS), by Charles Archaimbault, with an Afterword by Prince Boun Oum (Abridged Translation, by Simone B. Boas). 137 pages. January 1971. $4.00.

Number 79 CHINESE-THAI DIFFERENTIAL ASSIMILATION IN BANGKOK: AN EXPLORATORY STUDY, by Boonsanong Punyodyana. Cornell Thailand Project, Interim Reports Series: Number Thirteen. March 1971. 137 pages. $4.00.

Number 81 THAI TITLES AND RANKS, INCLUDING A TRANSLATION OF TRADITIONS OF ROYAL LINEAGE IN SIAM BY KING CHULALONGKORN, by Robert B. Jones. June 1971. 147 pages. $3.50.

Number 82 MAGINDANAO, 1860-1888: THE CAREER OF DATO UTO BUAYAN, by Reynaoldo C. Ileto. October 1971. 80 pages. $3.50.

Number 83 A BIBLIOGRAPHY OF PHILIPPINE LINGUISTICS AND MINOR LANGUAGES, with Annotations and Indices based on Works in the Library of Cornell University, by Jack H. Ward. Linguistics Series V. 557 pages. $6.50.

Number 84 A CHECKLIST OF THE VIETNAMESE HOLDINGS OF THE WASON COLLECTION, CORNELL UNIVERSITY LIBRARIES, AS OF JUNE 1971. Compiled by Giok Po Oey, Southeast Asia Librarian. December 1971. 337 pages. $6.50.

Number 85 SOUTHEAST ASIA FIELD TRIP FOR THE LIBRARY OF CONGRESS, 1970-71, by Cecil Hobbs. February 1971. 94 pages. $3.50.

Number 86 THE POLITICAL LEGACY OF AUNG SAN, compiled by and with an introductory essay, by Josef Silverstein. June 1972. 113 pages. $4.00.

Number 87 A DICTIONARY OF CEBUANO VISAYAN, Vols. I & II, by John U. Wolff. October 1972. Linguistics Series VI. 1200 pages. $8.00.

Number 88 MIAO AND YAO LINGUISTIC STUDIES, Selected Articles in Chinese, Translated by Chang Yu-hung and Chu Kwo-ray. Edited by Herbert C. Purnell, Jr., Linguistics Series VII. November 1972. 282 pages. $4.00.

Number 89 A GUIDE TO INDONESIAN SERIALS (1945-1970) IN THE CORNELL UNIVERSITY LIBRARY, compiled by Yvonne Thung and John M. Echols. January 1973. 226 pages. $7.00.

Number 90 BIBLIOGRAPHY OF VIETNAMESE LITERATURE IN THE WASON COLLECTION AT CORNELL UNIVERSITY, by Marion W. Ross. May 1973. 178 pages. $4.50.

Number 91 SELECTED SHORT STORIES OF THEIN PE MYING, Translated, with Introduction and Commentary, by Patricia M. Milne. June 1973. 105 pages. $4.00.

Number 92 FEASTING AND SOCIAL OSCILLATION: A Working Paper on Religion and Society in Upland Southeast Asia, by A. Thomas Kirsch. 1973. 67 pages. $3.00.

Number 93 FOREIGN AND DOMESTIC CONSEQUENCES OF THE KMT INTERVENTION IN BURMA, by Robert H. Taylor. 1973. 86 pages. $3.50.

CORNELL UNIVERSITY SOUTHEAST ASIA PROGRAM

IN PRINT (cont'd)

Number 94 THE PEASANT QUESTION (1937-1938), by Truong Chinh and Vo Nguyen Giap, translation and introduction by Christine Pelzer White. 1974. 102 pages. $4.00.

Number 95 ORIGINS OF THE PHILIPPINE REPUBLIC, Extracts from the Diaries and Records of Francis Burton Harrison, edited and annotated by Michael P. Onorato. June 1974. 258 pages. $6.50.

Number 96 SIAM'S POLITICAL FUTURE: DOCUMENTS FROM THE END OF THE ABSOLUTE MONARCHY, compiled and edited with introductions by Benjamin A. Batson. 1974. 102 pp. $4.00.

II. STUDY AND TEACHING MATERIALS - Obtainable from Southeast Asia Program, 120 Uris Hall, Cornell University, Ithaca, New York 14850

THAI CULTURAL READER, Book I, by Robert B. Jones, Ruchira C. Mendiones and Craig J. Reynolds. 1970. 517 pages. $7.00.

THAI CULTURAL READER, Book II, by Robert B. Jones and Ruchira C. Mendiones. 1969. 791 pages. $8.25.

INTRODUCTION TO THAI LITERATURE, by Robert B. Jones and Ruchira C. Mendiones. 1970. 563 pages. $7.00.

BEGINNING INDONESIAN, Part One and Part Two, by John U. Wolff. 1972. 1,124 pages. $15.00 per set. (Part One $8.50; Part Two $8.50) Tapes are available at extra cost.

Maps

Central Thailand. 7 x 10 inches; 34 km to 1 inch. Price $.25 each; $1.00 set of five.

A. 1. Jangwat Outline Map. 1955.
   2. By Amphoe. 1947.
   3. Population Density by Amphoe. 1947.
   4. Proportion of Chinese by Amphoe. 1947.
   5. Concentration of Chinese by Amphoe. 1947.

Thailand. 13 x 22 inches; scale: 50 miles to 1 inch, except B-10 as noted. Price $.25 each; $1.00 set of six.

B. 6. By Amphoe. 1947.
   7. Population Density by Amphoe. 1947.
   8. Fertility Ratios by Amphoe. 1947.
   9. Concentration of Chinese by Amphoe. 1947.
   10. Untitled (Amphoe Outline Map). 16 x 44 inches, in two parts, each 16 x 22 inches; scale: 27 miles to 1 inch.
   11. Jangwat Outline Map. 1955.

Ethnic Settlements. Prepared by Lauriston Sharp, L. M. Hanks, William Wohnus, and K. W. Wong, Cornell Thailand Project, 1965. 27 x 35 inches; scale: 1:10,000. Price $1.00 each.

1. Ethnic Settlements, June 1, 1964, Chiengrai Province (North of the Mae Kok River).
2. Ethnic Settlements, June 1, 1964, Chiengrai Province (North of the Mae Kok River)-Akha.
3. Ethnic Settlements, June 1, 1964, Chiengrai Province (North of the Mae Kok River)-Lahu.
4. Ethnic Settlements, June 1, 1964, Chiengrai Province (North of the Mae Kok River)-Lisu.
5. Ethnic Settlements, June 1, 1964, Chiengrai Province (North of the Mae Kok River)-Yao.

Films Rental Only. $15.00 per film.

BUA: A BUDDHIST ORDINATION IN BANG CHAN, THAILAND. 1954. One reel (400 feet), 16 mm. silent film, in color.

CORNELL UNIVERSITY SOUTHEAST ASIA PROGRAM

<u>Films</u> (cont'd)

DAWADUNGS: A DANCE OF THE SECOND HEAVEN. A Thai Classical Dance Performed by Miss Yibbhan Xoomsai. 1956. One reel (400 feet) 16 mm. sound film, in color.

OUT OF PRINT

SOUTHEAST ASIA PROGRAM DATA PAPERS:

Number 1   REPORT ON THE CHINESE IN SOUTHEAST ASIA, DECEMBER 1950, by G. William Skinner. 1951. 91 pages.

Number 2   A CENTRAL JAVANESE VILLAGE IN 1950, by Paul M. Kattenburg. 1951. 17 pages.

Number 3   AN ACCOUNT OF AN ACQUISITIONS TRIP IN THE COUNTRIES OF SOUTHEAST ASIA, by Cecil Hobbs. 1952. 51 pages.

Number 4   THAI CULTURE AND BEHAVIOR, An Unpublished War time Study Dated September 1943, by Ruth Benedict. 1952; third printing 1963. 45 pages.

Number 5   RURAL ORGANIZATION AND VILLAGE REVIVAL IN INDONESIA, by Ch. J. Grader. 1952. 15 pages.

Number 6   TEACHING AND RESEARCH RELATING TO SOUTHEAST ASIA IN AMERICAN COLLEGES AND UNIVERSITIES, by George McT. Kahin. 1952. 11 pages.

Number 7   LABOUR AND TIN MINING IN MALAYA, by Nim Chee Siew. 1953. 48 pages.

Number 8   SURVEY OF CHINESE LANGUAGE MATERIALS ON SOUTHEAST ASIA IN THE HOOVER INSTITUTE AND LIBRARY, by Giok Po Oey. 1953. 73 pages.

Number 9   VERB CONSTRUCTIONS IN VIETNAMESE, by William W. Gage and H. Merrill Jackson. 1953; reissued 1956. 14 pages.

Number 10   AN ACCOUNT OF THE JAPANESE OCCUPATION OF BANJUMAS RESIDENCY, JAVA, MARCH 1942 TO AUGUST 1945, by S. M. Gandasurbrata, Resident of Banjumas. 1953. 21 pages.

Number 11   ACCOUNT MADE OF A TRIP TO THE COUNTRIES OF SOUTHEAST ASIA FOR THE LIBRARY OF CONGRESS, 1952-1953, by Cecil Hobbs. 1953. 89 pages.

Number 12   POLITICAL INSTITUTIONS OF OLD BURMA, by John F. Cady. 1954. 6 pages.

Number 13   TADAGALE: A BURMESE VILLAGE IN 1950, by Charles S. Brant. 1954. 41 pages.

Number 14   THE VIET MINH REGIME: GOVERNMENT AND ADMINISTRATION IN THE DEMOCRATIC REPUBLIC OF VIETNAM, by Bernhard B. Fall. 1954; revised, enlarged edition 1956. 143 pages.

Number 15   SELECTED ECONOMIC DEVELOPMENT PROJECTS IN BURMA AND INDONESIA -- NOTES AND COMMENTS, by Charles Wolf, Jr. 1954. 25 pages.

Number 16   SOME OBSERVATIONS CONCERNING THE ROLE OF ISLAM IN NATIONAL AND INTERNATIONAL AFFAIRS, by Mohammad Natsir. 1954. 25 pages.

Number 17   MALAYA: A STUDY OF GOVERNMENTAL RESPONSES TO THE KOREAN BOOM, by John Paul Meek. 1955. 32 pages.

Number 19   THE PHILIPPINES: A STUDY OF CURRENT SOCIAL, ECONOMIC AND POLITICAL CONDITIONS, by Gerald D. Berreman. 1956. 55 pages.

Number 20   BIBLIOGRAPHY OF THAILAND, A Selected List of Books and Articles with Annotations by the Staff of the Cornell Thailand Research Project, by Lauriston Sharp, Frank J. Moore, Walter F. Vella and associates. 1956 (reissued 1957, without corrections or additions) 64 pages.

Number 21   THE STATUS OF RURAL LIFE IN THE DUMAGUETE CITY TRADE AREA PHILIPPINES, 1952, by Robert A. Polson and Agaton P. Pal. 1956. 108 pages.

CORNELL UNIVERSITY SOUTHEAST ASIA PROGRAM

OUT OF PRINT

Number 22 ASPECTS OF HEALTH, SANITATION AND NUTRITIONAL STATUS IN A SIAMESE RICE VILLAGE: STUDIES IN BANG CHAN, 1952-54, by Hazel M. Hauck and Associates. 1955. Cornell Thailand Project, Interim Reports Series: Number Two. 73 pages.

Number 23 THE REVISED UNITED STATES-PHILIPPINE TRADE AGREEMENT OF 1955, by Frank H. Golay, 1956. 61 pages.

Number 24 COURSES RELATED TO SOUTHEAST ASIA IN AMERICAN COLLEGES AND UNIVERSITIES, 1955-1956, by Barbara S. Dohrenwend. 1956. 30 pages.

Number 25 FACTORS RELATED TO ACCEPTANCE OF INNOVATIONS IN BANG CHAN, THAILAND, Analysis of a Survey Conducted by the Cornell Cross-Cultural Methodology Project, May 1955, by Rose K. Goldsen and Max Ralis 1957. Cornell Thailand Project, Interim Reports Series: Number Three. (Third Printing 1963) 72 pages.

Number 26 THE ROLE AND IMPORTANCE OF PHILIPPINE INTER-ISLAND SHIPPING AND TRADE, by Frederick L. Wenstedt. 1957. 132 pages.

Number 27 ON THE WAYANG KULIT (PURWA) AND ITS SYMBOLIC AND MYSTIC ELEMENTS (translated from the Dutch by Claire Holt) 1957. 37 pages.

Number 28 FIVE PAPERS ON THAI CUSTOM, by Phya Anuman Rajadhon. 1958. 19 pages.

Number 29 FOOD HABITS AND NUTRIENT INTAKES IN A SIAMESE RICE VILLAGE: STUDIES IN BANG CHAN, 1952-54, by Hazel Hauck, Saovanee Sudsaneh, Jane R. Hanks and Associates. 1958. Cornell Thailand Project, Interim Reports Series: Number Four. 129 pages.

Number 31 A BIBLIOGRAPHY OF INDONESIAN GOVERNMENT DOCUMENTS AND SELECTED INDONESIAN WRITINGS ON GOVERNMENT IN THE CORNELL UNIVERSITY LIBRARY, by Daniel S. Lev. 1958. 58 pages.

Number 32 RANTJAK DILABUEH: A MINANGKABAU KABA, A Specimen of the Traditional Literature of Central Sumatra. (Edited, translated and with an introduction by Anthony H. Johns) 1958. 152 pages.

Number 33 BIBLIOGRAPHY OF INDONESIAN PUBLICATIONS: Newspapers, Non-Government Periodicals and Bulletins, 1945-1958, at the Cornell University Library, by Benedict R. O'G. Anderson. 1959. 69 pages.

Number 34 BIBLIOGRAPHY OF SOVIET PUBLICATIONS ON SOUTHEAST ASIA, as Listed in the Library of Congress Monthly Index of Russian Acquisitions, by Ruth T. McVey. 1959. 109 pages.

Number 35 THE PHILIPPINE FEDERATION OF FREE FARMERS, A Case Study in Mass Agrarian Organization, by Sonya D. Carter. 1959. 147 pages.

Number 36 INDONESIANISASI: POLITICS IN A CHANGING ECONOMY, 1940-1955, by John O. Sutter. 1959. Four volumes. 1,312 pages.

Number 37 AMERICAN DOCTORAL DISSERTATIONS ON ASIA, 1933-1958, Including Appendix of Master's Theses at Cornell University, by Curtis Stucki. 1959. 131 pages.

Number 38 TWO PAPERS ON PHILIPPINE FOREIGN POLICY. The Philippines and the Southeast Asia Treaty Organization, by Roger M. Smith, The Record of the Philippines in the United Nations, by Mary F. Somers. 1959. 79 pages.

Number 39 MATERNAL AND CHILD HEALTH IN A SIAMESE RICE VILLAGE: NUTRITIONAL ASPECTS, Studies in Bang Chan, 1952-1954, by Hazel M. Hauck, Cornell Thailand Project, Interim Reports Series: Number Five. 1959. 70 pages.

Number 40 SOUTHEAST ASIA PUBLICATIONS SOURCES: AN ACCOUNT OF A FIELD TRIP, 1958-1959, by Cecil Hobbs, 1960. 145 pages.

Number 41 U HLA PE'S NARRATIVE OF THE JAPANESE OCCUPATION OF BURMA, by U Khin. 1961. 96 pages.

CORNELL UNIVERSITY SOUTHEAST ASIA PROGRAM

OUT OF PRINT

Number 42 THE JAPANESE OCCUPATION OF THE PHILIPPINES, LEYTE, 1941-1945, by Elmer Lear. 1961. 246 pages.

Number 43 TRENDS AND STRUCTURE IN CONTEMPORARY THAI POETRY, by James N. Mosel. 1961. 53 pages.

Number 44 THE MAN SHU (Book of the Southern Barbarians), translated by Gordon H. Luce; edited by G. P. Oey. 1961. 116 pages.

Number 45 OVERSEAS CHINESE IN SOUTHEAST ASIA--A RUSSIAN STUDY, by N. A. Simoniya. 1961. 151 pages.

Number 48 THE PACE AND PATTERN OF PHILIPPINE ECONOMIC GROWTH: 1938, 1948, and 1956, by Marvin E. Goodstein. 1962. 220 pages.

Number 50 AMERICAN DOCTORAL DISSERTATIONS ON ASIA, 1933-1962, INCLUDING APPENDIX OF MASTER'S THESES AT CORNELL UNIVERSITY, by Curtis W. Stucki. 1963. 204 pages.

Number 52 DRY RICE AGRICULTURE IN NORTHERN THAILAND, by Laurence C. Judd, Cornell Thailand Project, Interim Reports Series: Number Seven. 1964. 95 pages.

Number 53 SINGAPORE AND MALAYSIA, by Milton E. Osborne. 1964. (Second Printing 1967) 115 pages.

Number 56 SOUTHEAST ASIA VIEWED FROM JAPAN: A BIBLIOGRAPHY OF JAPANESE WORKS ON SOUTH EAST ASIAN SOCIETIES, compiled by Kenjiro Ichikawa. 1965. 150 pages.

Number 58 ETHNOGRAPHIC NOTES ON NORTHERN THAILAND, edited by J. R. Hanks, L. H. Hanks, and L. Sharp, Cornell Thailand Project, Interim Reports Series: Number Nine. 1965. 126 pages.

Number 59 THE NAN CHRONICLE, translated by Prasoet Churatana, edited by David K. Wyatt. 1966.

Number 63 A BIBLIOGRAPHY OF WESTERN-LANGUAGE PUBLICATIONS CONCERNING NORTH VIETNAM IN THE CORNELL UNIVERSITY LIBRARY (Supplement to Number 47), compiled by Jane Godfrey Keyes. 1966. 280 pages.

Number 66 THAI STUDENTS IN THE UNITED STATES: A STUDY IN ATTITUDE CHANGE, by Jean Barry, S. J., Cornell Thailand Project, Interim Reports Series: Number Eleven. 1967. 160 pages.

Number 76 BISAYAN FILIPINO AND MALAYAN HUMORAL PATHOLOGIES: FOLK MEDICINE AND ETHNO-HISTORY IN SOUTHEAST ASIA, by Donn V. Hart. April 1970. 96 pages.

Number 80 DEVELOPMENT AND CONFLICT IN THAILAND, by Joyce Nakahara and Ronald A. Witton, Cornell Thailand Project, Interim Reports Series: Number Fourteen. June 1971. 80 pages.

CORNELL MODERN INDONESIA PROJECT PUBLICATIONS

*No. 22 PAST AND FUTURE by Mohammad Hatta. 1960. 17 pages. (Translation)

*No. 23 AN APPROACH TO INDONESIAN HISTORY: TOWARDS AN OPEN FUTURE by Soedjatmoko. 1960. 22 pages. (Translation)

*No. 24 MARHAEN AND PROLETARIAN by Soekarno (Translated by Claire Holt). 1960. 30 pages.

No. 25 THE COMMUNIST UPRISINGS OF 1926-1927 IN INDONESIA: KEY DOCUMENTS edited and with an introduction by Harry J. Benda and Ruth T. McVey. 1960. (Second Printing 1969). 177 pages. $5.50. (Translation)

*No. 26 ASPECTS OF LOCAL GOVERNMENT IN A SUMBAWAN VILLAGE (EASTERN INDONESIA) by Peter R. Goethals. 1961. 156 pages. (Monograph)

*No. 27 SOME SOCIAL-ANTHROPOLOGICAL OBSERVATIONS GOTONG ROJONG PRACTICES IN TWO VILLAGES OF CENTRAL JAVA by Koentjaraningrat (Translated by Claire Holt). 1961. 76 pages.

*No. 28 THE NATIONAL STATUS OF THE CHINESE IN INDONESIA: 1900-1958 by Donald E. Willmott. Revised edition 1961. 152 pages. (Monograph)

*No. 29 SOME ASPECTS OF INDONESIAN POLITICS UNDER THE JAPANESE OCCUPATION: 1944-1954 by Benedict R. Anderson. 1961. 136 pages. (Interim Report)

*No. 30 THE DYNAMICS OF COMMUNITY DEVELOPMENT IN RURAL CENTRAL AND WEST JAVA: A COMPARATIVE REPORT by Selosoemardjan. 1963. 40 pages. (Monograph)

*No. 31 THE CHINESE OF SUKABUMI: A STUDY OF SOCIAL AND CULTURAL ACCOMMODATION by Giok Lan Tan. 1963. 314 pages. (Monograph)

*No. 32 PRELIMINARY CHECKLIST OF INDONESIAN IMPRINTS DURING THE JAPANESE PERIOD (March 1942 - August 1945) by John M. Echols. 1963. 62 pages. (Bibliography)

*No. 33 BANDUNG IN THE EARLY REVOLUTION, 1945-46: A SURVEY IN THE SOCIAL HISTORY OF THE INDONESIAN REVOLUTION by John R. W. Smail. 1964. 169 pages. (Monograph)

*No. 34 AMERICAN REACTIONS TO INDONESIA'S ROLE IN THE BELGRADE CONFERENCE by Frederick P. Binnell. 1964. 86 pages. (Interim Report)

*No. 35 PERANAKAN CHINESE POLITICS IN INDONESIA by Mary F. Somers. 1964. 62 pages. (Interim Report)

*No. 36 THE PROVISIONAL CONSTITUTION OF THE REPUBLIC OF INDONESIA by Prof. Dr. R. Supomo. Translated by Garth N. Jones. 1964. 104 pages. (Translation)

No. 37 MYTHOLOGY AND THE TOLERANCE OF THE JAVANESE by Benedict R. Anderson. 1965. (Second printing 1969) 77 pages. $3.50. (Monograph)

*No. 38 REPUBLIC OF INDONESIA CABINETS, 1945-1965 (With Post-Coup Supplement) compiled by Susan Finch and Daniel S. Lev. 1965. 66 pages. (Interim Report)

No. 39 PRELIMINARY CHECKLIST OF INDONESIAN IMPRINTS (1945-1949): WITH CORNELL UNIVERSITY HOLDINGS by John M. Echols. 1965. 186 pages. $3.50. (Bibliography)

*No. 40 THE TRANSITION TO GUIDE DEMOCRACY: INDONESIAN POLITICS, 1957-1959 by Daniel S. Lev. 1966. 298 pages. (Monograph)

*No. 41 A GUIDE TO INDONESIAN PERIODICALS, 1945-1965, IN THE CORNELL UNIVERSITY LIBRARY compiled by Yvonne Thung and John M. Echols. 1966. 151 pages. (Bibliography)

*No. 42 PROBLEMS OF THE INDONESIAN INFLATION by J. A. C. Mackie. 1967. 101 pages. (Monograph)

No. 43 STATE AND STATECRAFT IN OLD JAVA: A STUDY OF THE LATER MATARAM PERIOD, 16th TO 19th CENTURY by Soemarsaid Moertono. 1968. 174 pages. $3.00. (Monograph)

CORNELL MODERN INDONESIA PROJECT PUBLICATIONS

No. 44 OUR STRUGGLE by Sutan Sjahrir. Translated with an introduction by Benedict R. Anderson. 1968. 371 pages. $2.00. (Translation)

No. 45 INDONESIA ABANDONS CONFRONTATION by Franklin B. Weinstein. 1969. 94 pages. $3.00. (Interim Report)

No. 46 THE ORIGINS OF THE MODERN CHINESE MOVEMENT IN INDONESIA by Kwee Tek Hoay. Translated and edited by Lea E. Williams. 1969. $3.00.

No. 47 PERSATUAN ISLAM: ISLAMIC REFORM IN TWENTIETH CENTURY INDONESIA by Howard M. Federspiel. 1970. 250 pages. $7.50. (Monograph)

No. 48 NATIONALISM, ISLAM AND MARXISM by Soekarno. With an introduction by Ruth T. McVey. 1970. 62 pages. $3.00. (Translation)

No. 49 THE FOUNDATION OF THE PARTAI MUSLIM IN INDONESIA by K. E. Ward. 1970. 75 pages. $3.00. (Interim Report)

No. 50 SCHOOLS AND POLITICS: THE KAUM MUDA MOVEMENT IN WEST SUMATRA (1927-1933) by Taufik Abdullah. 1971. 257 pages. $6.00. (Monograph)

No. 51 THE PUTERA REPORTS: PROBLEMS IN INDONESIAN-JAPANESE WAR-TIME COOPERATION by Mohammad Hatta. Translated with an introduction by William H. Frederick. 1971. 114 pages. $4.00. (Translation)

No. 52 A PRELIMINARY ANALYSIS OF THE OCTOBER 1, 1965, COUP IN INDONESIA (Prepared in January 1966) by Benedict R. Anderson, Ruth T. McVey (With the assistance of Frederick P. Bunnell). 1971. 162 pages. $6.00. (Interim Report)

No. 53 THE EURASIANS OF INDONESIA: A POLITICAL-HISTORICAL BIBLIOGRAPHY. Compiled by Paul W. van der Veur. 1971. 105 pages. $3.50. (Bibliography)

No. 54 OLD JAVANESE (KAWI) by A. S. Teselkin. Translated and edited, with a preface by John M. Echols. 1972. 107 pages. $3.50. (Translation)

No. 55 REPORT FROM BANARAN: THE STORY OF THE EXPERIENCES OF A SOLDIER DURING THE WAR OF INDEPENDENCE by Major General T. B. Simatupang. 1972. $6.50. (Translation)

No. 56 GOLKAR AND THE INDONESIAN ELECTIONS OF 1971 by Masashi Nishihara. 1972. 56 pages. $3.50. (Monograph)

INDONESIA, a semi-annual journal, devoted to Indonesia's culture, history and social and political problems.

*Vol. 1, April 1966, *Vol. 2, Oct. 1966, *Vol. 3, April 1967 and *Vol. 4, October 1967

Vol. 5, April 1968, Vol. 6, Oct. 1968, $3.50 each, $6.00 both

Vol. 7, April 1968, Vol. 8, Oct. 1969, $4.00 each, $7.00 both

Vol. 9, April 1970, Vol. 10, Oct. 1970, $4.50 each, $8.00 both

Vol. 11, April 1971, Vol. 12, Oct. 1971, $4.50 each, $8.00 both

Vol. 13, April 1972, Vol. 14, Oct. 1972, $4.50 each, $8.00 both

Vol. 15, April 1973, Vol. 16, Oct. 1973, $4.50 each, $8.00 both

Vol. 17, April 1974, Vol. 18, Oct. 1974, $4.50 each, $8.00 both

CORNELL MODERN INDONESIA PROJECT PUBLICATIONS -- 102 West Avenue, Ithaca, New York 14850

*(Those preceded by an asterisk are out of print.)

*No. 1   THE NATIONAL STATUS OF THE CHINESE IN INDONESIA by Donald E. Wilmott. 1956.
          88 pages. (Interim Report)

*No. 2   STRUCTURAL CHANGES IN JAVANESE SOCIETY: THE SUPRA-VILLAGE SPHERE by D. H. Burger
          (Translated by Leslie H. Palmier). 1956. 38 pages. (Translation)

*No. 3   INDONESIAN WRITING IN TRANSLATION compiled and edited and with an introduction
          by John M. Echols. 1956. 178 pages. (Translation)

*No. 4   LIVING CONDITIONS OF PLANTATION WORKERS AND PEASANTS ON JAVA IN 1939-1940 by the
          Coolie Budget Commission. (Translated by Robert van Niel). 1956. 131 pages.

*No. 5   DECENTRALIZATION IN INDONESIA: LEGISLATIVE ASPECTS by Gerald S. Maryanov. 1957.
          75 pages. (Interim Report)

No. 6   THE INDONESIAN ELECTIONS OF 1955 by Herbert Keith. 1957. (Second printing 1971)
          91 pages. $3.50. (Interim Report)

No. 7   THE SOVIET VIEW OF THE INDONESIAN REVOLUTION by Ruth T. McVey. 1957. (Third
          printing 1969) 90 pages. $2.50. (Interim Report)

*No. 8   SOME FACTORS RELATED TO AUTONOMY AND DEPENDENCE IN TWELVE JAVANESE VILLAGES by
          Barbara S. Dohrenwend. 1957. 70 pages. (Interim Report)

*No. 9   PROBLEMS OF REGIONAL AUTONOMY IN CONTEMPORARY INDONESIA by John D. Legge. 1957.
          71 pages. (Interim Report)

*No. 10 STRUCTURAL CHANGES IN JAVANESE SOCIETY: THE VILLAGE SPHERE by D. H. Burger
          (Translated by Leslie H. Palmier). 1957. 17 pages. (Translation)

*No. 11 THE OFFICE OF PRESIDENT IN INDONESIA AS DEFINED IN THE THREE CONSTITUTIONS IN
          THEORY AND PRACTICE by A. K. Pringgodigdo (Translated by Alexander Brotherton).
          1957. 59 pages. (Translation)

*No. 12 DECENTRALIZATION IN INDONESIA AS A POLITICAL PROBLEM by Gerald S. Maryanov.
          1958. 118 pages. (Interim Report)

*No. 13 THE CALCUTTA CONFERENCE AND THE SOUTHEAST ASIA UPRISINGS by Ruth T. McVey. 1958.
          28 pages. (Interim Report)

*No. 14 THE BEGINNINGS OF THE INDONESIAN-DUTCH NEGOTIATIONS AND THE HOGE VELUWE TALKS
          by Idrus N. Djajadiningrat. 1958. 128 pages. (Monograph)

*No. 15 THE WILOPO CABINET, 1952-53: A TURNING POINT IN POST-REVOLUTIONARY INDONESIA
          by Herbert Feith. 1958. 212 pages. (Monograph)

No. 16   THE DYNAMICS OF THE WESTERN NEW GUINEA (IRIAN BARAT) PROBLEM by Herbert C. Bone,
          Jr. 1958. (Second Printing 1962) 182 pages. $3.00. (Interim Report)

*No. 17 ECONOMIC DEVELOPMENT AS A CULTURAL PROBLEM (Konfrontasi, Sept.-Oct. 1954) by
          Soedjatmoko. 1958. (Second Printing 1962) 28 pages. (Translation)

*No. 18 THE TOBA BATAK, FORMERLY AND NOW by J. Keuning (Translated by Claire Holt). 1958.
          24 pages. (Translation)

*No. 19 THE GO ERNMENT, ECONOMY AND TAXES OF A CENTRAL JAVANESE VILLAGE by Widjojo
          Nitisastro and J. E. Ismael (Translated by Norbert Ward). 1959. 37 pages.

*No. 20 THE POLITICAL CHARACTER OF THE INDONESIAN TRADE UNION MOVEMENT by Iskandar
          Tedjasukmana. 1959. 130 pages. (Monograph)

*No. 21 THE SOCIO-ECONOMIC BASIS OF THE INDONESIAN STATE: ON THE INTERPRETATION OF
          PARAGRAPH I, ARTICLE 38, OF THE PROVISIONAL CONSTITUTION by Wilopo and Widjojo
          Nitisastro. (Translated by Alexander Brotherton). 1959. 17 pages.